Fine WoodWorking *on* Proven Shop Tips

Fine WoodWorking *on* **Proven Shop Tips**

Selections from
Methods of Work,
edited and drawn by
Jim Richey

 The Taunton Press

Cover art by Jim Richey

First printing: January 1985
Second printing: August 1985
Third printing: March 1986
Fourth printing: February 1987
Fifth printing: November 1987
Sixth printing: June 1988
Seventh printing: September 1989
Eighth printing: August 1990
Ninth printing: January 1993
International Standard Book Number: 0-918804-32-9
Library of Congress Catalog Card Number: 84-052095
Printed in the United States of America

A FINE WOODWORKING Book

FINE WOODWORKING is a trademark of The Taunton Press, Inc.,
registered in the U.S. Patent and Trademark Office.

The Taunton Press
63 South Main Street
Box 5506
Newtown, Connecticut 06470-5506

Contents

1 Introduction

2 Measuring & Marking

6 Benches & Vises

12 Clamps

20 Gluing

23 Bending, Steaming & Drying

26 Joinery & Wooden Threads

34 Sanding & Scraping

37 Shop Aids & Construction Tips

42 Finishing

48 Sharpening & Grinding

54 Pulls, Latches & Hardware

58 Homemade Handtools

66 Radial-Arm Saw Jigs & Fixtures

70 Tablesaw Jigs & Fixtures

80 Bandsaw Jigs & Fixtures

84 Drill Press Jigs & Fixtures

90 Router Jigs & Fixtures

102 Sander Jigs & Fixtures

104 Lathe Jigs & Fixtures

114 Planer Jigs & Fixtures

118 Index

Introduction

Back in 1976, one R.P. Gwinn from the unlikely spot of Golf, Illinois, wrote a letter to the then-new *Fine Woodworking* magazine. He had a suggestion for a regular feature:

> It has to do with tricks amateurs and professionals learn by trial and error, or by sharing successes and failures of others, or by accident. I suspect your readership would respond with a multitude of suggestions. Selection of two or three items per issue should develop into a unique library of information over a period of time.

The editors thought it a good idea, so in the next issue they began a column called *Methods of Work*. And Gwinn was right. The readers did respond with multitudes of suggestions. The column quickly became an established, well-read feature. A couple years later I came on the scene (working out of my Oklahoma home) to help edit and illustrate the ideas. Our fear in those days was that the number of good woodworking methods was finite, that next month's mailbox would be empty. After all, each of us could number on one hand the good tricks we knew. But over the years, suggestions have poured in at the rate of three or four for each one we have room to publish.

This matter of numbers created a continuing agonizing problem for those of us who had to sift through and select ideas to publish. Of course, we tried to screen using such criteria as broadness of interest, ingenuity, simplicity and communicability. But when fifty shop tips met the criteria and there was room for only twelve, a second level of selection came into play that was somewhat personal and subjective. Nonetheless, in reviewing the Methods we selected over the years (and have now collected in this book), I think our batting average was pretty high. It's easy to be a good hitter when you have a lot of fat pitches.

Gwinn was right on another count. After eight years the material published in the Methods column has indeed become a unique library of information. Unfortunately, until now, the library has been dispersed across forty or so back issues of *Fine Woodworking*. This book, *Proven Shop Tips*, remedies the inconvenience by compiling into one organized volume the best ideas from past issues. As a group the tips, jigs and tricks presented here range far and wide across the woodworking landscape. There are methods for drying green wood and for polishing a finish, and for every operation in between. There are jigs to enhance every tool in the shop. There are more ideas for clamps than you can shake a homemade dowel at. Taken individually, each of these tips can stand alone, a tribute to the ingenuity and innovation of its author. These are real solutions to real woodworking problems, devised by real woodworkers.

In addition to the four hundred woodworkers who authored this book, a few other acknowledgments are in order. John Kelsey, Rick Mastelli, Deborah Fillion and Jim Cummins, all editors at The Taunton Press, put much energy and care into combing the burrs out of my oftentimes rough material and worrying each miniature article into its published form. A few of the illustrations in this book were drawn by Joe Esposito. And, to Mr. R.P. Gwinn of Golf, Illinois, thanks.

Jim Richey, editor, Methods of Work

Measuring & Marking

Chapter 1

Beam compass

A beam compass is a handy tool, but trammel points are expensive to buy. My own version costs less than $2 and takes about two hours to make. The beam is milled from two pieces of ½-in. Baltic birch plywood, 1¾ in. by whatever length you want. The dado for the nut to slide in is cut to the

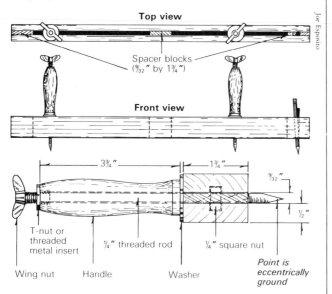

Top view

Spacer blocks
(⁹⁄₃₂″ by 1¾″)

Joe Esposito

Front view

3¾″ 1¾″

⁹⁄₃₂″

½″

T-nut or threaded metal insert

¼″ threaded rod

¼″ square nut

Wing nut   Handle   Washer

Point is eccentrically ground

inside of both pieces. The sides of the beam are joined at the ends and on center with three spacer blocks 1¾ in. square. In one of the end blocks drill a ⁵⁄₁₆-in. opening, in which a pencil will be wedged.

The handles can be turned from maple, birch, beech or similar hardwood. Drill a ⁹⁄₃₂-in. hole for the rod, and insert a ¼-in. *T*-nut in the top. The rods are ¼-in. dia. by at least 8 in. Allow extra threading for resharpening the point, because this is not tempered steel. Grind the point eccentrically (off center) for fine adjustments. Then solder a wing nut on top of the rod.

Now thread the rod through the *T*-nut in the handle and the square nut that rides in the dado cut into the beam until the point is exposed about an inch on the underside of the beam. Slide both points to the desired arc (⅛-in. tolerance), then tighten the handles. With the wing nuts, you can fine-adjust the radius to the exact dimension. To mark with the pencil, raise one of the points above the pencil point. The only radius you can't get is from the pencil to the center block. In this case I remove one of the points and thread the pencil through the square nut by pushing down and twisting at the same time. The beam compass can also be used as a panel gauge if you attach a fence to the end.

—*Michael Lynch, San Francisco, Calif.*

Archimedean marking gauge

This marking gauge employs a simple bar-locking system consisting of one moving part. The shape of the bar is an adaptation of the Archimedes spiral—actually it is a scroll

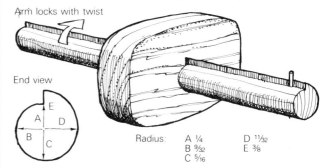

Arm locks with twist

End view

E
A D
B C

Radius: A ¼   D ¹¹⁄₃₂
           B ⁹⁄₃₂   E ⅜
           C ⁵⁄₁₆

curve made up of tangential circular arcs. Make the bar and fence from a close-grained hardwood such as beech. A slight twist of the bar will hold it securely, and a reverse twist will release it for adjustment. —*John Arthey, Southampton, Ont.*

Drawing an ellipse

Here's how to draw all or part of an ellipse with a lath and a framing square. First, lay out the major and minor diameters of the ellipse on the workpiece, and clamp a framing square on these lines with its outside corner at the center. Install a pencil in a hole near one end of the lath, and measuring from the pencil, drive two brads through the lath, one at distance A from the pencil, the other at distance B. Clip off the brads

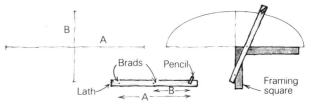

B

A

Brads   Pencil

Lath

A   B

Framing square

so that they don't protrude more than the thickness of the square. If you swing the lath, keeping one brad riding the top edge of the square and the other brad riding the side edge, you will scribe one-quarter of the ellipse. Flip the square, re-clamp, and repeat the procedure to complete the ellipse.

—*Frank Grant, Round Pond, Maine,*
and Matt Longenbaugh, Darrington, Wash.

Adjustable curve

To make this adjustable curve, start with a piece of fine, straightgrained hardwood—hickory is best. Cut a ¼-in. thick strip about 36 in. long and 1½ in. wide. Now taper the strip

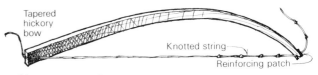

Tapered hickory bow

Knotted string

Reinforcing patch

to ¾ in. wide and ³⁄₃₂ in. thick at one end. Glue a reinforcing patch on the thin end and saw a small notch in each end of the piece. To complete the curve tie a series of knots in a string and string up the curve like a bow. Unstring the curve when it's not in use. —*Floyd Lien, Aptos, Calif.*

Triangle tips

An architect's 45° triangle is inexpensive and handy around the shop. Attach a ½-in. x ½-in. strip of walnut along the hypotenuse with No. 2 R.H. brass wood screws to make a miter square. Take care not to cut into the edge of the triangle when you scribe with a metal instrument.

—*Dwight G. Gorrell, Centerville, Kans.*

Drafting a smooth curve

Several years ago a Danish carpenter showed me this method of drawing a smooth curve to fit a given width and height. Start by driving three nails, one at the top and one at each end of the space where you will construct the curve. Now tack two sticks together—one parallel to the base and the oth-

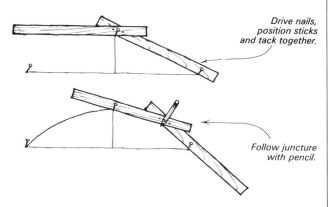

Drive nails, position sticks and tack together.

Follow juncture with pencil.

er riding two of the nails: the one at the top and one at one edge. Put a pencil at the juncture of the sticks and let the sticks slide over the nails as you mark the curve. Repeat the same procedure on the other side to complete the curve.
—*Thomas Baird, Woodland, Calif.*

Trueing framing squares

Here's a method for trueing a framing square using just a hammer and center-punch. First test to determine if your square is true by drawing a straight line three to four feet long. Then, with the tongue on the line, draw a pencil line alongside the blade. Flip the tongue over and bring the square into the corner of the two lines just drawn. If the square is true, the lines will be right alongside both tongue and blade.

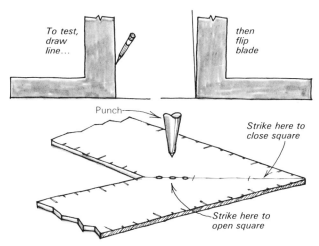

To test, draw line...

then flip blade

Punch

Strike here to close square

Strike here to open square

But if the lines don't coincide, here's how to regain a true 90°. At the heel, draw a line from the inside corner to the outside corner and divide the line into thirds. Place a center-punch on the line in the center of either the inner third or the outer third. By striking the punch in the outer third you spread the metal and cause the square to close (decreasing the angle). By striking the punch in the inner third you will open the square (increasing the angle). Rap the punch smartly with a hammer, as you would to leave a starting hole for a drill. Naturally, check the square after each adjustment is made.
—*Robert C. Amirault, South Thomaston, Maine*

Marking tips

Old furniture that is to be taken apart, repaired and reassembled must be marked so that the pieces can be easily identified. Since surface marks will be obliterated by stripping and refinishing chemicals, it is best to use indentation marks. I mark all pieces before disassembly, and always on the underside. I mark only one end of the male/tenon member close to the female/mortise member. I use one set of chisel marks with the grain, then one set across the grain, then tiny nail-set marks. Next I use X marks or any combination of the above.
—*Price G. Schulte, St. Louis, Mo.*

Circle division table

During my forty years as a modelmaker, I have used this circle division table many times. I know of no faster method to divide a circle into several equal parts. To use the table, just pick the number of divisions you want from the 'No. of spaces' column. Multiply the selected 'Length of chord' times the diameter of your circle and set a divider to this reading. Then simply walk the dividers around the circle, marking each point. If you're working with small circles, it helps to have a rule divided in hundredths to set the dividers accurately.
—*Ray Elam, Los Gatos, Calif.*

No. of spaces	Length of chord	No. of spaces	Length of chord	No. of spaces	Length of chord	No. of spaces	Length of chord
3	0.8660	28	0.1120	53	0.0592	78	0.0403
4	0.7071	29	0.1081	54	0.0581	79	0.0398
5	0.5878	30	0.1045	55	0.0571	80	0.0393
6	0.5000	31	0.1012	56	0.0561	81	0.0388
7	0.4339	32	0.0980	57	0.0551	82	0.0383
8	0.3827	33	0.0951	58	0.0541	83	0.0378
9	0.3420	34	0.0923	59	0.0532	84	0.0374
10	0.3090	35	0.0896	60	0.0523	85	0.0370
11	0.2818	36	0.0872	61	0.0515	86	0.0365
12	0.2588	37	0.0848	62	0.0507	87	0.0361
13	0.2393	38	0.0826	63	0.0499	88	0.0357
14	0.2224	39	0.0805	64	0.0491	89	0.0353
15	0.2079	40	0.0785	65	0.0483	90	0.0349
16	0.1951	41	0.0765	66	0.0476	91	0.0345
17	0.1837	42	0.0747	67	0.0469	92	0.0341
18	0.1736	43	0.0730	68	0.0462	93	0.0338
19	0.1645	44	0.0713	69	0.0455	94	0.0334
20	0.1564	45	0.0698	70	0.0449	95	0.0331
21	0.1490	46	0.0682	71	0.0442	96	0.0327
22	0.1423	47	0.0668	72	0.0436	97	0.0324
23	0.1362	48	0.0654	73	0.0430	98	0.0321
24	0.1305	49	0.0641	74	0.0424	99	0.0317
25	0.1253	50	0.0628	75	0.0419	100	0.0314
26	0.1205	51	0.0616	76	0.0413		
27	0.1161	52	0.0604	77	0.0408		

These figures are for a 1-in. diameter circle. For other sizes, multiply length of chord by diameter of circle desired.

Centerfinder for woodturners

This Plexiglas centerfinder will be useful to woodturners who split odd-shaped workpieces from the log. To make the gauge, first mount a piece of scrap wood to the faceplate and trim it to a round disc. Now attach a piece of ⅛-in. thick clear Plexiglas to the scrap-wood disc and scribe a series of target-like circles into the face of the

Plexiglas through its protective paper. Drill a center hole to fit your favorite scratch awl. To complete the gauge, spray the grooves with a colored enamel, drill a hang-up hole in one corner and remove the paper. To use the gauge, hold it on the end of irregular stock and adjust it until the largest possible circle falls completely over wood. Then mark the center.
—*Nels Thogerson, Ames, Iowa*

Centerfinders—three variations on a theme

An old organ-builder friend showed me this handy home-made guide for center-drilling holes in the edges of boards to be doweled and edge-glued. The device consists of five sticks of hardwood screwed together in the configuration shown.

The sticks should pivot so that the device collapses like a parallelogram. For the drill guide, fit the center strip with a bolt ⅛ in. larger than the bit size. Then, using a drill press for

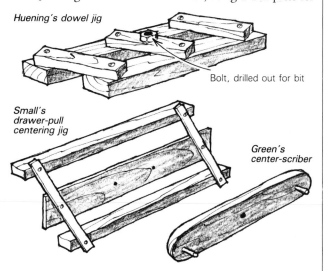

Huening's dowel jig

Bolt, drilled out for bit

Small's drawer-pull centering jig

Green's center-scriber

accuracy, drill a pilot hole through the bolt using a bit one number larger than the bit you intend to use for doweling. To use, first align the edges of the boards and mark off the dowel locations with a square. To center the dowels, set the device to straddle each board's edge and squeeze the parallelogram shut. Then slide the device to each mark, and drill.

—*John Huening, Seffner, Fla.*

Here's a self-centering jig for boring drawer-pull holes. The pivoting sticks should be made long enough to span your widest drawer. The center plate may be fitted with drill-bit guide bushings or just small holes for marking with an awl.

—*J.B. Small, Newville, Pa.*

This old-time gadget is handy for center-scribing boards. Install dowel pegs at the ends of the device and drill a hole in the center for a pencil point. —*Larry Green, Bethel, Conn.*

Approximating angles

Here's a surprisingly accurate procedure to estimate angles using only a rule and a compass. First, draw a circle with a radius of 5¾ in. Now say you want a 10° angle. Mark off two points one inch apart (a 1-in. chord) on the circumference. Join the two points with the center of the circle, and the

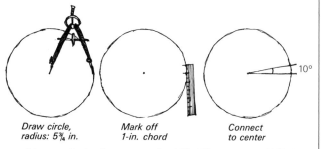

Draw circle, radius: 5¾ in.

Mark off 1-in. chord

Connect to center

10°

resulting angle is almost exactly 10°. If you want 20°, just lay out two 1-in. chords (not one 2-in. chord). Use fractions of an inch or just split the distance by eye for angles less than 10°. For large angles lay out multiples of 60° (using the compass set to the circle's radius), then add or subtract 1-in. (10°) slices to get the angle you want.

—*Jules Paquin, Laval, Quebec*

Using chalk

When working the darker woods like walnut or rosewood, pencil lines and even scribe marks have a distressing way of fading into the vagaries of color and grain. The woodworker can waste a lot of time relocating his mark, or worse, cutting what he thought was his mark, only to discover it to be a color change inches from the desired point. A piece of chalk can be a great help. The faintest scribe mark, dusted with yellow or white chalk, jumps out dramatically and makes accurate cutting a certainty. One can also use chalk for setting out dimensions on lumber prior to rough-sizing. If you are like me, and indecision is a habit, you can easily brush off the chalk.

—*Christopher Murray, Richmond, Va.*

Superellipse

The superellipse is a contemporary classic curve of unusual grace used on some Scandinavian tabletops. Its simple geometric derivation enhances its aesthetic appeal. The superellipse has the equation:

$$(x/A)^n + (y/B)^n = 1$$

A is half the width and B is half the length of the superellipse; n is a constant of 2, 4, 6, 8, etc. If n is 2, the equation produces a standard ellipse or a circle (if A equals B). As

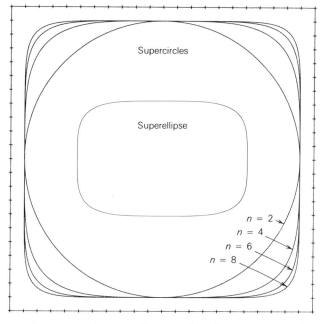

Supercircles

Superellipse

n = 2
n = 4
n = 6
n = 8

you increase n, the superellipse tends to become rectangular, yet there are no straight segments. Thus you can mathematically generate intermediate shapes between an ellipse and a rectangle by choosing an appropriate value for n.

The easiest way to apply supercircles and superellipses to an actual tabletop is by the squares method. Use the grid marks on the drawing to divide it into a number of squares. Mark the length and width of the tabletop with the same number of divisions, which will form a grid of rectangles. When you copy the supercircle to the rectangular grid, it will stretch the supercircle into a scaled superellipse.

—*James Potzick, Potomac, Md.*

EDITOR'S NOTE: For more information on the superellipse and on Piet Hein, the Dane who discovered and named it, see Martin Gardner's ''Mathematical Games'' column in the September 1965 issue of *Scientific American* (213:222+).

Drilling a dowel

If you have a lathe, it's easy to bore a centered hole in the end of a dowel. You can also do it on the drill press or radial arm saw, if you have a drill bit the size of the dowel to be bored and a block of scrap wood. First clamp the scrap underneath the drill chuck, and bore a hole the size of the dowel. Without disturbing the block, press the dowel into the hole. Change to the smaller bit and drill your hole—it's automatically centered.　　　　　—*Larry Green, Bethel, Conn.*

Checking a miter square

I am getting weary of buying 45° miter squares from mail-order catalog firms and receiving ones of 44° or 46° instead. Veneering does not permit such a variance. The angle of a miter square can be checked with a perfect straightedge (a wide piece of carefully jointed ¾-in. maple will do) and a draftsman's triangle with an angle of exactly 90°.

First (A) place the miter square against the straightedge, as shown in the drawing below. Then (B) position the 90° angle of the triangle against the extended leg of the miter square. With the triangle secured, (C) flop the miter square to the other side of the triangle. Slide it against the straight-

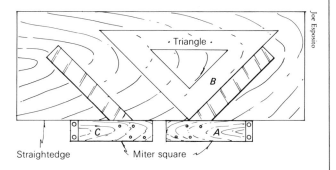

Straightedge　　　Miter square

edge until it meets the triangle. Any resulting angle between the miter square and the triangle is twice the error angle of the miter square.　　　　　—*C. Edward Moore, Bowie, Md.*

Benches & Vises

Chapter 2

Shaving horse #1

The design of this dumbhead shaving horse, suited to working both long and thick stock, was handed down to me by some old-timers. It is made mostly from oak timbers and can be completed in a couple of days.

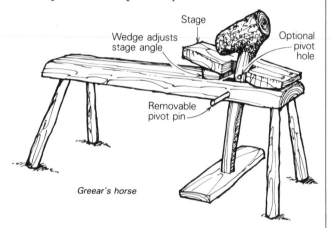

Stage
Wedge adjusts stage angle
Optional pivot hole
Removable pivot pin

Greear's horse

First split and hew a 5-ft. long, red oak log sap-side-up for the top of the bench. The heart side of a split log is harder to smooth and doesn't take the weather as well. Split the legs from an oak billet that is drier than the top, shape them with a hatchet, and mortise them into the bottom of the bench. For stability, cut or bore the mortises so the legs splay out, and use fox (blind) wedges for a tight fit. Hew the stage (the working platform) from a 3-ft. long, split oak log, and peg or bolt it to the bench at the far end. Taper the width of the stage toward the front (about 4 in.) so that the handles of the drawknife—and your fingers—have good clearance. Belly the underside of the stage in front of the pins and support its front edge with a wedge, so you can vary the working angle of the stage.

The "dumbhead" is a short section of hickory trunk with 3 ft. of limb left attached to act as a lever. Cut a mortise in the right side of the stage and hew the branch to fit it, being sure to flatten the limb at an angle so that the trunk section aligns over the stage. The fulcrum is a removable peg—you can make a series of pivot holes to adjust the horse for the thickness of your stock. Tusk-tenon a large pedal to the end of the limb.

This design is for right-handed people. Long pieces of wood, such as shovel handles, are positioned to the left of the dumbhead lever and pass comfortably under the shaver's right arm. A left-handed person would want to move the mortise for the dumbhead lever to the left side.

—*Delbert Greear, Sautee, Ga.*

Shaving horse #2

To make a shaving horse quickly with a chainsaw and broad ax, select a 6-ft. long hardwood log, 8 in. to 10 in. at the butt. Snap parallel lines down the log, halving the circumference. Saw kerfs down to the snap lines every 3 in. or 4 in., stopping 2 ft. from the butt end. Hew the chips out with the broad ax. Next hew out the remaining 2 ft. to act as a stage, angling it and tapering it as shown—the front of the work

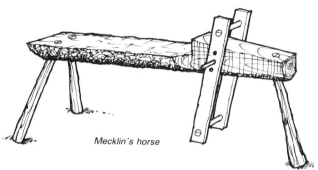

Mecklin's horse

area should be less than 6 in. wide, to clear the drawknife handles. Make three 2-ft. long legs, and mortise them into the bench at an angle for stability. Now you have the basic work area shaped. It can be smoothed with adze or plane. Spend time on the work area to ensure that it is flat and true.

Traditionally, the head extends through a mortise in the work area. However, I prefer the "ladder-rung" head shown. With this setup you can work a long piece of wood unencumbered by the neck of the traditional head. Also, the ladder-rung head holds larger pieces of wood. Make the head out of two 2-ft. long 1x3s and two 1-in. dowels glued and wedged in the 1x3s. The head pivots on a $\frac{5}{8}$-in. linchpin through the bench. Drill additional holes in the 1x3s as you experiment with the horse. If you wish, add a more elaborate pedal to the bottom of the head frame. Now you're ready to make excellent kindling. —*John Mecklin, Cherryfield, Me.*

Outdoor workbench

I needed a small outdoor bench for fair-weather work outside my shop and demonstrations at the county fair. To make the bench I cut a beefy slice of oak tree and mounted it on three legs canted outward. For the "vise," I fitted the bench with holes for my cast-iron hold-down (available from Woodcraft Supply, P.O. Box 4000, Woburn, Mass.

01888, and other suppliers). I bored a 2-in. hole into the top of the bench clear through to the bottom (so rainwater wouldn't collect in the hole). Then I plugged the top 2 in. of the hole with hardwood and centerbored the plug to fit the hold-down shaft. I flattened a place on the side of the oak slice and fitted a plug as above so I could use the hold-down to clamp work vertically. The arrangement works surprisingly well. —*J.B. Small, Newville, Pa.*

Planing stand

To hold boat planks and decking for planing and beading, we use what must be the world's simplest workbench. It con-

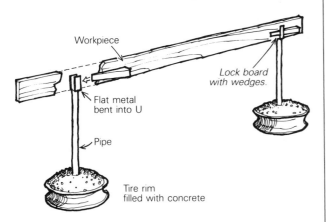

sists of two stands made from concrete-filled wheel rims, some 1½-in. pipe, a couple of pieces of flat steel bent into U-shape, and a couple of wedges. The stands are very stable (approximately 150 lb. each), yet they can be easily tilted and rolled wherever needed. One advantage of the stands is that you can work a plank from both sides—there's nothing in your way anywhere. —*Kim Aaboe, Halifax, N.S.*

Saw-sharpening stand

For those who prefer to sharpen their own handsaws, this sharpening stand is a winner. A wooden tightening bar,

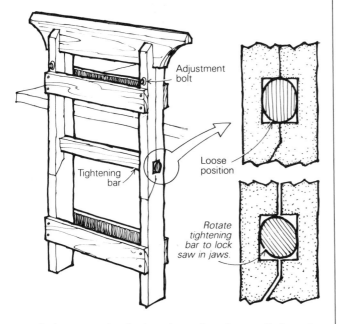

worked to an oval at both ends, wedges the stand's jaws shut on the sawblade when turned. The two adjustment bolts near the saw holders act as pivots. They should be tight enough to hold the saw in place before the tightening bar is turned. I'm 5 ft. 8 in. tall and the 44-in. height is comfortable for me.

When you sharpen, you normally have to maintain two different angles: tilting the file up in the air a little, and also angling it toward the tip of the saw. Here's a trick: Instead of worrying about both angles, just tilt the saw stand so that it leans against the bench. Then you can concentrate on the angle toward the tip while you hold the file level. —*Brian Johnson, Sacramento, Calif.*

Carver's stand

Woodcarvers will find this carver's stand useful—especially for sculpture and figures in-the-round. An old bowling ball at the heart of the stand forms what is, in essence, a universal joint. The carver can rotate his work or incline it at any angle, thus permitting easy access to all areas of the carving. Hardware consists of a long lag bolt mounted through the bowling ball into the work and two 24-in. long, ½-in. threaded steel rods. When the carver has his work in the desired position, he simply tightens nuts on the threaded rods to lock the bowling ball in position and also to make the stand rigid.

—*M.B. Hansen, Huntsville, Texas*

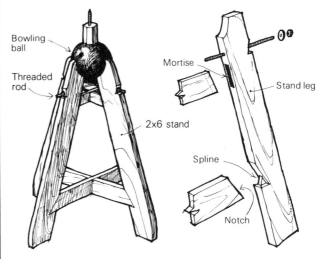

Sawing and assembly work station

Here's a shop aid that let me put three different sets of sawhorses out to pasture. It makes a strong, portable work station for sawing, sanding, assembly and other operations. Simply flop the box to position the work 24 in., 30 in. or 36 in. off the floor, whichever is convenient. Construct the unit by screwing together six dowel-joined frames.

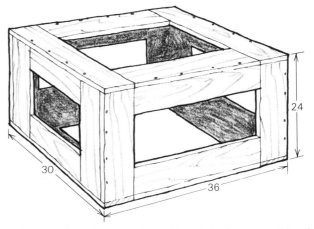

As a final touch, paint three sides of the box—one side of each of the three sizes. Always turn a painted side down when you work. Debris from the floor will become embedded only in these painted surfaces, and you'll never have to risk scarring your workpiece by putting it on a surface that's been on the floor. —*Bill Nolan, Munising, Mich.*

Inexpensive workbench

This simple workbench uses two pipe clamps for the vise. The size of the bench, quality of material and construction

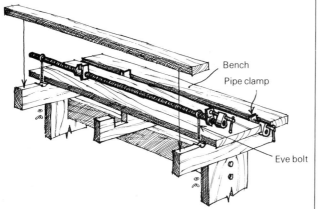

Bench

Pipe clamp

Eye bolt

design can all be varied to suit the needs of the builder. My choice is the trestle-leg design shown; others may want to use four corner legs to provide a mounting location for a leg vise. The major drawback to this design is the non-adjustable dog height. To overcome this problem, preset the dog height at ¼ in. or ½ in. Then, to surface thin stock, shim it off the table with thin plywood. —*J. Butler, Hubbardston, Mass.*

Folding cutting table

Here is a simple, useful rack for supporting large plywood panels when cutting with a hand-held power saw. It also doubles as a gluing table and, with a sheet of plywood on top, as a spacious worktable. When you are not using it you can fold it, scissor-like, into a compact unit for storage in a corner of the shop.

Material consists of 24 ft. of 2x2 construction-grade fir, eight carriage bolts (¼ in. x 2½ in.) and four lag screws (¼ in. x 3 in.). Cut the fir into two long strips (72 in.) and four cross-beams (36 in.). Bolt the cross-beams to the long strips on 20-in. centers and 6 in. from each end. Countersink the carriage bolts a full ¾ in. into the cross-beams to clear the

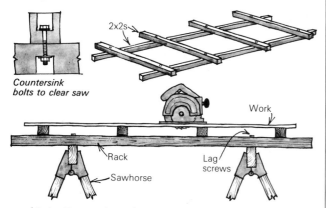

2x2s

Countersink
bolts to clear saw

Work

Rack

Lag
screws

Sawhorse

sawblade. Fasten the rack to two wooden sawhorses with the four lag screws centered 12 in. from each end of the long strips. —*Stephen Wysocki, Colton, Calif.*

Two-level rolling worktable

I made this rolling worktable to ease the logistics of constructing a full set of kitchen cabinets in my small (18-ft. by 18-ft.) workshop. Since then I have found it to be the ideal companion to the traditional cabinetmaker's workbench when space is limited. Built square, level and strong it provides an excellent base for moving cabinets and furniture into or out of the work stream. Or, with the crossbars in place, the work-

table can be used at waist height for moving production pieces from machine to machine. As a bonus, it stores away without taking up much room.

Four 360° heavy-duty casters support a 40-in. by 40-in. finger-joined or dovetailed frame of 2x3 hardwood, gusseted with ¾-in. plywood at each corner. Add a couple of 1x3 crossbraces if needed. Screw and glue the ¾-in. plywood top to the frame, then paint and wax it to make it easy to clean up spilled glue and finishes. Next add two pockets on each of two opposite sides, as shown, to accept the ends of the four hardwood 1x3 uprights. Slot the top of each upright to slip into the two appropriately notched crossbars. These four uprights and two crossbars can be assembled in about 30 seconds to produce a table-height workhorse. —*Norman Odell, Quathiaski Cove, B.C.*

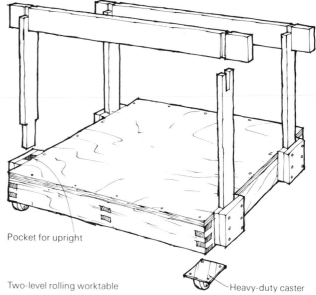

Pocket for upright

Two-level rolling worktable

Heavy-duty caster

Portable sawhorse

This sawhorse design doesn't look very strong, but it will stand up to all but the most demanding jobs. Because they are light and fold flat, the horses are perfect to take along to the job site. You'll wonder how you put up with those awkward 2x4 horses for so long.

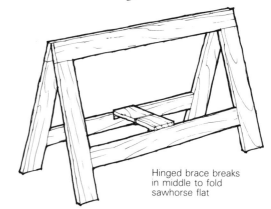

Hinged brace breaks
in middle to fold
sawhorse flat

I used white pine for all parts, and doweled the joints. You could certainly make a stronger horse by using oak or maple and joining parts with mortise and tenon. After three years of service, however, my dowel joints are still tight. Make sure the hinges don't stick up above the top rail of the sawhorse, and be careful not to cut into the hinges when you work. —*Brad Schwartz, Huntington Beach, Calif.*

Two plywood dollies

Struggling with sheets of plywood is a real strain on my back, so I built this plywood dolly that makes handling those sheets easy. When I bring plywood to my shop in my pickup truck, I wheel the dolly up to the back of the truck with the cradle locked in the horizontal position. Then I slide the plywood from the truck onto the dolly with the long edge of the sheet resting against the foot. To tilt the cradle for transporting I just tap the locking bar with my foot to allow the cradle to swing to the vertical position. The cradle, when loaded with plywood, is almost evenly balanced but with a little more weight on the side with the foot. That way the cradle always tips the right way. When I wheel the plywood up to the saw, I tilt the cradle back to the horizontal position where the locking bar falls into a notch and locks. Since the dolly is the same height as my saw I can feed the plywood directly into the saw from the dolly. —*R.W. North, Burbank, Calif.*

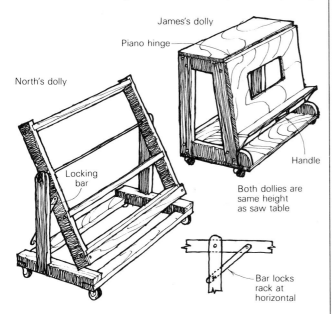

North's dolly

Locking bar

James's dolly

Piano hinge

Handle

Both dollies are same height as saw table

Bar locks rack at horizontal

I've used the dolly sketched above right for years to handle large, heavy panels. I use it to tilt the panels up to the top of my table saw and unload panels from my truck. It also serves as a roll-around stepladder and a portable work surface. —*Ben James, Jacksonville, Fla.*

Making stationary tools portable

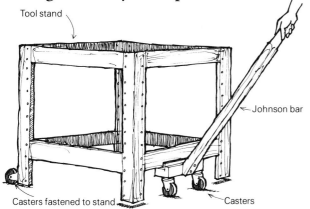

Tool stand

Johnson bar

Casters fastened to stand

Casters

I do my woodworking in the garage, so when I'm through for the day the tools must be moved to make room for the car. For this I use a homemade Johnson bar—a small two-wheel trolley. I made the Johnson bar from heavy-duty casters, a short length of angle iron and a couple of pieces of scrap wood. I insert the trolley under the tool stand, and lever the handle down to jack up the tool stand on its own set of two fixed casters. —*Jerome A. Jahnke, Milwaukee, Wis.*

Folding saw-dolly

I have to share my shop space with an automobile and other "foreign objects" so from time to time I have to move my

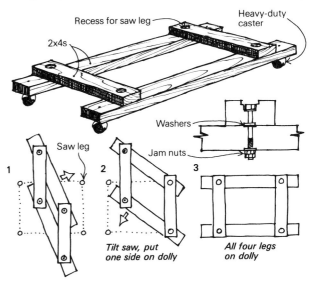

Recess for saw leg

Heavy-duty caster

2x4s

Washers

Jam nuts

Saw leg

1   2   3

Tilt saw, put one side on dolly

All four legs on dolly

table saw, which is on a four-legged, sheet-metal stand. To avoid having to drag the saw across the floor, I made a dolly that collapses like a pantograph. The folding action allows me to load the saw on the dolly one side at a time as shown in the sequence above.—*Robert E. Warren, Camarillo, Calif.*

Portable benches

Shown below are two valuable additions to my shop. The sawhorse on the left is fitted with a small bench vise. I keep small power tools in the tray, and store hand tools in the drawers below. Because of the three legs and the extra weight

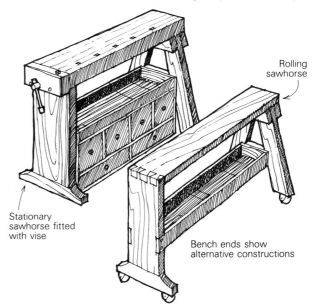

Rolling sawhorse

Stationary sawhorse fitted with vise

Bench ends show alternative constructions

the horse is very stable. A short board can be clamped between the dogs. For longer work, the caster-fitted second horse rolls easily into position to support the distant end. —*S. Grandstaff, Happy Camp, Calif.*

Portable table saw

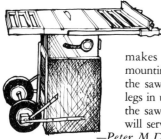

I have fitted wheels to my table saw, as shown in the sketch at left. The arrangement makes the saw portable (without mounting it on a dolly), but allows the saw to sit on its own four stable legs in use. You can fit handles under the saw table, or extended fence rails will serve the same purpose.

—Peter M.D. Darbishire, Hensall, Ont.

Homemade bench vise

Unless you're lucky enough to own a European workbench with well-designed, sturdy vises, you are likely relying on inadequate ways of holding your work. Most commercially available wood vises are too small. And it is awkward to hold workpieces vertically because the center screw is in the way.

My alternative to the commercial vises is shown in the sketch below. It is a simple, inexpensive, effective means of

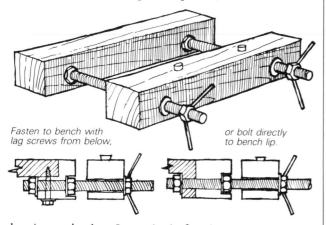

Fasten to bench with lag screws from below,

or bolt directly to bench lip.

keeping work where I want it. At first the two wing-nut vise screws might appear to be inconvenient, but in most cases you can hold narrow stock by tightening only one screw. In fact, because of the independent movement allowed by two screws, it is routine to secure work with non-parallel sides.

The feature that has been most useful is the ability to hold panels up to 17 in. wide in a vertical position right down to the floor. This feature is invaluable for planing end grain and cutting dovetails and tenons.

I made my vise from two 24-in. lengths of 4x4 scrap hardwood, salvaged from a freight skid, and two 19-in. long sections of 1-in. threaded rod with matching nuts and washers. A friend spot-welded the wing handles on two of the nuts. You could epoxy the nuts into wooden wings instead. Be sure to angle the handles away from the jaw.

Drill 1-in. holes in the rear jaw, but drill $1\frac{3}{16}$-in. holes in the front jaw to allow for free jaw movement. Be sure to align the holes properly. I clamped both jaws together and drilled through one jaw, allowing the tip of my drill bit to register the hole in the other jaw.

—Joe Loverti, Miamisburg, Ohio

Leg vise

For years I have admired in museums and photographs those sturdy, simple contraptions I call leg vises. They are mounted at one end of a bench, in front of and parallel to its front leg, and are as high as the top of the bench. This type of vise was prevalent in old woodshops both in this country and abroad. A day at a bench equipped with one and you begin to understand its previous popularity and question its present scarcity.

This vise can be adjusted to hold at various angles and gains much of its holding power from simple leverage. It is capable of holding much larger pieces of wood, both in width and thickness, than most commercial bench vises can. Because the bottom of the front jaw is on the floor and the rear jaw is the bench itself, it is quite stable (or as stable as your bench) and will withstand great abuse from pounding. With the addition of a few holes and a peg or two in the other front leg, you can support long boards on edge. Hardware can be had from $15 to $20 from well-stocked tool suppliers such as Woodcraft Supply Corp., P.O. Box 4000, Woburn, Mass. 01888. But for less than half that price you can have a leg vise with features that standard bench screws don't allow.

You will need a piece of wood about $3\frac{1}{2}$ in. by $3\frac{1}{2}$ in. by the height of your bench, a pipe-clamp or bar-clamp fixture, a piece of pine 1 in. by 4 in. by 12 in., a dowel, a couple of wood screws and a few hand tools. For wood I've used common 4/4 fir, but anything you have will work. Softwoods can be fitted with hardwood faces at the inside top for better wear. The lower adjustment shown in the diagram works the same as the second screw on a handscrew works. It enables you to keep the vise faces parallel, or at the angles you need. The hole in the upper part of the vise must be elliptical to allow for changes in the relationship of the pipe to the jaw. These changes take place only vertically, so the width of the ellipse should match the outside diameter of the pipe, usually $\frac{3}{4}$ in. I bore two holes at 75° off horizontal, intersecting at the center of the wood. This gives a round hole in the center of the piece and ellipses at the outer edges. Cutting two parallel holes also works but is sloppy.

With this bar-clamp system, you get quick action by releasing the bar at the stationary fixture behind the bench leg. Simply pushing closes the vise on whatever is in it. A quick, short twist of the crank and all is secure.

—Craig Schoppe, Arlington, Vt.

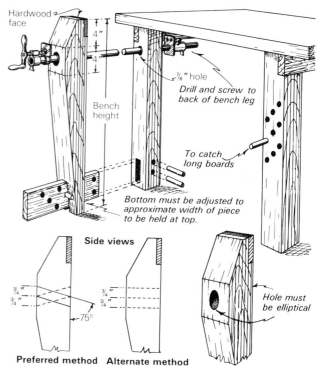

Hardwood face

4"

4"

Bench height

$\frac{7}{8}$" hole

Drill and screw to back of bench leg

To catch long boards

Bottom must be adjusted to approximate width of piece to be held at top.

Side views

$\frac{3}{4}$"
$\frac{3}{4}$"
75°

$\frac{3}{4}$"
$\frac{3}{4}$"

Preferred method   Alternate method

Hole must be elliptical

Improved leg-vise adjustment

On all the leg vises I've seen, to change the jaw opening you have to wiggle a pin out of a hole near the floor and fiddle it back into the next hole. Here's a design with fixed pins you can work with your foot—just step on the adjustment foot and it disengages, then kick the bottom of the moving jaw to where you want it.

The trick is to make the adjustment foot not out of wood but out of ¼-in. aluminum plate scavenged or from a sheet-metal dealer. To make the slots, drill a series of holes in the plate and saw into them from the edges with a hacksaw or a bandsaw. You can saw most aluminum alloys on the bandsaw with regular wood-cutting blades. Aluminum tends to grab drill bits, so clamp the adjustment foot down before you begin drilling. —*Geraldo Bennuccio, Oakland, Calif.*

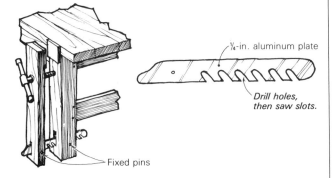

¼-in. aluminum plate

Drill holes,
then saw slots.

Fixed pins

Holding dogs

For those woodworkers who want to use a piece of hardwood in place of ready-made bench dogs made of metal, there is a problem of holding them in the rectangular hole in the work-

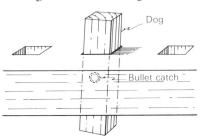

Dog

Bullet catch

bench. A perfect solution is the bullet half of a bullet catch. The spring inside the bullet exerts enough force to hold the dog in place. —*Edmund H. Anthon, Akron, Ohio*

Plastic collars for bench dogs

This round bench-dog design is the simplest I've seen and yet provides additional benefits. Make the dog by slipping a short length of transparent plastic laboratory tubing over one end of a ½-in. or ¾-in. dowel. If the tubing is the right size, it will hold tight without glue. If loose, fasten the collar to the dowel with rubber cement. The compliant plastic adjusts to non-parallel edges and firmly grips odd-shaped pieces. It won't mar even soft woods, and if damaged by an errant chisel (which emerges unnicked from the encounter), the collar is easily replaced.

—*Thomas K. Dykstra, Rochester, N.Y.*

Auxiliary vise

When I acquired a large European workbench, I decided to make an auxiliary vise similar to the one made by Ulmia. Held in the right-hand end vise, the auxiliary vise clamps thin

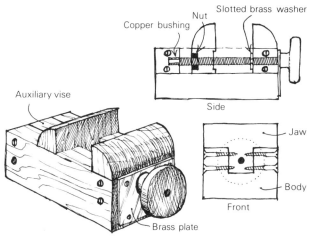

Copper bushing

Nut

Slotted brass washer

Side

Auxiliary vise

Jaw

Body

Front

Brass plate

boards or molding for planing. My version uses maple, a piece of ⅛-in. thick brass, a small handwheel and a length of ordinary ⅜-in. threaded rod.

Make the body of the vise by cutting a 1-in. channel in a maple 2x3. Or glue up two or three pieces of maple into a *U*. Attach the fixed front jaw and the end block with bolts or screws driven in from the sides. Screw the brass plate to the front of the vise to prevent wear by the knob and threaded rod. Drill a hole through the vise and install the threaded rod and movable jaw as shown in the sketch. I reduced the diameter of the end of the rod and bushed the end block with copper tubing. Recess a nut into the back side of the movable jaw and pin the nut in place with a couple of fine screws, or epoxy it. To keep the threaded rod from slipping out of the vise, file a notch around the rod just inside the front jaw and force a slotted brass washer around the notch as a retainer. Recess the front of the movable jaw to accommodate the washer. —*Ralph Luman, Virginia Beach, Va.*

Improved wooden dog

A couple of years ago, we furnished our Tage Frid style workbenches with these maple dogs. They are strong, easy to make and adjustable to any height.

Cut the dog to rough shape, sizing it for a loose fit. Then drill a hole through the dog so that it won't split when you wedge it open. Next cut the dog's body with a bandsaw to the drilled hole. Wedge layers of thin veneer in the kerf until the two halves are flared enough to hold the dog securely.

—*Michael L. Sandiland and
Phil Holland, Vancouver, B.C.*

All-wood bench dogs

Here's a simple, inexpensive way to make bench dogs of wood, including the spring. First cut the dog to shape, as shown in the drawing at right. Then saw a kerf at the lower end of the dog and insert a wooden tongue of the same thickness as the sawcut. Simply press the tongue into place, don't glue it. When it breaks, it will be easy to replace.

—*Michel Petrin, Ste.-Marie Salome, Quebec*

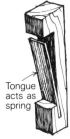

Tongue
acts as
spring

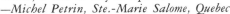

Clamps

Chapter 3

Making clamps

For many people who aren't professional cabinetmakers, wooden clamps are in the luxury-tool class. Good commercially made handscrews cost at least $10 in the 8-in. size. Materials to make one cost less than $2.

Make the jaws from maple or another dense hardwood. The ½-in. holes must be carefully drilled square to the jaw surface and the same distance apart. The spindles are 5⁄16-in. steel bar. Thread one end 5/16-18 right-handed, and the opposite end 5/16-18 left-handed. Make the 5-in. long

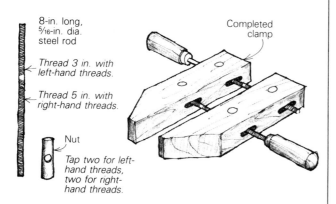

8-in. long, 5⁄16-in. dia. steel rod

Thread 3 in. with left-hand threads.

Thread 5 in. with right-hand threads.

Nut

Tap two for left-hand threads, two for right-hand threads.

Completed clamp

thread right-handed on one spindle, and left-handed on the other. The 3-in. thread is also reversed. Make the nuts from ½-in. round bar. Be sure the tapped holes are square to the axis of the bar. Small file handles will work well if you don't have a lathe. Drill through the ferrule and spindle and insert a small pin after assembly.

—*Richard E. Price, Seattle, Wash.*

Inexpensive homemade clamp

When you run out of clamps and money at the same time, these simple old-timers can be quickly made from wood scraps and an old leather belt. Make up several sizes of end-blocks to keep the front jaws roughly parallel.

—*Larry Humes, Everson, Wash.*

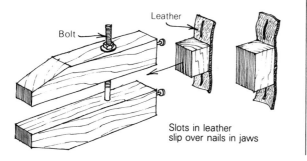

Leather

Bolt

Slots in leather slip over nails in jaws

Deep-throat clamp

If you need a deep-throat clamp and none is available, substitute a conventional C-clamp and two blocks of wood arranged as in the sketch below. Though direct pressure is less than with expensive specialty clamps, the system works fine for gluing inlays, guitar bridges and other simple joints.

—*Bob Osbahr, Tucson, Ariz.*

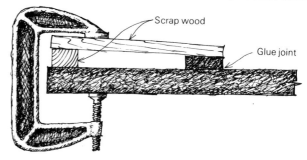

Scrap wood

Glue joint

Toolmaker's clamp

I've seen several wooden clamp designs—but none similar to what machinists know as a toolmaker's clamp. It is constructed like a standard wooden clamp but uses fixed bearing surfaces in place of the left-handed threaded rods and the barrel-nuts. Because the toolmaker's clamp uses standard hardware-store threaded rod, it is much easier to build. Only a right-hand tap and drill bits are needed to complete the metal work.

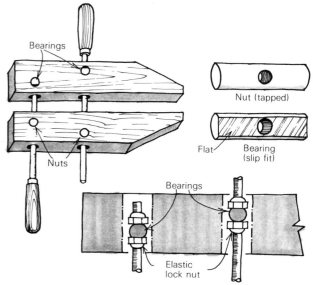

Bearings

Nut (tapped)

Flat

Bearing (slip fit)

Nuts

Bearings

Elastic lock nut

Although the barrel-nuts can be made from either brass or steel, make the bearings out of brass (steel would soon gall the thrust surfaces). File a flat on each side of the two bearings and turn the flat toward the side that takes the thrust. The thrust-nuts that bear up against the bearings must be locked into position on the threaded rod. I found that elastic lock-nuts work well, but a pair of jam-nuts or a single nut brazed to the threaded rod could be substituted.

Both barrel-nuts must be located in one jaw and both bearings in the other jaw to get the standard tightening and loosening rotation. It will take twice as many turns to close the toolmaker's clamp, but you get twice the clamping force for the same tightening torque.

—*Larry Pagendarm, Santa Clara, Calif.*

And more clamps

Perhaps some readers might be interested in making some adjustable clamps entirely of wood, as I have done. The dimensions can be varied to suit one's needs.

These clamps don't operate quite like the metal-threaded ones since both screws are right-handed. However, I have found them to be quite satisfactory. In use one tightens the

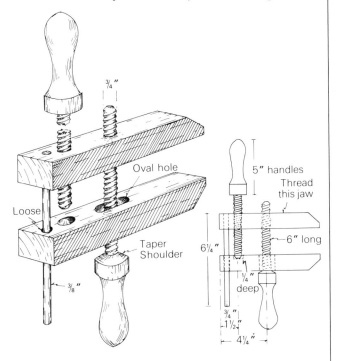

inner screw to clamp the work, then secures the jaws by spreading the outer screw. The small dowel serves as a guide rod to keep the loose jaw in alignment. The hole in the loose jaw should be oval to permit angular pieces to be clamped. Of course, hard maple or other dense wood should be used.
—*Arvle E. Marshall, Watkinsville, Ga.*

Clothespin clamps

I make heavy-duty clothespin clamps from two hardwood sticks (½ in. square by 7 in. long), a short ⅝-in. dowel fulcrum, and a heavy rubber band (about ¼ in. by 4 in. long). The dowel fulcrum fits in slight hollows filed in the sticks about one-third the way from the front. Dull the sharp edges of the sticks, then double the rubber band around the two sticks in front of the fulcrum as many times as possible.

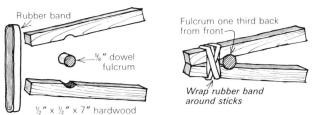

I use this clamp as described for gluing the linings onto the sides of musical instruments. But by making a few changes the same basic clamp can be used for other applications. For example, different jaw capacities or parallel-jaw clamping can be achieved by using different sized fulcrums. The weight of the rubber band can be varied for more or less clamping pressure. The jaws can be notched to clamp unusually shaped work. —*Bart Brush, Cherry Valley, N.Y.*

Less is more

I have any number of expensive, cumbersome, time-consuming holddown clamps for carving, but this rig beats them all. I discovered it while visiting China last summer. It's an easy

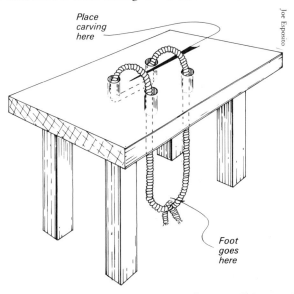

way to hold down a piece that has to be moved frequently, for carving and fine work. It even could be made deluxe with straps and a foot rest. —*W.D. Young, Scotch Plains, N.J.*

Gripping thin wood

When I hand-plane thin wood on edge, it often gets away from me. This V-cut support block is like having an extra hand. I screw the block to the bench or fit it with dowels that mate with holes in the benchtop. You should arrange the dowels near the mouth of the V and angle them back slightly so the block won't shift as you plane.

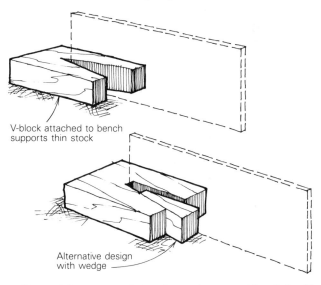

You might try a variation by cutting one side of the V parallel to the work and using a wedge for a positive grip. A pull on the workpiece releases the wedge.
—*Percy W. Blandford, Stratford-Upon-Avon, England*

Picture-frame clamp

This is my no-cost solution for clamping a picture frame: Clamp all four pieces at once with a length of nylon cord. Measure the outside perimeter of the frame and tie a non-slip knot so the cord will just fit around. Then use four or more scrap blocks between the cord and the frame to stretch the cord tight and draw up the joints. Pieces of cardboard or leather folded over the corners prevent the cord from digging in. If the frame twists when tensioned, place

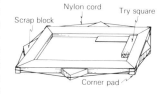

a weighted piece of plywood on top—after you have tested the squareness of the frame. (Try the procedure dry first, to spot bad joints). On narrow frames, use eight blocks, all located near the corners. With white glue, heavy clamping pressure is not required to make a solid, lasting joint.

—*Duane Waskow, Marion, Iowa*

Another no-cost picture-frame clamp

My modification of Duane Waskow's picture-frame clamp (above) uses a tourniquet to apply pressure at the glue joints. To make the clamp, cut four *L*-shaped clamping blocks from ¾-in. pine and groove the outside edges of the blocks a little wider than the rope diameter. Then round, smooth and wax the grooves to minimize friction. Cut or drill a circular area at the inside corner of the blocks to allow for slight inaccuracies (which accumulate at that point) and to permit excess glue to escape. When you're ready to glue, place a piece of waxed paper under each block to prevent it from becoming glued to the frame.

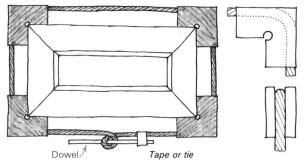

Dowel   *Tape or tie*

For the rope, choose something with a little stretch—I use ⅛-in. nylon. Tie a loop in the rope just long enough so that it can barely be snapped over the blocks. This will hold the frame together while final adjustments are made in the glue joints. When the joints are right, twist a dowel onto the rope and turn it to produce whatever pressure is desired. The leverage is tremendous so don't overdo it. It's a good idea to put a weight on the frame while you're applying pressure. If one corner comes up a little, the whole assembly may twist and fly apart.

When the pressure is sufficient, tape or tie the dowel to the rope. Always maintain a tight grip on the dowel—it can unwind with surprising force.

—*H.N. Capen, Granada Hills, Calif.*

One-clamp frame clamp

This picture-frame clamp beats anything else I've tried. Make the device from ¾-in. thick, 2-in. wide hardwood strips. I covered the hardwood with smooth Formica for extra strength and for freer action of the parts. You'll need four 16-in. legs, two 4-in. connectors and four 2-in. discs notched to hold the corners of the frame.

To use, determine the positions of the notched discs on the

legs through a dry run. When everything is ready, apply pressure to the frame using a parallel-jaw wooden clamp across the center connectors.

—*John L. Van Scoyoc, Bartlesville, Okla.*

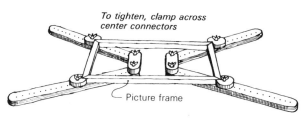

Quick-adjust picture-frame clamp

The key to this quick-adjust picture-frame clamp is the split-nut tighteners, tapped cylinders, which can be opened to disengage from the threaded rod and slid close to the corner

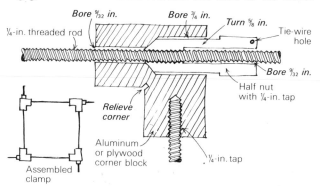

blocks. This allows the clamp to be tightened at any size with only a few turns. The corner blocks can be made from either plywood or aluminum (try the high-school metal shop for casting work). To make the split-nuts, center two pieces of ⅜-in. by ¾-in. by 2-in. cold-drawn steel in the four-jaw chuck of a metal lathe. All operations can be made from this initial setup, except boring the relief and the tie-wire holes. To keep the nut halves in mating pairs, pass a short piece of braided flexible cable (used on radio and TV drum drives) through each nut half and secure each wire end with a ball of solder.

—*Brad Dimon, Swanton, Vt.*

Quick-adjust picture-frame clamp-nut

To make this clamp-nut, tap a ¾-in. section of ¾-in. aluminum or steel rod. Then cut through the tapped hole on an angle with an end-mill cutter to clear the threads. Use a ¹⁷⁄₆₄-in. end-mill cutter for a ¼-in. tap and a ²⁵⁄₆₄-in. cutter for a ⅜-in. tap.

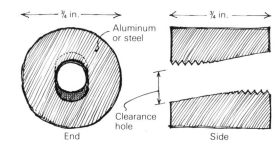

To use, tilt the nut on the threaded rod and slide into position for quick adjustment. Then straighten out the nut for fine adjustment and locking. The nut works well not only on picture-frame clamps but also in other locking-knob or quick-adjust situations.

—*Walter W. Yaeger, Maple Shade, N.J.*

Bench clamp

My clamping device extends the top (for holding and clamping) of a small workbench. It can be used in conjunction with a tail vise on the opposite end of the bench or alone with dog holes drilled on line with the clamp head device.

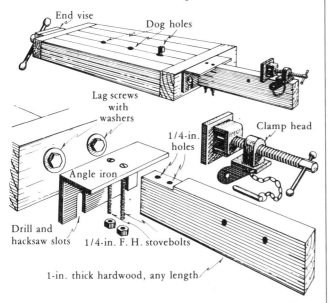

I used 3-in. angle iron 6 in. long with the slots drilled and hacksawed 1 in. from either end. The 3/8x4-in. lag screws were driven through the slots into the end of my workbench so that the angle iron is flush with the top. Tightening and loosening the lag screws facilitates rapid installation and removal. Wooden bars of various lengths are handy for different projects. —*Robert Bessmer, Averill Park, N.Y.*

Horizontal vise

This horizontal vise, installed on a workbench, is indispensable for sanding, routing, carving and planing. For many operations it holds the work better than bench dogs. The vise consists of three simple parts: a bench screw, an oak jaw and a wooden step-block. Mount the bench screw's nut to the bench from the bottom so that the surface will be flat if you remove the vise. Cut the 2-in. thick jaw about 20 in. or so

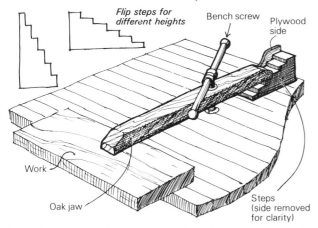

long. Drill an oversize hole in the jaw about 7 in. from the back and fasten the bench screw through the hole. Bandsaw the step-block from a 4x4. Cut the steps taller one way than the other so you can flip the block and use it both ways. To keep the back end of the jaw from slipping off the sides of the step-block, glue a piece of plywood to each side.
—*Pendleton Tompkins, San Mateo, Calif.*

Homemade bar clamps

You can never have too many bar clamps. But a woodworker's cash usually goes toward tools and machinery, leaving clamps for another day. The homemade model below, though made from light, cheap material, will do most (though not

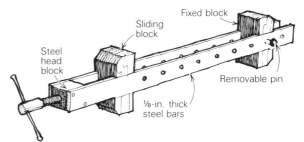

all) things a bar clamp will do. The two bars are made of mild steel, 3/4 in. wide by 1/8 in. thick. Clamp the two bars together and drill 1/4-in. holes spaced 1 1/2 in. apart. Make the head block from a 3/4-in. cube of steel tapped for a 3/8-in. threaded rod. With the head block carefully lined up and clamped in position, fasten it to the bars by welding, brazing or riveting.

Make the 2 1/4-in. by 1-in. by 1-in. sliding block and the fixed block from any dense hardwood. Cut a 1/8-in. deep groove on each side of the blocks to give a sliding fit between the bars. Drill a shallow 3/8-in. hole in the sliding block to take the end of the threaded rod. So the rod won't continually bore its way into the wood, force a pellet of 3/8-in. steel into the bottom of the hole.

Braze a short length of pipe onto the end of the threaded rod and drill it to accept a tommy bar of 1/4-in. steel rod. Peen the ends of the tommy bar to keep it from falling out of the hole. In use, the work is slid between the bars to ensure even clamping pressure, and the fixed block is moved and pinned in the appropriate place for the width of the work.

This clamp will handle work up to 3/4 in. thick and perhaps 24 in. wide. The clamp could be scaled up using heavier materials for thicker or wider applications.

An alternative use for the clamp is to prevent "spelching" (the splitting off of the end grain during hand planing). Move the clamp to the edge of the board so its blocks are flush with the end grain. The clamp may be used many times before its wood blocks need replacing.
—*Robert Wearing, Shropshire, England*

Rubber clamps

Over the years I have refinished several old pieces with delicate curved surfaces and very hard-to-redo finishes, where normal clamps just won't work well. I tried string tourniquets with not too great results. Aviation bungee cord worked well but is expensive and hard to find. Now I use tire tubes cut in long ribbons. Bound around any surface, they conform to shape and apply a very satisfactory even pressure. The more wraps, the more pressure. I cut ribbons about 1 1/2 in. wide, stretch each wrap as tightly as I can and tie off the end with an overlap. —*C. H. Dimmick, Sparta, N.J.*

Gain two clamps

In exchange for a little ingenuity you can gain two large-capacity, versatile clamps: your drill press and lathe. Just clamp the work between quill and drill-press table or between headstock and tailstock (remove centers).
—*Michael Bavlsik, Paterson, N.J.*

Homemade bench-top clamp

An inexpensive and fast-acting clamp for securing work to jigs and bench tops can be made from a bolt, a straight mending plate of corresponding strength, a wing nut, two washers, a nut and a wedge. Choose a bolt of sufficient diameter for your application. If the wood in which the clamp is to sit is thick enough and a permanently protruding bolt will not be objectionable, a hanger bolt will make installation simpler. If you have to, enlarge the first hole from one of the ends of the mending plate to allow a loose fit with the bolt. Then bend the mending plate about 20° or so at the location of this hole.

To use, unscrew the wing nut so the work and a protective scrap piece can pass below the shorter bent edge of the mending plate. Keeping the bent section parallel to the work surface ensures even pressure and reduces the chances of marring the work. To engage the clamp, simply push in the wooden edge.

To unclamp, first press on the thinnest part of the wedge

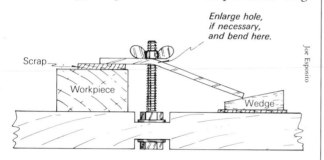

Enlarge hole, if necessary, and bend here.

Scrap

Workpiece

Wedge

Joe Esposito

and rotate that point far enough to let you get your fingers below the plate. Then ease the pressure by lifting up the plate and withdrawing the wedge.

—*Blake Raines, Springfield, Pa.*

Bench-top clamps

My bench has two rows of holes, along the front and back edges. These accommodate lengths of ¾-in. pipe, standing vertically, each fitted with extension-clamps of the Sears variety. Two or more clamps may thus be mounted in conjunction with cross members for clamping frames, boxes, chests or chairs in gluing position. Four or more clamps form a light-duty veneer press against the bench top.

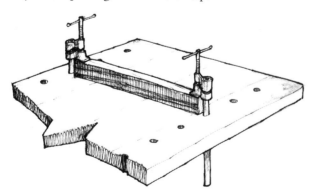

The advantage of this gluing method is that the work is always held true and square because the bench is a flat reference surface.

The holes for the pipe clamps are spaced about 8 in. apart. A crosspiece between two clamps may be used as a bench stop in conjunction with the stop on the tail vise, thereby holding long pieces of wood on the bench.

—*Harold F. Lathrop, Milan, Ill.*

Blocks for pipe clamps

To avoid the frantic search for clamping blocks while gluing up, I have designed blocks that remain in place on my pipe clamps. I cut a hole in the block the same diameter as the

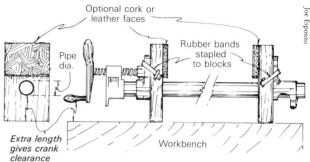

Optional cork or leather faces

Pipe dia.

Rubber bands stapled to blocks

Extra length gives crank clearance

Workbench

Joe Esposito

pipe. The block slides onto the clamp and is held in place with a rubber band, making it easy to remove. I made the blocks longer on the bottom to allow for the swing of the crank when the clamp is set on the bench and tightened. The blocks extend above and beyond the clamp to distribute pressure over a wide area, and to make a wider base for the clamp to rest on when set on the workbench. —*David Raynalds, Eugene, Ore.*

Magnetic pipe-clamp pads

The best pipe-clamp pads I've seen were made by facing hardboard with sticky-back magnetic tape. The hardboard is hard enough to resist deforming yet soft enough to not mark softer woods like walnut and mahogany. The magnetic tape holds the pads in place better than a third hand, yet the pads are easily removed. Magnetic tape (I used 3M Plastiform brand) can be obtained locally at sign shops and some hardware stores, or it can be mail-ordered from Woodcraft Supply, PO Box 4000, Woburn, Mass. 01888.

—*Mike Graetz, Lakeland, Minn.*

Clamping wide boards

In bookcase construction and other large-carcase work, it is often necessary to join wide boards in an *H*. Without special clamps it is difficult to achieve the necessary clamping pressure. This simple crowned caul, used with ordinary bar clamps, solves the problem.

To make the caul, select a 1-in. thick, 2-in. wide block as

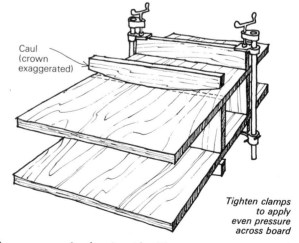

Caul (crown exaggerated)

Tighten clamps to apply even pressure across board

long as your lumber is wide. Plane a crown on one edge, leaving the center high and each end about a degree lower. Now lay the caul, crown edge down, across the width of the board to be clamped. As you apply pressure to each end with bar clamps, the end-gaps will close, resulting in even pressure across the joint. —*David Shaffer, Silvercliff, Colo.*

Clamping boxes

Clamping and squaring large box pieces can be a problem. The pressure of the clamps will often pull the piece out of square at the critical moment of final tightening. The first hint is quite obvious but often forgotten: Get all the parts ready to glue and assemble, have all your clamps extended to the length you will need, and tape your softwood clamping blocks either to the work or to the clamp faces before applying any glue. Proper preparation will always save precious time.

After assembling, tighten opposing clamps in small increments. When the pieces are just snug, measure the diagonals

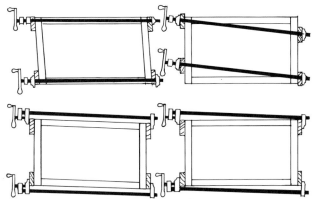

Out-of-square boxes, left, can be aligned by repositioning clamps to oppose the pull, as shown at right.

for squareness. A folding rule with a slide extension is indispensable here. If the work is out of square, move the clamps slightly to oppose the pull, i.e., make the clamps pull more parallel to the longer diagonal. A very small movement will make a lot of difference.

This process becomes much more complicated if all four sides of the rectangle are open and being glued at once. But I have clamped together a post-and-rail crib with all four sides openwork and no top or bottom. Using eight clamps, I pulled it square in all directions at once. A final hint, which most know: Don't wipe the glue. It will be much easier to chip it off the surface than to sand it out of the pores later.
—George Pilling, Springville, Calif.

Clamping with bedsprings

Old bedsprings make excellent—and cheap—clamps for hard-to-clamp jobs, such as clamping veneer on curved surfaces. They can also be used for small solid wood patches. Springs can be cut to a variety of sizes, then bent to put pressure in the exact spot needed. A piece of Saran wrap and a block of wood placed over the veneer will give more even clamping pressure, without marring the work. A word of caution: Bedspring clamps can suddenly spring off, if wrongly placed.
—Robert S. Friedensen, Winston-Salem, N.C.

Long clamps

For an extra-long clamp, thread the ends of two pipe clamps and join them together with a pipe coupling.
—Murray Godfrey, Moncton, N.B.

Vacuum clamping system

If you have a central dust-collection system in your shop, a simple addition to it will provide a useful clamping system. Cut a 5-in. hole through the top of your bench, rabbet the

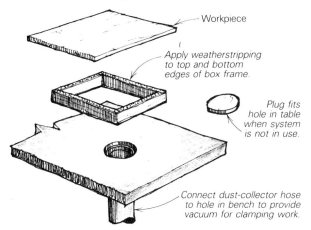

Workpiece

Apply weatherstripping to top and bottom edges of box frame.

Plug fits hole in table when system is not in use.

Connect dust-collector hose to hole in bench to provide vacuum for clamping work.

edge of the hole with a router, and cut a hardwood plug to fit flush—it will leave the bench smooth when you're not using the clamp. Connect your dust-collection system to the bottom of the hole with whatever piping is necessary.

To use the clamp, make a box frame, and cover the top and bottom edges with self-adhesive foam weatherstripping. Place the box on the bench over the hole, place the workpiece on top of the box, and turn the vacuum on. The workpiece will be held firmly for edge-routing, sanding and other operations, with nothing to obstruct work on all four edges. Because of the padding offered by the weatherstripping, this is an ideal way to hold flat panels for sanding between coats of finish. The hole in the bench has a side benefit: it makes cleaning shavings off the bench easier and faster.
—Mac Campbell, Harvey Station, N.B.

Spur dogs for clamping miters

Here is a method that allows you to clamp up mitered edges. The method is based on a spur dog, a device that provides a perch for C-clamps and spreads clamping pressure evenly over the joint. To make the dogs, cut several pairs of 3-in. sections from a length of 1-in. angle iron. In each section, hacksaw two 5/16-in. deep slots about 1/2 in. from each end of one side. Bend the two tabs down about 3/32 in. and file the spurs sharp, as shown in the sketch.

Spur dog

To use, spread glue on both faces of the miter and press together for a light tack. Tap the two (or more) dogs into place and clamp. The spurs enter the wood grain about 1/8 in. and therefore leave small scars on the wood. These scars can be removed by rounding over the corner, or they can be closed up some by steaming. You might decide to simply tolerate them.
—Peter Bird, Midhurst, Ont.

Spanish luthier's clamp

I know of no simpler, cheaper or more convenient method to clamp up edge joints than the Spanish luthier's technique for joining guitar tops and backs. Though intended for thin wood, the technique is easily adaptable to any thickness, width or length required. All that is needed are several long wedges, a few 1x2s (longer than the work is wide) and a length of ¼-in. rope.

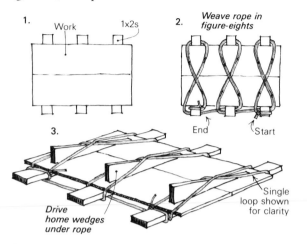

When the work is ready to be glued, lay it on the 1x2s as shown. Tie the rope to the right-hand stick and weave it over the work and around both ends in a figure-eight. The diagram above shows one figure-eight loop for clarity but several are necessary. Moving to each 1x2 in turn, repeat weaving the figure-eights, tying off the rope on the last stick.

Now insert the wedges under the middle of the figure-eights and drive them home with a mallet. This will apply clamping pressure without danger of the wood buckling and damage to the edge. Wax the wedges and 1x2s to prevent their being glued to the work by squeeze-out. The whole process is fast, but it's advisable to practice a few times to get the hang of the rope weaving.

—*Douglass Peoples, Arlington, Va.*

Clamping a scarf joint

A scarf joint can be securely clamped as shown: After spreading the glue, tack the pieces to be joined with pin brads (#16/18) cut to ¼ in. long. Then sandwich the pieces be-

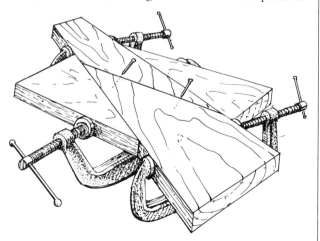

tween wedges made of soft, wet wood. While one C-clamp applies pressure directly on the surfaces to be joined, two others hold the wedges in position.

—*Price G. Schulte, St. Louis, Mo.*

Clamping segmented turning blanks

Worm-screw hose clamps make good, inexpensive gluing clamps for segmented turning blanks or other cylindrical gluing jobs. The clamps are available in hardware and automotive supply stores in sizes up to 6 in. in diameter. For larger diameters simply screw two clamps together head-to-tail, or cut the band and install steel wire to extend the clamp's

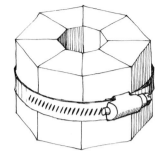

circumference. Marks and dents can be avoided by placing cardboard or wooden pads between the clamp and the work.

—*W. L. Chess, Washington, Conn.*

Assembling staved cylinders

Here's a method based on the principle of canvas-backed tambours that simplifies the assembly of staved cylinders. Lay the staves side by side on a flat surface and carefully align the ends. Apply rows of tape (I use 2-in. wide plastic tape) to the outside surface. Turn the assembly over, apply glue to the stave edges and roll up the cylinder. Apply a strap clamp to complete the job.

—*Pope Lawrence, Santa Fe, N. Mex.*

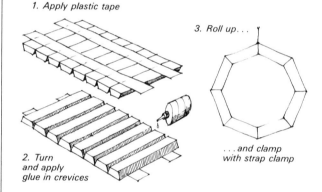

Veneering cylinders

Paul Villiard in *A Manual of Veneering* makes two suggestions, among others, for veneering cylinders. (1) Use photographic print flattening solution to make the veneer flexible; and (2) clamp the veneer by wrapping the veneered cylinder in several layers of friction tape.

After veneering a large tapered cylinder, I offer these comments: (1) The print flattening solution produced very good results on a wavy and brittle zebrano veneer 1/28 in. thick. (2) As an alternative to friction tape, I used strips of rubber bicycle inner tube. The strips are cut about ½ in. to ¾ in. wide from an old tube. The strips should be cut as long as possible in a continuous cut around the tube. The strips are then stretched as tightly as possible around the veneered cylinder after gluing. I found I was able to get a much tighter wrap with one layer of rubber than with several layers of tape. And the rubber strips are reusable and virtually free if discard tubes are used.

—*David J. Lutrick, Seattle, Wash.*

Veneering with sandbags

The easiest way to apply even pressure on veneer being glued to a curved surface such as a serpentine drawer front is to use several pillow sacks filled with sand. Store the sandbags near the stove. Their warmth will shorten the glue-curing time.

—*Stanton James, El Paso, Tex.*

Veneering convex workpieces

Here is an alternative to a custom-fitted caul for veneering curved work. The device will cope with a wide range of convex forms, is quickly made in any size and requires much less material and construction effort than a specially shaped caul.

Take a piece of hardwood slightly longer than but not quite as wide as the item to be veneered. Tap the board for wooden screws to provide pressure along the midline at about

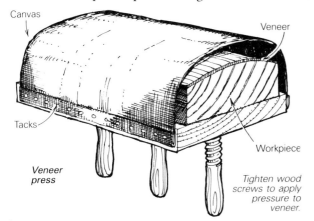

Canvas

Veneer

Tacks

Veneer press

Workpiece

Tighten wood screws to apply pressure to veneer.

6-in. centers. (You could use wedges or threaded rods and nuts if you have no threading tools.) Tack a strip of stout canvas along both edges to form a tube as shown in the illustration. Place the veneered workpiece in the tube and tighten the screws. A glance at the open ends will show when the tube is taut and has clamped the veneer against the base. Put aside to dry. Tubes of various sizes can be built up sharing the same wooden screws.

—*R.W. Shillitoe, Ilkley, West Yorkshire, England*

Holding irregular shapes

A simple pegboard table will help hold irregular shapes in place. All you need is a sheet of ¼-in. pegboard for the top, a can of ¼-in. dowels in various lengths and a can of softwood wedges. Put the work anywhere on the pegboard, press in the dowels around the piece and take up the slack with the wedges.
—*Dennis J. Teepe, Lawrence, Kan.*

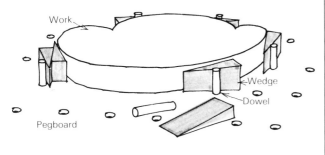

Work

Wedge

Dowel

Pegboard

Gluing

Chapter 4

Repairing cracks

In the process of repairing furniture or using seasoned lumber we occasionally encounter a split board. Depending on the severity of the crack and the value of the lumber, it is sometimes desirable to repair the crack. A vacuum cleaner, masking tape, clamps and glue can accomplish this. Tape over the crack, down the end of the board and on the underside of the crack. The object is to create a vacuum.

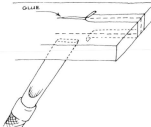

With a crevice tool on the vacuum cleaner, suck the glue into the crack while slowly peeling back the masking tape. Add glue while sliding the crevice tool out to the end of the board. Once the crack is filled with glue, clamp the split closed. The viscosity of the glue is usually sufficient to prevent it from being sucked into the vacuum cleaner hose. To be safe, remove the hose as soon as glue is visible on the underside. A little experimentation will show you how much time, glue and tape to use.

—*Ray Schwenn, Jamesville, N.Y.*

Edge gluing without clamps

Here's how I edge-glue boards using wide masking tape rather than clamps. First be sure your boards mate perfectly; the finished joint is no better than the initial fit. Now with the boards on a flat bench top, pull the joint together and run a strip of tape down the joint, spanning the crack with the tape. Turn the boards over, pull the boards to the edge of the bench and let one board drop a wee bit. Put glue in the open crack and flex the boards like a hinge until the joint is covered with a layer of glue. Slip the boards back on the bench,

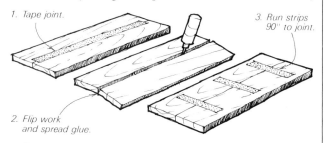

1. Tape joint.

2. Flip work and spread glue.

3. Run strips 90" to joint.

pull the joint together hand-tight and, after pausing a few seconds to allow the excess glue to squeeze out, run two or three strips of tape across the joint at 90°. A distinct advantage of this technique is that the boards don't slip out of position as they sometimes do under clamps.

—*V.L. Luther, Tarrant, Ala.*

BRUCE HOADLEY COMMENTS: Luther's system would, as he suggests, be no better than the quality of surfacing and even-

ness of glue spread. I can believe that a strong joint could be attained, but I don't believe it would consistently equal the strength of a clamped joint. However, most glue joints are far stronger than they need to be.

Aside from the strength issue, the taping approach has some important advantages in handling. First, it indexes and holds the pieces conveniently. Second, it enables both surfaces of the joint to be spread simultaneously while controlling the excess from dripping. Third, it eliminates the squeeze-out from at least one face of the assembly, which could be extremely beneficial in later stages. In summary, I think the idea has advantages that would pay dividends when combined with more standard clamping methods.

No-mess epoxy mixing

To mix small amounts of epoxy, simply squeeze equal amounts of resin and hardener into the corner of a plastic sandwich bag. Twist and mix the two until a uniform color appears. Then puncture the bag with a pin and squeeze out the glue. No clean-up is required—just throw the bag away. —*Edgar E. Gardner, Nashua, N.H.*

Darkening glue lines

Glue lines of polyvinyl and aliphatic resin glues (white and yellow) can be darkened with tincture of iodine. This will turn the glue a dark purple, perfect for walnut and dark mahogany. It should be applied after wet sanding as it does not penetrate deeply, but it does go through oil nicely. I have also had good results using it under lacquer.

—*Richard S. Newman, Rochester, N.Y.*

Printers' brayer spreads glue

The best glue spreader I've found is a printers' brayer, a soft-rubber roller available from art supply stores in widths from 1½ in. to 6 in. You don't even have to wash it clean—just roll it over a scrap to get most of the glue off. Next time you use it, any residue will disappear.

—*Floyd Foess, Federal Way, Wash.*

Glue tool for sockets

In assembling doweled joints it is difficult to gauge the right amount of glue for the sockets. If you put in too much, the trapped glue acts as a hydraulic fluid, preventing the joint from pulling up. This simple tool solves the problem by assuring each socket has just the right amount of glue.

Select a short length of dowel the same size as the pins you're using and, with the dowel chucked in a drill, sand slightly undersize. Then saw a narrow kerf through the axis

slightly longer than the hole is deep. To use, apply glue to the sockets, then insert the kerfed dowel in each and twist. The tool squeezes excess glue out of the hole and evenly coats the socket. —*Duane C. Marks, Waltham, Mass.*

Glue-up rack

This inexpensive glue-up rack keeps edge-glued stock perfectly flat under the pressure of bar clamps. The rack is made from industrial framing channel which is available under several trade names (Super Strut and Kindorf are two) at electrical and plumbing-supply houses. You'll need two lengths of channel, four $\frac{3}{8}$-in. spring nuts (made especially for use with the channel), two homemade hold-down boards and other hardware as shown in the sketch.

To make the hold-down boards, glue two 1x3s together with $\frac{1}{2}$-in. spacers between. Plane a slight curve on the bot-

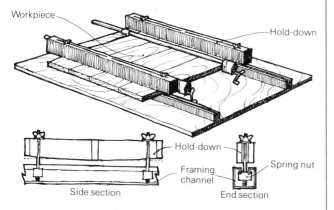

Workpiece

Hold-down

Hold-down

Framing channel

Spring nut

Side section

End section

tom so pressure will be even along their length. Assemble the rack as shown. To use, slide the spring nut/threaded-rod assembly right up against the edge-glued workpiece. Tighten the wing nuts to apply downward pressure and flatten the workpiece. —*Lloyd Winters, Ft. Wayne, Ind.*

Gluing table

A most functional and sturdy gluing table is made of angle irons bolted to a wooden base. Dressers, tabletops and wide boards for beds are easily glued up using such a table. The construction allows easy application of clamps, and the spe-

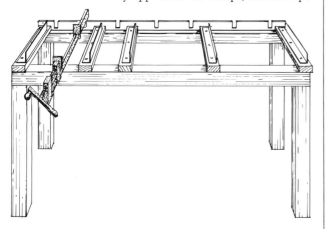

cially notched board at the back even holds bar clamps erect and up against the underside of the boards while you align and level them with one hand and crank the clamp with the other. If the vertical face of the angle iron is too narrow, it must be built up to make room for easy placement of clamps, since at least one will go on the underside of the board. Glue dribbles are easily cleaned off the irons with a few smacks of a hammer after they've dried.

—*James B. Small, Jr., Newville, Pa.*

Palette knife

The best tool I've found for applying glue is a small, flexible artist's palette knife. —*Phil Loomis, Enfield, N.H.*

Toothbrush for glue

I offer the following two tips for spreading glue in holes for dowels and on flat surfaces, as in edge-gluing. For dowel holes, take a piece of pipe cleaner and fold it in half. Put glue into the hole and work it on the sides with the pipe cleaner. Use the pipe cleaner to put glue on the dowels. For edge-gluing, apply a bead of glue from the container and use a toothbrush to brush an even layer of glue on and into the surfaces to be joined. Do not forget to wash out the toothbrush before you brush your teeth; discard the pipe cleaner.

—*Arthur Witt, Jr., Columbia, Mo.*

Spreading glue with a pad painter

The pad painters sold for painting trim are excellent glue spreaders. Their short fibers and stiff backing let you apply a smooth coat of glue faster than with a brush. Dip the pad into a shallow pan of glue or just use the pad to spread glue straight from the bottle. —*Chuck Lakin, Waterville, Maine*

Cut sticks for spreaders

For years I had trouble spreading just the right amount of glue on the edge of boards. Fingers are messy, brushes get hard and the glue bottle's applicator leaves blobs. Recently I discovered that a short, thin piece of scrap will even out the glue perfectly. The sticks work so well it's worth cutting a supply of the 5-in. long, $\frac{1}{8}$-in. thick, $\frac{1}{2}$-in. wide applicators to have on hand. —*Jon Gullett, Washington, Ill.*

Popsicle sticks for glue

The old familiar Popsicle sticks work well for spreading glue. These inexpensive sticks are available in large quantities from craft stores or from restaurant suppliers as coffee stirrers.

—*Larry Joseph, Alva, Okla.*

Glue spreader for lamination

This glue spreader makes easy the tedious job of covering thin laminations with just the right amount of glue. The heart of the spreader is a cork-covered cylinder. The cork has the right

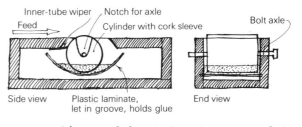

Inner-tube wiper

Notch for axle

Cylinder with cork sleeve

Feed

Bolt axle

Side view

Plastic laminate, let in groove, holds glue

End view

texture to pick up and deposit the right amount of glue. Make the spreader frame from plywood. Cut a semicircular groove in each side of the frame to hold a piece of plastic laminate which acts as a glue reservoir. Notch the sides of the frame so the glue-spreader cylinder can be removed for cleaning. Tack a piece of rubber inner tube to the frame so that it will scrape excess glue from the cylinder as it rotates. I use a commercial white glue mixed with water to get a better consistency for spreading.—*Rod Davidson, Port Angeles, Wash.*

Masking out squeeze-out

Glue squeeze-out problems can be avoided by covering areas near joints with masking tape. Carefully place the tape during final assembly so that it covers the area but doesn't get caught in the joint. This technique is especially useful on the inside corners of joints (drawers, boxes, etc.) where cleanup is a problem. —*Tim Rodeghier, Highland, Ind.*

Removing excess glue

Very often excess glue is not discovered until stain is applied to a project. Then it is not only difficult to remove, but the stain tends to appear darker in the spot where the glue was removed. This is especially true for polyvinyl resin (white) glue, which dries transparent and is difficult to see.

Many of us were taught years ago that excess glue around a joint or on the surface of stock should be wiped off with a wet rag. This is one of the worst things to do—it tends to dilute the glue and washes some of it into the pores where it cannot be sanded off. A better solution when gluing stock together is to allow the glue to gel for five or ten minutes, then scrape it off with a putty knife. Excess glue in difficult-to-clean areas, such as leg and rail joints where the rail or apron is set in from the edge of the leg, presents a challenge, especially for the beginner. A method I use is to dry-clamp first, apply a thin coating of paste wax around the outside of the joint, then remove the clamp, take the joint apart, apply the glue and reclamp. When the glue has dried the excess can easily be removed by lifting with a putty knife or chisel. The wax can be cleaned by washing the area with paint or lacquer thinner, or cleaning solvent. All will remove the wax without raising the grain or staining the wood.

Another good practice prior to staining that will make defects such as glue stains, dents or scratches stand out is to wipe the entire project with a rag that has been saturated in paint or lacquer thinner, or cleaning solvent. The defects should be noted by marking lightly with a pencil. When the surface is dry the areas can be scraped with a hand scraper and/or sanded. —Eric Schramm, Los Gatos, Calif.

Homemade glue bottle

Woodworkers who use white or yellow glue and favor a brush applicator will appreciate this homemade glue bottle. It's unbreakable, practically spill-proof and free. Just cut off the top of a plastic bottle at the shoulder, invert and press in place. As you use the glue be sure to push the top down to eliminate air in the container. Most glue drips will run back into the bottle, but those that don't will peel off easily.
—Carl E. Roos, Pottsville, Pa.

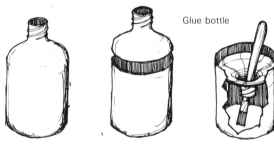

Glue bottle

Plastic bottle   Cut off top at shoulder.   Invert top, press in.

Bending, Steaming & Drying

Chapter 5

Wooden blanket for ribbed bending form

This flexible wooden blanket puts to bed the problem of form squeeze-marks on curved laminated panels. Used in

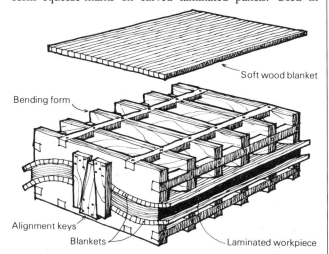

Soft wood blanket

Bending form

Alignment keys

Blankets

Laminated workpiece

pairs (one above, one below), the blankets evenly distribute the pressure between the ribs of the form and smooth out small irregularities.

To make the blankets, saw ½-in. sq. strips of a soft wood (I used basswood) and string them together with wire. Cut enough strips so the blankets are a couple of inches wider and longer than the workpiece. Drill the wire holes through the strips on a drill press using a fence and stops to ensure the holes are lined up. Drill the holes a little oversize. This makes stringing easy and allows the strips to move freely as they adjust under pressure to the contours of the bend.

In use I place a piece of ⅛-in. plywood or cardboard between the blanket and the laminated panel to further smooth out the pressure. Form alignment is critical to an accurate curve, so I use indexing fingers (two on the top mated with one on the bottom) as shown in the sketch.

—*Robert Thomason, Providence, R.I.*

Tank steamer

I have bent many chair rockers, back boards and splats, as well as wooden hoops, with the simple, safe steamer described here.

It is a 12-in. by 60-in. hot-water tank with the top cut out. It has wrap-around insulation and a plywood lid with a soft rubber gasket. A 10-lb. weight holds down the lid. The tank sits on building tiles, and an electric hot plate is set between them. Presoaked wood is suspended above the water line on twine string. A caution: When removing wood, raise the lid slowly and away from you to avoid the hot steam. For longer wood, a downspout could be attached to the tank.

—*Albert J. Gnaedinger, Pocahontas, Ill.*

Pipe steamer

A simple and cheap steamer for bending wood can be made using a pressure cooker and some ordinary pipe fittings. Screw out the center post of a pressure cooker. A Presto brand cook-

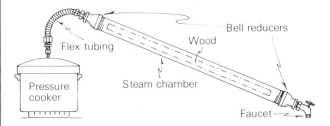

Flex tubing

Pressure cooker

Wood

Bell reducers

Steam chamber

Faucet

er has ¼-in. pipe threads; others may be different. Purchase adapters for this fitting so it will connect with ½-in. flexible (ribbed) tubing, and a pipe nipple and bell adapter to bring the other end out to fit a 2-in. pipe. A piece of 2-in. pipe about 50 in. long makes an excellent steam chamber. The length should be an inch more than the longest piece you plan to bend; you can always lengthen the chamber by adding couplings and more pipe. Use another bell reducer on the other end, then put on a faucet to regulate the amount of steam and drain excess water. I use our kitchen pressure cooker; all these fittings cost less than $15.

Cut and shape the wood the way you want it to be finished, then put it in the chamber and screw on the bell reducer and faucet assembly. Fill the pressure cooker to about 2 in. from the top, tighten all fittings, screw into the top of the cooker, and open the faucet. After it starts to steam, close this valve so the water drips out but just a small amount of steam escapes. Never close the valve all the way, or an explosion could occur. A piece of straight-grained wood ⅝ in. thick should easily bend around a form for a Windsor chair after thirty minutes of steaming.

If you use a pressure canner that has a gauge on it, you can safely steam wood with pressurized steam. For safest operation, remove the gauge and attach your steam tube to that hole, leaving the rocker assembly in place. Fit the gauge on at the end of the steam chamber by using a pipe tee and reducing bushings. Using the end valve as a regulator and keeping an eye on the gauge, you can generate superhot steam up to 240° F (at 15 lb. pressure). Ten pounds will cut the steaming time approximately in half. Watch the gauge at all times and be sure that the pressure cooker's safety valve is clean. Always let some steam escape through the end valve to keep the superheated steam flowing around the wood.

—*George Pilling, Elgin, Ariz.*

Bending wood without steam

Here's how to bend wood using a solution of hot water and Downy fabric softener. First build a container of black 6-in. ABS pipe by cementing a cap on one end and putting a removable cap on the other. Don't try regular PVC pipe; it won't hold up to high temperatures. The length of pipe can be whatever fits your need.

Mix one part Downy to twelve parts water, and heat the solution to boiling. Put the wood to be bent in the container and pour in the hot solution. Seal the open end of the container. It is important to keep the container warm. Here in California, I set the pipe out in the sun. On cloudy days I've sat the pipe next to a mirror and heated it with sunlamps. Leave the wood in the hot solution for a minimum of one hour. You'll find that wood softened in this solution will hold its shape better and not snap in the bending process. The solution turns thin wood to spaghetti.

—*David Ferguson, San Clemente, Calif.*

Proven Shop Tips   23

Bending iron

I teach high-school woodworking and for the past two years have had the students design projects that require bent wood. I have tried soaking and steaming with limited results, so I designed and built a simple bending iron from an aluminum bar and an old steam iron. The wood is wet with a sponge only where it is to be bent. This eliminates the staining and raised grain caused by soaking or steaming, and it can be glued immediately if it is not wet too much. My students have used the iron to bend wood up to ⅛ in. thick for projects ranging from guitar and dulcimer sides to fishing nets.

Start with a 6-in. length of round aluminum bar, and hacksaw it in half lengthwise. Sand the cut surface smooth on an aluminum oxide belt, and file all the edges smooth. Pick two steam holes on the sole of the iron, drill them out and thread them to accept #10/32 machine screws. Drilling elsewhere on the sole risks breaking into the heating element. Thread only as deep as the original steam holes, else the tap may bottom out and break off. Now locate these holes on the bottom of the aluminum block, drill through with a ¼-in. diameter bit for clearance, and countersink the top of the holes for the flathead screws. The screwheads may need to be

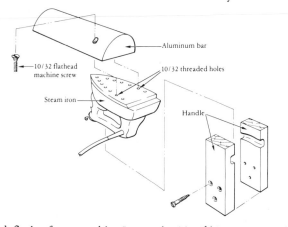

Aluminum bar

10/32 flathead machine screw

10/32 threaded holes

Steam iron

Handle

filed flush after assembly. I started with 1½-in. screws and ground them to length so they would tighten in the threaded holes without bottoming. Finally, groove two chunks of 2x4 to fit around the handle of the iron, so it may be clamped upright in the vise. —*David G. Johnson, Hanover, N.H.*

Check-free drying for green bowls

If you hesitate to turn bowls or other lathe projects from green log slices because of the checks and cracks that develop as the wood dries, here's a cure that is effective, free, uses no chemicals and requires no kiln. The secret is to bury your project in wood chips while it dries. During the rough turning of the bowl I accumulate a fair amount of green wood chips. I add chips left over from previous projects—all the chips I can find. I dump the chips in a box and bury my bowls in them, leaving at least a couple of inches of chips around all sides. I bury the bowl again after each work session and, after the project is completed, I leave it in the chips for a month. That's it. Sound too simple? Apparently the chips absorb the moisture from the green workpiece without letting it dry too fast. I have used this procedure with a large number of projects using several species of wood without a single failure.
—*William Wisniewski, Albion, Pa.*

Tin-can drying oven

If you have a stack of wood air-drying in the shop, chances are you have used this test to determine the moisture content of the wood: Cut a small sample from the wood, weigh the sample (I use a caloric scale), then dry the sample in the kitchen oven (until it doesn't change weight). Percent moisture is then calculated by dividing weight loss by final weight.

Unfortunately, the procedure ties up the oven for a day and, depending on the species being dried, fills the house with a disagreeable odor. These problems can be eliminated by a simple and inexpensive oven made from tin cans and heated by a 25-watt light bulb.

The model shows a 2-lb. coffee can (5 in. dia. by 6½ in. tall) as the inner container, and a large photographic-film container (7 in. dia. by 12 in. tall) as the outer container. The size and shape of the cans are not important—just so there's enough room for the wood samples and at least 1 in. of space between the inner and outer cans. Fill this space with fiberglass wool to retain the heat.

In operation, the heated, moist air rises through the chimney and is replaced by outside air drawn through the three tubes at the bottom. After a 20-minute heat-up period, adjust the temperature to about 112°F to 120°F by opening or closing the damper in the chimney. If the outside air temperature does not change drastically, the temperature inside the oven will remain relatively constant over the 24-hr. drying period with no need for a thermostat.

To solder the parts together, first file the surfaces clean, and

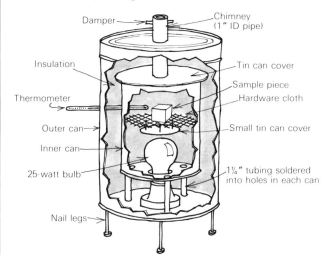

Damper

Chimney (1″ ID pipe)

Insulation

Tin can cover

Sample piece

Hardware cloth

Thermometer

Outer can

Small tin can cover

Inner can

25-watt bulb

1¼″ tubing soldered into holes in each can

Nail legs

tin with solder. Using soldering paste or acid as flux. Since tin cans are already tinned, soldering is easy.

The illustrated oven is designed for rather small wood samples. If you want to dry larger samples, the same design can be scaled up to a larger oven requiring, perhaps, a 40-watt or larger light bulb. —*H. Norman Capen, Granada Hills, Calif.*

Microwave drying

I dry green-wood bowls in my microwave oven, which heats the water clear through the wood and causes it to steam from the pores. I remove the metal faceplate and screws from the bowl, then set the oven on a low to medium setting, and run one minute on, one off, for about ten minutes, letting the moisture out of the oven from time to time. Bowls will change shape about as much as they would in air-drying, but I haven't had any crack yet. —*Robert Kick, Houston, Tex.*

Steam-bending jig

An inexpensive jig for steam-bending or bent laminations can be rigged up using an ordinary automobile bumper jack to supply the clamping force. First weld U-bolts to either end of a flexible steel strap of about the same length and width as the stock to be bent—I used a 36-in. by 1½-in. section of

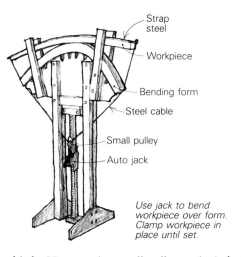

Strap steel

Workpiece

Bending form

Steel cable

Small pulley

Auto jack

Use jack to bend workpiece over form. Clamp workpiece in place until set.

band-saw blade. Now attach a small pulley to the jack. With the jack installed in the jig framework so that its force is directed away from the bending form, thread wire rope through the pulley and the jig framework, then attach it to the U-bolts with steel rope reinforcing loops and rope clamps.

Place the steamed or laminated material to be bent between the relaxed strap and the bending form head, then use the jack to pull it around the form. Clamping from the tightest point on the curve outward to each end will ensure perfect laminations. The form is secured to the jig with four bolts; other forms may be easily substituted.

—*Steve Voorheis, Missoula, Mont.*

Preserving green bowl blanks

To eliminate checking on green bowl blanks, simply store them in your freezer until you're ready to turn. I even use the freezer for storing work in progress if I'm interrupted before completing the rough-turning. This method is especially useful if you have a large number of green blanks and don't have time to rough them out so that they will dry properly. For long-term storage, wrap the blanks in plastic bags to avoid freezer burn and surface drying.

Another advantage of the method is that the frozen blanks turn without building up heat at the cutting edge—your gouge will need sharpening less frequently. Also, spalted wood, soaked and frozen, holds together much better.

—*Joel N. Kutz, Brockport, N.Y.*

Joinery & Wooden Threads

Chapter 6

Book-matched box

This simple book-matching technique yields a box with perfectly matched grain at all four corners. The system requires the rough lumber to be only as long as one side and one end of the box, but thick enough to resaw.

First resaw the box lumber. The inside surfaces match, so reverse them to become the outside of the box. Now cut the sides and ends sequentially, keeping all the waste to one end as shown in the sketch. Assemble the box as you like. I prefer the dramatic matched effect of mitered corners, with spline reinforcements for strength. —*Sam Bush, Portland, Ore.*

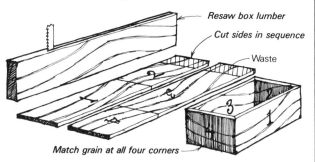

Resaw box lumber

Cut sides in sequence

Waste

Match grain at all four corners

Springboard applies squeeze

In the small custom furniture shop where I worked some time ago, we glued solid oak edging to the unsightly edges of fibercore, oak-veneer panels. Because this required a bar clamp every 8 in. for a tight joint, we soon depleted our supply of clamps, time and patience. My solution is a springboard which applies even pressure to the edging using far fewer clamps. Cut the springboard about 20 in. long from ¾-in. thick, 1½-in. wide hardwood (I used red oak for its resiliency in bending). Plane the middle of the

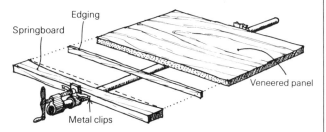

Springboard

Edging

Veneered panel

Metal clips

front edge to produce a concave shape, about ¼ in. deeper in the center than at the ends. Fasten with screws a couple of sheet-metal fingers to the back edge to hold the springboard in position on the clamp face while you're adjusting the work to be glued. As you tighten the bar clamp and close the gap, pressure will equalize along the concave face of the springboard.

—*Michael Mikutowski, South St. Paul, Minn.*

Hammer-eye joint for chair spindles

The best way to join brace spindles to back bows in Windsor chairs is a hammer-eye joint, shown at right. This joint is tapered top and bottom, glued, and wedged from the top. Flare the bottom of the hole with a taper reamer and the top with a round file, taking care to enlarge the top hole only with the grain, so it will fit the elliptical shape of

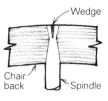

Wedge

Chair back

Spindle

the wedge-expanded spindle. To taper the ends of the spindles, I use a "precision pencil sharpener" made from a rabbet plane clamped or screwed to a block of wood, as shown at left. Drill a hole through the block and ream the hole at an angle, so the reamed edge is parallel to the surface of the block. Now plane down the block until about ¹⁄₁₆ in. of the hole is exposed. Screw or clamp a rabbet plane over the

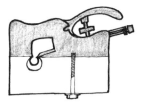

reamed part of the block so that the plane's blade will shave the spindles to shape. Run each spindle about ½ in. beyond the blade, so its tip will be round, ready for wedging, rather than tapered. —*David Sawyer, E. Calais, Vt.*

Making wooden checkers

Here's my method for making wooden checkers on the drill press. First grind the point off a 1½-in. spade bit. Only one side of the bit cuts, so grind it to the shape shown in the sketch and sharpen. Grind the other side of the bit back so it won't touch. Next, make a wooden jig with a ¼-in. deep, 2½-in. wide channel as shown. Install a ¼-in. dowel near one edge. Clamp the jig to the drill-press table, aligning the dowel with the centerline of the chuck.

Use 2½-in. wide, ⁵⁄₁₆-in. thick material for the checker blank (I use walnut and maple). Drill ¼-in. registration holes along one edge of the checker blanks, making sure the holes are the same distance from the edge as the ¼-in. dowel is from the edge of the jig. Place the blank in the jig with a hole over the dowel. Set the drill press at its fastest speed and lower the bit ⅛ in. or so into the blank. You may have to experiment with depth to get the checkers to stack right. After shaping the top sides of all the checkers with the spade bit, use a fly cutter to cut almost through the blank. Grind

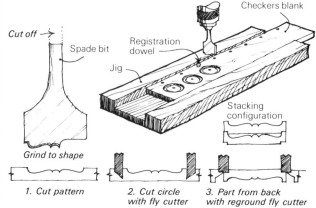

Cut off →

Spade bit

Checkers blank

Registration dowel

Jig

Stacking configuration

Grind to shape

1. Cut pattern

2. Cut circle with fly cutter

3. Part from back with reground fly cutter

another fly cutter so it will cut square, turn the blanks over and part the checkers with a shoulder as shown above. The shoulder of one checker should mate with the shaped cavity in the top of another for stacking.

—*Larry W. Brewer, Roanoke, Va.*

Checkerboard

Here's how I build a 16-in. checkerboard with a tenth of the work and time of the individual-square method.

First, saw and joint three strips of light wood and three strips of dark wood (like walnut and birch), each exactly 2 in. wide and 19 in. long. Now saw one strip dark and one strip light, 3 in. wide by 19 in. long, and joint one edge of these wider pieces. Edge-glue these eight strips together, alternating dark and light. Put the 3-in. strips on the outside, to build in a buffer strip for clamping.

When the glue has dried, square up one end, saw one wide (2½-in.) strip, then saw and joint six 2-in. strips. You should have one wider strip left over, making eight in all. Reverse four of the strips end for end and glue up. You will end up with an oversize 16-in. board that needs only to be sawn to size. This approach leaves the grain in all squares running the same direction. To build a board with alternating grain in adjacent squares, glue up a 19-in. wide, 10-in. long board of either the dark or light wood. Slice three 2-in. by 19-in. strips, and one 3-in. by 19-in. strip off the end grain. To avoid problems with end-grain butt joints, you could use thin (¼-in.) stock and laminate the completed board to ½-in. plywood. —*G. Vander Stoep, Pittsfield, Ill.*

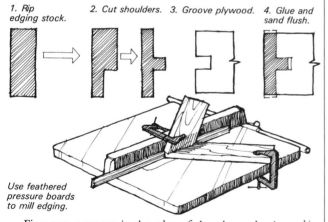

Glue up alternating strips. Slice. Turn every other strip end for end.

Laminate to plywood for extra strength.

Tongue holds edge-banding

This method for edging plywood is simple yet produces a very strong joint. The idea is to key the edge banding to the plywood via a simple tongue-and-groove joint, so there is no movement when you clamp up.

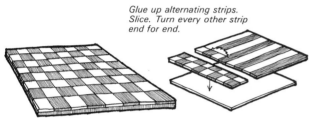

1. Rip edging stock.   2. Cut shoulders.   3. Groove plywood.   4. Glue and sand flush.

Use feathered pressure boards to mill edging.

First rout a groove in the edge of the plywood using a ⅛-in. slotting cutter bit. Take care to center this groove. To make the edging, rip solid stock into thin boards, ¼ in. thick and 13⁄16 in. wide. Using finger boards on the table saw as shown in the sketch, cut a shoulder on each side of the edging to produce a tongue that fits snugly in the plywood slot. It will take you a couple of tries to get the blade set at just the right height, but once it's set you can mill a hundred feet of edging very quickly. To complete, spread glue on the edging and clamp up. Later sand down the slightly thicker lip of the banding flush with the plywood.
—*V. Spiegelman, Los Angeles, Calif.*

Flush rule joint for oval tables

Simon Watts wrote that he does not like "oval-shaped drop-leaf tables because the curve crossing the rule joint makes part of the joint project in an unsightly way." I agree that the projection is unsightly, but there's a simple solution that makes the rule joint flush in both the open and closed positions: bevel the edge of the table top.

Figure 1 shows how the corner of a rule joint projects when the leaf is lowered. The edge of the table continues to curve whereas the top corner of the rule joint swings down in an arc perpendicular to the line of the rule joint. But if the edge of the table is beveled at angle *a* determined from the tangent to the oval at the rule joint, the lower edge of the table top is farther out on a radius than the top corner of the leaf. When the leaf drops (figure 2), the edge and the corner match.

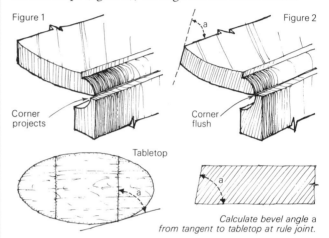

Figure 1

Figure 2

Corner projects

Corner flush

Tabletop

Calculate bevel angle a from tangent to tabletop at rule joint.

Recently I made a drop-leaf table incorporating this method and was pleased with the result. Later I visited Williamsburg and noticed that many of the oval drop-leaf tables of colonial times also have beveled edges. So, my idea is far from original. —*James H. Smith, Champaign, Ill.*

Improved tusk-tenon joint for bed frame

The traditional tusk-tenon joint is well suited to joining bed side rails to headboard and footboard in all respects save one—the protruding parts are real shin-kickers. To overcome this problem, I designed an internally wedged joint which is no more difficult to make and works quite well. From the

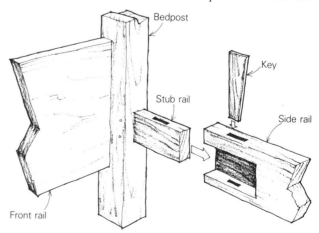

Bedpost

Key

Stub rail

Side rail

Front rail

outside you see only the ends of the key. The secret of the joint is a stub rail mortised into the bedpost, pinned through the cheeks for strength. The stub rail fits into a short slot cut in the back of the bed's side rail. There it is locked in place by a key driven in from the top. —*Stefan During, Texel, Holland*

Cutting splines

This simple technique for cutting snug-fitting splines reduces the time and eliminates the frustration of the trial-and-error approach. First mount in the table saw a fine-

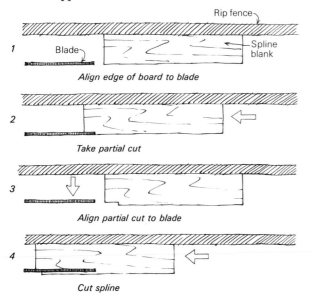

1. Align edge of board to blade

2. Take partial cut

3. Align partial cut to blade

4. Cut spline

tooth plywood blade, to be used for the entire process. Cut the spline grooves, for a ¾-in. spline, just slightly deeper than ⅜ in.

To cut the splines, make a partial cut (½ in. or so), removing one full, exact saw kerf from the edge of the ¾-in. spline stock. Now readjust the rip fence so that the left side of the blade is aligned with the right side of the previous kerf cut. Pass the stock through the blade to make a spline the exact size of the grooves. —*Thomas S. North, Bloomfield, Conn.*

Miniature log-house joint

This simple little jig makes joints on dowels or short tree branches for a miniature log house. Choose a drill bit the same size as the dowels or sticks to be used in the house, then

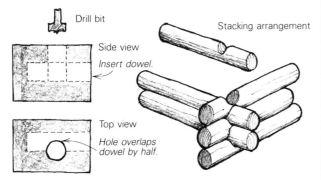

Drill bit

Side view

Insert dowel.

Top view

Hole overlaps dowel by half.

Stacking arrangement

drill a block of wood from two sides, with the second hole overlapping half of the first. To use, insert a dowel in the first hole and use the other as a guide for the drill bit. Note that the distance between the overlap and the end of the first hole will determine the overhang of the miniature logs.

—*Gerald Robertson, Angus, Ont.*

Banding plywood

Plywood can be easily and neatly edge-banded using a 90° flute shaper cutter (Rockwell #09-106) and cutoffs from solid stock. Adjust the shaper to cut a notch centered in the edge of the plywood and deep enough to cut into, but not through, the edge of the veneer on each face. If the cut is too deep, the

cutter tends to fuzz up the end grain of the veneer or else chip it loose. For the band, rip triangular strips from solid stock of about the same thickness as the plywood. These strips can usually be made from scraps from the ripsaw if you choose pieces with two surfaces jointed at a right angle. Unless the bands are cut from the edge of a board, it is probably safer and easier to rip these narrow triangles on a band saw. Glue the strips into the notches, and trim the excess on a table saw, jointer or by hand plane. The jointer or table saw will need some sort of spacer, a piece of ¼-in. plywood, for example, to prevent the corner of the band from causing an uneven cut.

If more than two parallel edges of the plywood are to be banded, all of the edges can be notched at the same time and

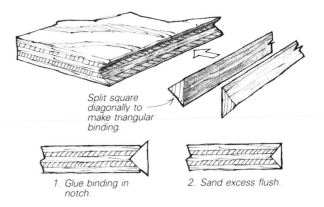

Split square diagonally to make triangular binding.

1. Glue binding in notch.

2. Sand excess flush.

the bands mitered at the corners, or two parallel edges can be notched, banded and trimmed before the notches are cut into the other edges. The second procedure leaves two small triangles of end grain exposed on two edges of the plywood.

If the band is trimmed carefully, which is not difficult to do, it is not visible on the face of the plywood, and the picture-frame look that usually accompanies edge bands is avoided. Because the notch provides a large surface area for gluing, the band is exceptionally strong. The solid wood edge makes hinges mounted on plywood doors more secure, for example, and provides a reasonably strong glue surface for plywood-to-plywood butt joints and the like.—*David Landen, Chapel Hill, N.C.*

Figure flows over edge

Here's how to edge-finish plywood and match color and grain exactly. Buy enough plywood so you can saw strips from the edge and ends of the panel slightly wider than the plywood is thick. Now saw off the face veneer from the strips using a thin-

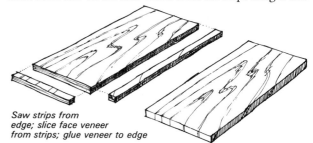

Saw strips from edge; slice face veneer from strips; glue veneer to edge

rim plywood blade on a table saw. To prevent the veneer from falling through the gap between blade and table insert, tape a piece of ¼-in. plywood to the saw-table top and elevate the blade through it. If you are careful in sawing the veneer, you can match the edge strips with the face to create a continuous grain pattern that's quite attractive. Glue the strips in place, then sand off the slight overhang. —*Floyd L. Lien, Aptos, Calif.*

Wedges clamp edges

On a recent platform-bed project I needed to glue ¼-in. oak strips to the edge of a plywood panel. Only two of my bar clamps were long enough for the job. Luckily I hit on a way to combine the two clamps with a double-wedge clamping method I use in guitar construction. I simply clamped a stur-

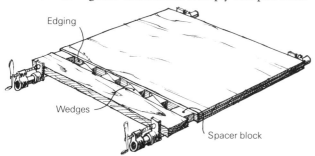

Edging

Wedges

Spacer block

dy oak 1x4 to the edge I wanted to glue, separating the board from the edge with two spacer blocks. The resulting gap left room all along the edge to drive home pairs of wedges. The system worked better than I expected. I was able to control the clamping pressure at many points along the edge without wrestling with a lot of clamps.

—*Willis Overholt, Wichita, Kans.*

Heat speeds glue cure

I use a hot-water clamp-table to speed up edge-gluing on plywood cabinet parts. When I clamp the plywood and edge strip to the rectangular steel tube (maintained at 160°F by circulating hot water) the plastic resin glue sets in 15 to 20 minutes. I trim the just-glued piece while the next one sets.

The device consists of a hot-water tank, a pump, hoses, fittings, a table and the 48-in. rectangular tube. Two points of caution: Use a pump designed for hot water (check with demolition companies—they salvage these pumps from old buildings) and install a pressure-relief valve. The valve is especially important if your system is closed, as is mine. Cover the work table with plastic laminate and wax so the glue will chip off easily after it has set. Leave a space between the rec-

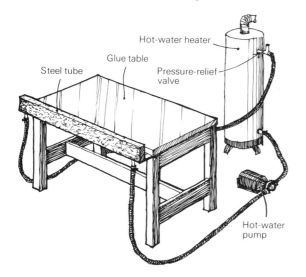

Hot-water heater

Glue table

Steel tube

Pressure-relief valve

Hot-water pump

tangular tube and the table so that you can adjust the edging and leave an overhang on the bottom.

To use, apply glue to both surfaces, position the strip, then bring the edge against the hot tube. Start clamping with the plywood angled up slightly so the bottom glueline is tight but there's a gap on top. Apply pressure until the gap closes.

—*Richard Esteb, Olympia, Wash.*

Wedged loom joint

I devised a wedged half-lap joint to replace the tusk-tenon joint traditionally used in loom construction. The joint fills all the requirements I wanted: it can be taken apart, won't vibrate loose, is easy to make and finishes flush and neat. In my version the joint members are made up from two face-glued planks. The double-plank approach greatly simplifies cutting the joint and fitting the mortise to the tenon.

To make the joint, start with one of the four boards that will later form the mortise. Crosscut the board with the miter gauge set at 88° and the blade angled at 15° to make both sides of the mortise (flop one board). Miter the end of the tenon backup board at 30° and then cut a 30° notch in the mortise back-up board. The mitered end should wedge tightly into the notch.

To make the tenon, first locate and drill a large hole on the tenon's centerline. This hole helps prevent the joint from cracking and allows the tenon walls to flex. Next bevel the sides of the tenon at 15° and cut the angled slot for the wedge. The sides of the tenon should be left parallel. Later the wedge will spread them to fit the angled mortise.

Glue the tenon to its mitered backup board. Place this member in position on the mortise backup board and fit the

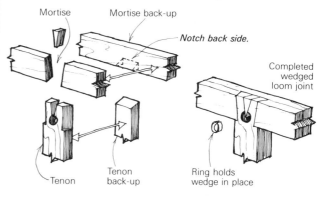

Mortise

Mortise back-up

Notch back side.

Completed wedged loom joint

Tenon

Tenon back-up

Ring holds wedge in place

two mortise pieces against the sides of the tenon; the mortise pieces touch the tenon only at its shoulder. Mark the position of the mortise pieces, remove the tenon member and glue the mortise pieces in place. After the glue sets you're ready to assemble the joint and tap in the wedge.

I recommend you oven-dry the wedges for two hours or so before you drive them in. This will reduce the chance of their shrinking and needing to be driven in further after you've trimmed them flush. Even so, leave the wedges in place for a few weeks before finishing flush. If the wedges persist in loosening, cut a short section of brass tubing the same diameter as the tenon hole. Cut a tapered section out of the ring so that, when inserted in the hole, it bites the wedge where it enters the hole.   —*Irving Sloane, Brussels, Belgium*

Splint joint

To splice pieces of ash splints for chair seats, first soak the splints to make them pliable. Then, with a leather punch,

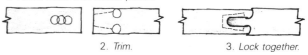

1. *Punch holes with leather punch.*

2. *Trim.*   3. *Lock together.*

punch holes in the splints and trim the ends to the shape shown in the sketch. This procedure achieves the same result as the traditional method (knife and chisel), but it's faster, easier, and handier in tight places. And the rounded edges resist splitting while the seat dries and tightens.

—*Bruce Herron, Ganges, Mich.*

Easy stretcher joint

One of the easiest stretcher-to-post joints (used on European workbenches and machinery stands) is to butt-join the parts using two bolts engaging captured nuts. The simple joint eliminates the precision fitting required with mortise and tenon. In fact, with this joint, bolt holes should be bored oversize to accommodate adjustments or inaccuracy. Twin bolts keep the joint tight and the members perpendicular,

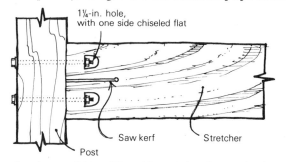

1¼-in. hole, with one side chiseled flat

Saw kerf   Stretcher

Post

but there's a problem: The wide stretcher is restrained cross grain against the post, making it prone to splitting.

Here's a solution to the problem: Pre-split the end of the stretcher by sawing a kerf down the middle of the stretcher for 3 in. or 4 in. The split is an adaptation of twin tenons. The slot allows the wood to move across its width, relieving the stresses from changes in humidity. Drill a hole through the stretcher at the end of the slot so that splitting forces are distributed around the circumference of the hole rather than focused at one point. —*Richard Starr, Thetford Center, Vt.*

Invisible edge joint

When I edge-join hardwood boards, I plane the edges by eye, then do one additional step—a technique I borrowed from the dental practice used to fit teeth and plates together. With the boards flat on a workbench, I fold ordinary typewriter carbon paper, place it between the edge surfaces and rub the boards back and forth against each other. Any high spots or edge misalignments show up as black smudges. I snick them off with a plane set to cut a very fine shaving. Then I repeat the procedure until I have an even smudge all along the edge. The result after gluing is a joint that is almost invisible, except for differences in grain pattern.

—*James V. Ralston, Murray Hill, N.J.*

Drawer joint

This rarely seen drawer joint is my favorite for fine furniture. Properly fitted, it is strong and attractive. The initial cuts, made on the table saw, are similar to those used for the familiar drawer joint. Then cut the tenons with a backsaw, chopping out the waste with a chisel. Tap the tenons into the

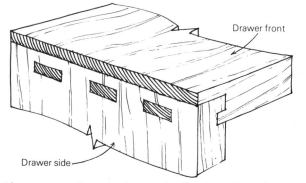

Drawer front

Drawer side

side groove and mark the mortise locations. Complete the mortises with a small drill, coping saw and file.

—*John W. Wood, Tyler, Tex.*

Decorative door joint

This homemade barrel-nut adaptation uses short sections of ½-in. ID iron pipe and captured ⅜-in. hex nuts. I installed several of these fasteners in an old weathered door to pull

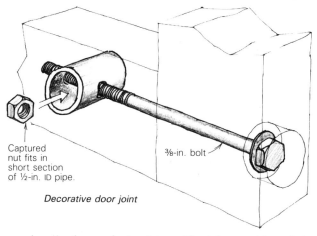

Captured nut fits in short section of ½-in. ID pipe.

⅜-in. bolt

Decorative door joint

together the loosened glue joints. The joint would work in other applications as well, such as machine stands and workbench carriages. You can plug the holes in the pipe after the bolt is tight, allowing the metal to show like an inlaid ring.

—*Jack Niday, Balboa Island, Calif.*

Jointing decorative strips

When fitting out a project with decorative wood strips and binding (on a guitar or violin, a marquetry frame, or a fancy box) a most difficult operation is making tight butt or miter joints between the strips—especially if the wood is white. A little jig, which I call a miter block, surmounts this problem. It will produce good, flat gluing faces on the ends of the strips at 90° or 45° (or whatever angle you design it for), and will also trim them to perfect length.

The block itself is a square of metal or dense hardwood (say 2 in. by 2 in. by 6 in.), with opposite faces parallel and all four faces mutually square. One end of the block is cut at 90° and the other at 45°. It is placed on a flat base, and the purfling (decorative) strip, rough-trimmed and marked for length, is placed (usually vertically) against the block's side and the base, and held securely in place with a straight caul. The left hand holds both block and caul so that the strip's end protrudes slightly past the end of the block. The right hand holds a small, straight sanding stick (a high-quality metal nail file is best) against the end of the block (the guide), and works the stick to and fro, sanding the end of the

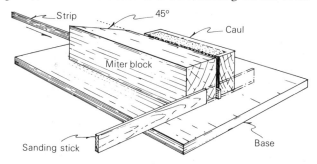

Strip   45°   Caul

Miter block

Sanding stick   Base

strip until it is flush with the block's end and the length mark is reached. Sandpaper glued to the caul grabs the strip so the left hand can feed it into the moving sanding stick. The process is complicated to describe, but a cinch to carry out. By changing the orientation of the block, both inside and outside miters can be obtained. The block can be used for pearl, ivory and other inlay materials as well. —*William D. Woods, Phoenix, Ariz.*

Cutting corner bridle joints

This procedure eliminates the tedious fence adjustments and frustrating $\frac{1}{32}$-in. errors that go with cutting open mortise-and-tenon joints on the table saw. It is based on a thin auxiliary fence or shim that's exactly as thick as the saw kerf of the blade you're using. The shim stock, made of thin plywood (door skin) or surfaced from solid stock, should be as wide as your fence is tall, and should be long enough to clamp to your fence—say 8 in. by 16 in.

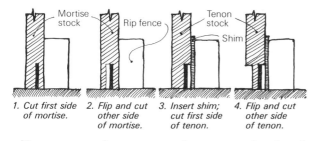

1. Cut first side of mortise.
2. Flip and cut other side of mortise.
3. Insert shim; cut first side of tenon.
4. Flip and cut other side of tenon.

To use, set up the saw to cut the open mortise. Saw the mortise as usual by passing both cheeks of the stock over the blade. Do not adjust the fence to saw the tenon. Simply clamp the shim to the fence and saw out the tenon—first one face, then the other. The shim repositions the tenon stock just to the other side of the cut line. The joint will be just right.

—*John F. Anderson, Bottineau, N.D. and Ivan Hentschel, Kingston, N.J.*

Doweling *T*-jig

A *T*-jig, used in doweling edge joints, ensures alignment of dowel pins and holes. Boards joined with the jig will mate better on the finish side, and sanding or planing misaligned joints is virtually eliminated. The jig's bar and leg are made of steel. High-carbon steel is best (anneal for machining, then harden later), but cold-rolled, mild steel will do. Wood will wear too fast. Drill common-dowel-size holes ($\frac{1}{4}$ in. and $\frac{3}{8}$ in.) in the center of the $\frac{3}{4}$-in. bar on each side of the leg. Two allen-head machine screws secure the leg to the bar.

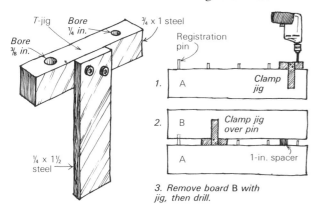

3. Remove board B with jig, then drill.

In use, the *T*-jig serves as both a gauge (all the pin holes are equidistant from the face) and a copier (the pin holes are mated from one edge to the other). First use the jig to drill all the pin holes in board *A*. Clamp the leg of the jig to the face of the board. No exact measurement of pin locations is needed—the holes in board *B* will be copied from the pins in board *A*. Install an extra-long registration pin in the first hole and regular-length pins in all the other holes.

Now clamp the jig to board *B* (leg to face) and drill the registration pin hole. Place the *T*-jig over one of the regular-length pins on board *A*, leg up, and fit the registration hole over the registration pin. Clamp the jig in place on board *B*, remove the board and drill. Repeat this operation for each pin

in turn. Cut and use 1-in. spacer blocks to aid the pin-copying process.

After all the holes are drilled, trim the registration pin to size, spread glue on the joint and press the boards together, keeping the ends even as the boards go together.

—*Wallace Smith, Newport Beach, Calif.*

Greeno interlock joint

The development of a genuinely new wood joint is worthy of notice. In the shop of Jerry Green, the furniture maker with whom I apprenticed, we often worked with a tropical wood called partridge wood. Dramatic color made the wood popular, but it was prone to checking and honeycombing in thicker dimensions. Green's designs, nevertheless, frequently called for 2-in. and thicker material, so we laminated $\frac{3}{4}$-in. stock. Capitalizing on this, Green invented this highly deco-

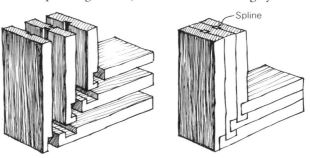

rative, extremely rigid and (since it requires only one setup) easy-to-machine joint. Because the joint is self-locking, it must be assembled while laminating. After the glue sets, scrape and belt-sand the surfaces. To register the laminated boards we often added splines, as shown in the sketch.

In memory of its inventor, we call this joint the Greeno interlock joint. —*John W. Kreigshauser, Kansas City, Mo.*

Three-member lap joint

Here's a variation of the lap joint I discovered while trying to find a way to connect three stretchers on a three-legged table. The joint is attractive and strong. Each member overlaps the other two members with a large edge-grain glue surface.

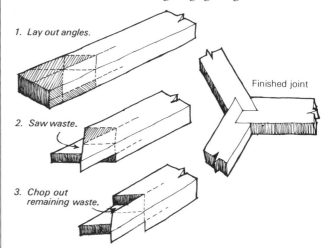

1. Lay out angles.
2. Saw waste.
3. Chop out remaining waste.

Finished joint

To lay out the joint scribe a centerline on both faces and both edges of all pieces. Set a bevel gauge to 60° and use it to mark the diagonal lines shown in the sketch. Saw away what waste you can, then finish chopping out the waste with a chisel. Take care to keep the glue surfaces flat and the edges that show crisp.

By changing the angle of the layout you can adapt this joint to any number of members, odd or even.

—*David Nebenzahl, Flagstaff, Ariz.*

Making dowels

Although I often need oak or walnut dowels, they're not readily available where I live. Not owning a lathe, I resurrected an ancient but effective dowel-making method that uses a simple jig and hand plane. Dowels made this way are, in my opinion, superior to those made by driving blanks through a steel sizing plate.

Construct the dowel-holding jig by ripping several V-grooves in a 2x6. A variety of groove depths will allow a wide range of dowel sizes. Screw a stop on one end of the 2x6. Place a square dowel blank in a groove and plane the top corner. Turn and plane repeatedly until the blank is oc-

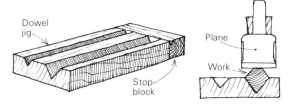

tagonal. Successive turn/plane cycles will result in a nearly round dowel, which can then be finished with sandpaper. One small drawback—the blanks must be flipped end for end as the grain direction changes. —*Frederick C. Wilbur, Shipman, Va.*

Dovetail template

This homemade dovetail template was found among my deceased grandfather's effects. Its origin is uncertain, but it's permanent and probably better than a bevel gauge. It can

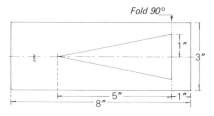

easily be duplicated with a 3-in. by 8-in. piece of thin aluminum (an offset printing plate is the right thickness), a steel rule and an X-acto knife. Draw a line 1 in. from and parallel to the bottom edge, then scribe a triangle with the desired tail and pin angles (I use a 1:5 slope). Cut out the triangle with the knife, using the rule as a guide, fold the aluminum at the base of the triangle, and there's your template. The triangle may be truncated at its top to leave a shorter piece to work with. —*Roger Schroeder, Amityville, N.Y.*

Dovetail marking setup

This setup for scribing pin sockets in hand-dovetail construction eliminates hand-held slipping and repositioning problems. Put a spacer block under a handscrew on the workbench. Align the two workpieces, tighten the handscrew, then lock the whole in position with a C-clamp.
—*Richard Kendrot, Windsor, N.Y.*

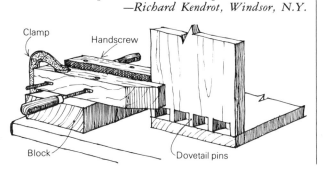

Dovetail square

I do a considerable amount of hand-dovetailing and find an adjustable bevel or protractor a bit awkward. Since pin and tail angles remain constant (I use 12°), I have made a square at that angle that is very easy to use. Mine is made from well-cured cherry with ³⁄₁₆-in. birch pins. The body is a laminate of two ¼-in. thick cheek pieces, 6 in. long, and two ⅛-in. center pieces, 3 in. long, cut at 12° on the inner ends. The blade

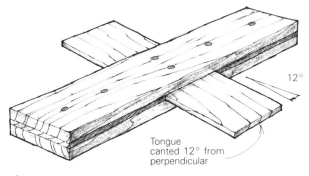

is ⅛ in. thick and 6 in. long.

I assembled my tool dry in clamps to drill the pin holes, then I removed the blade and pinned the body together dry. After trimming the ends smooth, I lapped all the working edges, including the blade, with 220-grit paper placed on a surface plate.

Reassemble with glue and clamp, and you have a handy tool that never has to be set or checked, and can easily be flopped to pick up the other angle.
—*Don Kenyon, Naples, N.Y.*

Cutting dovetails on the scroll saw

Traditional "hand" dovetails can be cut quickly and accurately on the scroll saw or band saw. The scroll saw gives a finer, more accurate cut than the band saw—especially if a thin, 32-point blade is used.

First, lay out the pins following the traditional method. Cut one side of the pins by tilting the scroll-saw table to the proper angle (8° to 14°). Then tilt the table the other way, cut the other sides of the pins and chop out the waste between with a chisel.

Some saw tables (especially on band saws) don't tilt in both directions. This problem is easily solved by building a clamp-on auxiliary table that can be reversed to get both angles.

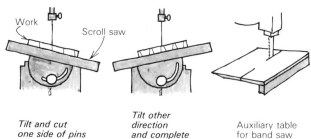

The tails, scribed from the pins, are easily cut by returning the saw table to the horizontal position. By sawing away most of the waste between the tails, only a bit of chisel work is needed to complete the joint.
—*Gustave Kotting & David Haber, Grantsville, Md.*

Trimming dovetails

With through dovetails it's accepted procedure to cut the joints a bit long and trim the ends flush after gluing. The fastest method I've found for trimming the slight overhang is to use a router equipped with a carbide-tipped, ball-bearing flush-trim bit. Start the cut at the very corner to prevent the bit from grabbing at the beginning. Always feed against the direction of the cutter rotation. After routing, a light planing or sanding will complete the job.

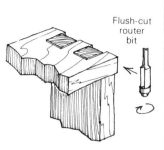

Flush-cut router bit

—*Don Herman, Brecksville, Ohio*

Sliding dovetail bookends

Most furniture designed to hold books doesn't. Shelves must be filled with books end to end or pairs of movable bookends must be used. I make integral, sliding bookends from the same wood as the bookshelf. Cut ½-in. dovetail keys across the bottoms of matched blocks. Then rout a mating dovetail

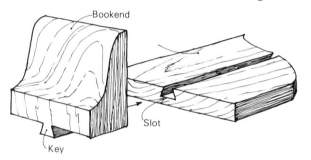

Bookend

Slot

Key

slot in the shelf end to end. The fit of key to slot should be smooth but not loose. Allow for swelling during humid seasons. Slide the bookends into the slot prior to assembly. Books placed between the bookends supply the necessary leverage to jam the key tight in the slot. Bookends can be easily repositioned if book tension is relaxed.

—*Rick Kramer, Beech Creek, Pa.*

Threads in end grain

When tapping wooden threads with a homemade or commercial steel tap, good clean threads can be gotten only when tapping perpendicular to the grain of the wood. It sometimes is necessary in the design of a certain project to tap directly into end grain, as in a turning, in which case the threads will be torn out. However, the tap can be sharpened so that the wood fibers on the inside surface of the pilot hole are cut before the root of the thread, thus not tearing out the whole thread.

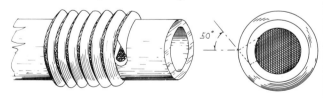

50°

Looking at the end view of the tap, it is filed so that the angle of the two cutting edges is sloped back from the radial position. This could be anywhere from 40° to 50°. A 45° file can be used to rough-form the inside bevel of the cutter. The edge can then be finished with a small slip stone.

—*William Stockhausen, Northville, Mich.*

Cutting wooden threads

To cut perfect wooden threads, immerse the dowel in hot paraffin for ten minutes prior to threading. Thread while the dowel is still warm. The shavings roll out of the die in a neat string, leaving a perfect thread base.

—*Al Grendahl, St. Paul, Minn.*

Sizing

When cutting threads in end grain, an aid to preventing tear-out that will give clean-running threads is to "size" the wood. After drilling the hole in the end grain, coat the hole with a watery glue (polyvinyl acetate, plastic resin, etc.) thin enough to penetrate the fibers. Less tear-out will occur during the tapping. Afterwards apply more coats of sizing to harden the wood further.

Sizing so applied increases the toughness of any running or bearing surface.

Another use of sizing is to raise the grain. Before the final sanding, apply a thin wash coat of sizing. Avoid thermoplastic adhesives (the white and yellow glues) because they soften with friction and load up abrasive paper. Brown glue such as Borden's or Weldwood plastic resin sands and hardens the wood especially well. Another way to raise the grain is with thin shellac or lacquer. When it dries, the sizing "keeps" the wood fibers and grain raised, so they can be sanded away. If a better surface is not immediately noticed, the improvement may well be apparent after several months of humidity fluctuation.

—*C.B. Oliver, Durham, N.H.*

Sanding & Scraping

Chapter 7

Homebuilt vertical sander

This homebuilt vertical belt sander performs well and is easy on the tool budget. All you need to drive a standard 1-in. by 42-in. belt the proper 1500 to 2000 FPM (surface feet per minute) is a small 1725-RPM motor, a 3-in. to 4-in. drive pulley, and two slave wheels installed on a frame with a tensioning device.

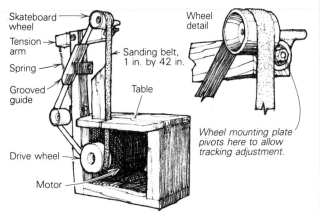

Skateboard wheel
Tension arm
Spring
Grooved guide
Drive wheel
Motor
Sanding belt, 1 in. by 42 in.
Table
Wheel detail
Wheel mounting plate pivots here to allow tracking adjustment.

A satisfactory drive wheel can be turned from wood, or fabricated from a tuna can with both ends cut out. Take a small pulley that fits your motor shaft and epoxy it in the center of the can, being careful not to cover the setscrew on the pulley. For greater traction, wrap the circumference of the drive wheel with duct tape.

For weight and strength, construct the frame from 2-in. thick hardwood. Plywood will suffice for the table. The tensioning arm should fit the vertical support with a pivoting bridle-joint arrangement.

Scavenge the slave wheels from an old skateboard and, using the existing hardware if possible, fasten one wheel to the tensioning arm 12 in. to 15 in. above the drive wheel. Fasten the other slave wheel to the back of the vertical support. Make sure the wheels are attached so that they can pivot to allow the small adjustments needed for alignment and perfect belt-tracking. Other construction details are shown in the sketch. —Leon O. Beasley, Lafayette, La.

Ersatz sanding disc

A tire valve stem makes a cheap, simple and flexible mounting for sandpaper. Cut the stem from the tube, glue on sandpaper and chuck the stem in a drill press or portable drill. I use the discs to sand irregular bowls. —Bart Brush, Cherry Valley, N.Y.

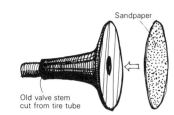

Sandpaper
Old valve stem cut from tire tube

Contour sander

This shopmade sander for lathe work and curves uses a length of abrasive cloth tensioned, bowsaw fashion, by a twisted

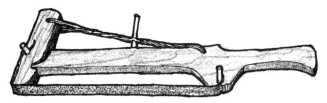

cord. The abrasive cloth, which can be purchased in ¾-in. or 1½-in. width rolls, is clamped into the sander with tight-fitting dowel pegs. —Richard Tolzman, Excelsior, Minn.

Hand sander

Strip from sanding belt

Here's an inexpensive, quick-to-make hand sander that's effective for smoothing out gouge marks on curved surfaces or for rounding off a sharp edge. You will need some scrap plywood, a used belt from a belt sander and a little contact cement.

First, cut the plywood into an 8-in. to 12-in. long hacksaw shape. Tear a strip from an old sanding belt as wide as the plywood you use and a couple of inches longer than the frame you cut. Spread a little contact cement on the back of the strip and along the bottom surface of the frame and press the abrasive strip along the bottom of the handle to the front.

When completed, the sander has an open section with a little give for sanding curves and a rigid section for sanding flat surfaces. The rounded ends are designed for sanding concave surfaces. By changing the shape of the frame, the applications are virtually endless. When the abrasive is dull, just pull off the old strip and glue another on.
—Richard Neubauer, Jr., Cincinnati, Ohio

Sanding block for beaded edges

On a recent mantle clock project I needed to sand the beaded edges without rounding the crisp corners or flawing the uniform curvature of the bead. Hand sanding with a folded sheet of sandpaper just would not do. I made a reverse-image sanding block by routing a cove into a small piece of wood. Then I cut strips of sandpaper and glued them to the cove with 3M's feathering disc adhesive. This adhesive, used by auto body workers to attach abrasive discs to disc sanders, was excellent for my purpose. Since it remains tacky, I could attach new strips of sandpaper as the old strips wore out without reapplying the adhesive. It also works well for attaching wooden protective pads to the jaws of the C-clamps and bar clamps. —John Searles, Xenia, Ohio

Long-lived sanding strips

Narrow strips of sandpaper used to sand turnings or curved objects tend to tear, cutting less efficiently the shorter they get, until they are so many useless pieces of expensive paper.

Fiberglass strapping tape
Sandpaper strip

To make them last longer, back them with fiberglass strapping tape; they'll be virtually untearable.
—J.S. Gerhsey, Lake Ariel, Pa.

Sanding device

To sand holes or a flat surface, take a ¼-in. rod—the length depends on the depth of the hole or the width of the surface. Cut a slot down the center to hold a piece of sandpaper. Cloth paper is best, and you can use old sanding belts. Then

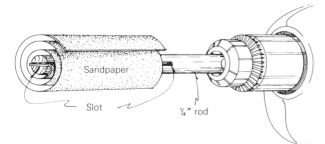

chuck the rod in a ¼-in. electric drill. Make sure the paper is wound the right way. The paper sands as it flaps. When the edge wears, it can be trimmed off.

—*T. L. Trudell, Saginaw, Mich.*

Sanding mop

To sand hard-to-get-at spots, make a sanding mop from a nut-and-bolt arbor and a handful of small pieces of sandpaper. Overlap the sandpaper like shingles around the arbor and chuck it in a drill. The irregular edge eliminates the hard sanding line produced by rubber-backed discs.

—*Allan Adams, San Francisco, Calif.*

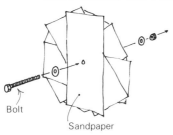

Sanding canoe paddles

This setup speeds up the tedious job of rounding canoe paddle shafts. I suspect it has other applications as well.

To start, turn a wooden cylinder 18 in. long and 3 in. in diameter. Wrap it with masking tape, building it up in the middle to form a crown. This will help center the sanding belt as you work. Then turn a sanding belt inside out and place it over the wrapped cylinder.

I prepare the handle by squaring off a blank, then chamfering the corners, except where the blades will be glued on. I

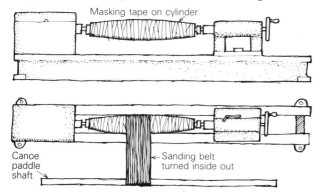

then stick the handle into the sanding-belt loop, pull tight and sand round. It will take a little practice at first, but eventually you will be able to make a difficult task simple.

—*Wright E. Bowman, Jr., Honolulu, Hawaii*

Sanding small pieces in the clothes dryer

Here's a way to sand the corners off small pieces of wood. My method does not even require a frame.

I needed radiused edges on both ends of a thousand ½-in. long pieces of ½-in. diameter dowels. I lined the insides of three 5-lb. plastic peanut-butter buckets with 100-grit sandpaper, tossed in about 350 dowels per bucket and secured the lid with masking tape. Then I put the buckets into my clothes dryer along with a couple of heavy towels to aid the tumbling action. I set the dryer to air fluff and turned it on. In only ten minutes the job was done.

To protect your dryer, be sure to use only "soft" containers, secure the lid, add towels and use a no-heat setting.

—*Marilyn Warrington, Tiro, Ohio*

Block sander from sanding belt

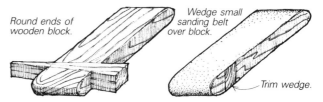

With the wedge-tightened block shown here, you can use small sanding belts as block sanders. The tight belt makes for better sanding action, and because cloth sanding belts are of a better quality than abrasive paper, the blocks last a long time. You can shape the end profiles for inside sanding, too.

—*Robert J. Harrigan, Cincinnati, Ohio*

Sandpaper sizer

Everybody may know this one already, but you don't need scissors and a ruler to cut up sandpaper to fit your electric

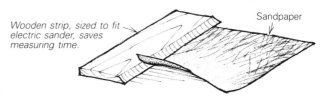

sander—just make a sharp-edged wooden strip the size of your sander's paper, place it on the sandpaper, and tear the sheet to size. —*Harry D. Stumpf, West Point, N.Y.*

How to fold sandpaper

An old paint salesman showed me how to get the most out of a sheet of sandpaper. Fold the sheet in half in both directions. Then tear the sheet halfway through on the short fold line.

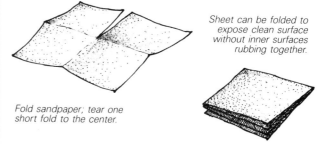

Now fold the sandpaper up into a four-layer sanding pad. The sheet can be refolded different ways to expose a fresh surface. None of the sanding surfaces rub against each other, which results in a longer-lasting sanding pad.

—*Steve Chastain, Bellingham, Wash.*

Stopping sandpaper gumming

If your sandpaper loads up with residue when you're sanding wood that has been stripped, for example, throw some pumice-stone powder on the work. The paper will keep working and won't load up, and the abrasive will stay sharp longer. Add more pumice as needed.

—Jon Gullett, Washington, Ill.

Homemade cabinet scraper

Cabinet scrapers can be made to special shapes from old hand or power saw blades. Cheap saws seem to work as well as good ones. The ideal thickness is about $\frac{1}{32}$ in., and 3 in. by 5 in. is a nice size. After cutting out the scraper with tin snips—little nibbles will do a better job than big bites—hammer the edge to remove irregularities. With the scraper flat on an oilstone, rub to flatten the edges and continue the process begun with the hammer. Next, drawfile the edge in a vise,

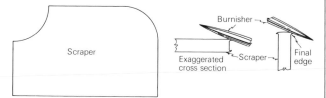

Scraper

Burnisher

Exaggerated cross section

Scraper

Final edge

then back to the stone, then draw the stone along the edge as you did the file. The object is to produce a sharp, square edge. Next, turn the edge with a piece of steel—a burnisher is best but a drill shank will work, as will an auto valve stem—anything hard and smooth. Hold the scraper horizontally, with the end of the edge you are working on braced against your chest. Then, pressing hard, draw the tool along the whole edge; reverse direction and do the other side. Then hold the scraper vertically away from your body and turn the edge down. The edge can be renewed several times by turning it down before you need to use the stone again.

—John Owen, Isaacs Harbor, N.S.

Glass scraper

Microscope slides work very well as scrapers, particularly in tight places like the interiors of small boxes, or drawers. When the edge is fresh, they cut beautifully, and though they lose the edge faster than a metal scraper, they are disposable and don't require the time spent on resharpening. I've found that so-called petrographic slides (27mm x 46mm) are sturdier than biological slides (25mm x 75mm). One supplier (of many) is Buehler, Ltd., 41 Waukegan Rd., PO Box 1, Lake Bluff, Ill. 60044.   *—John Reid, Amherst, Mass.*

Recycling old blades as scrapers

An excellent cabinet scraper can be made from a section of a 1-in. or wider bandsaw blade. Just cut the blade to 9-in. lengths, grind off the teeth and round the ends to get the shape you need. Because the blade flexes you can scrape hard-to-finish surfaces like handrails and cabriole legs.

—John E. Freimuth III, Peoria, Ill.

Hacksaw scrapers

I recycle 12-in. power hacksaw blades as scrapers. When you grind the teeth off the blade, the resulting scalloped edge (from the wavy set) can be used for fast, rough stock removal. Reserve the other edge for finish work.

—Girvan P. Milligan, Carmel, N.Y.

Shop Aids & Construction Tips

Chapter 8

Fold-away ladder

Needing some form of access to an overhead storage area, I rejected a stepladder (shaky and dangerous) and permanent stairs (loss of valuable shop space). The solution was a sturdy,

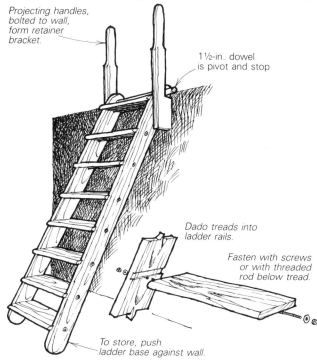

Projecting handles, bolted to wall, form retainer bracket.

1½-in. dowel is pivot and stop

Dado treads into ladder rails.

Fasten with screws or with threaded rod below tread.

To store, push ladder base against wall.

shop-built, fold-away ladder. It is always there when it's needed and a simple pull locks it into place. Because the steps are wide (more like stair treads) and the slant is not so steep (20° from vertical), the ladder is safe and reassuring to use. The projecting handles at the top make the most unstable phase of descent—mounting the ladder at the top—hardly more precarious than descending your front porch steps. With few changes you could adapt the design for over-the-side access or through-the-ceiling access.

—*William Lego, Springfield, Va.*

William Lego's fold-away ladder is a good idea, which I've used a few times in construction and remodeling. But his 1½-in. dowel running through the top of the ladder is a tripper at the worst possible spot. I suggest blocks screwed to the outside of each riser, leaving the passage unobstructed.

—*Dick Alexander, Lakeville, Conn.*

Plywood rack

For those whose shop lacks the space to flat-stack sheets of plywood, here's a vertical rack that will neatly contain the sheets and prevent the warping that results from merely leaning the sheets up against a wall.

—*Bruce Bozman, Addison, N.Y.*

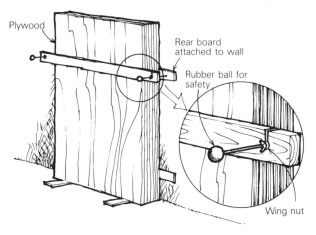

Plywood

Rear board attached to wall

Rubber ball for safety

Wing nut

Jig indexing mechanism

This indexing mechanism can be incorporated into a variety of woodworking jigs for the table saw, drill press, overarm router, and other machines where accurately spaced cuts, dadoes or holes are required. The idea was originally given to me by Herman Kundera, a knowledgeable woodworker from San Bruno, Calif.

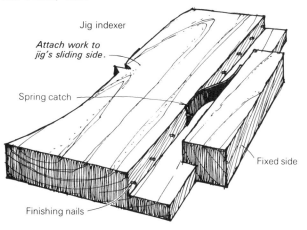

Jig indexer

Attach work to jig's sliding side.

Spring catch

Fixed side

Finishing nails

The mechanism consists of a spring catch mounted to the jig's fixed or base side and stops of finishing-nail heads set in the sliding side of the jig. The locations of the catch and the nails can be reversed if it's more convenient. For precise, accurate spacing, predrill holes for the finishing nails with a slightly undersized bit. Vary the nail spacing as required for the particular job at hand. Although I made my spring catch from a piece of hacksaw blade (anneal for bending and drilling, then reharden and temper), any thin piece of metal would make a serviceable catch. Fasten the catch to the jig with a roundhead screw.

In using the jig you will slide one part against the other. The spring will ride up and over the nail head and then click down. When you feel the spring click, move the jig back until the spring catch registers against the nail. Now you're ready to proceed with cutting, drilling or whatever.

—*Donald M. Steinert, Grants Pass, Oregon*

Handsaw storage rack

This shop-built saw holder provides a convenient place to store handsaws and straightedges that may be leaning against a wall or lying about in your workshop. To use it, slip the saw in from the bottom and give it a tug down to

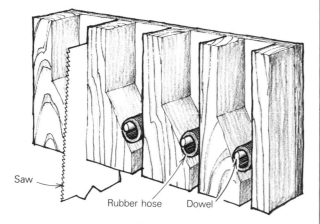

Saw

Rubber hose   Dowel

wedge it in place. I used ½-in. plywood for the back of the rack and 2-in. material for the partitions. I found that rubber hose from an automobile heater works better for the grippers than plastic garden hose, which is too smooth. The dimensions aren't critical, but if the dowels are too high, the hose won't pinch the sawblade. If they are too low, the hose jumps to the floor when you remove a saw. Trial and error will find the happy medium.

—*Kim Anderson, Loyalton, Calif.*

Laminated plywood storage bracket

To store plywood in our new shop, we built a laminated bracket that doesn't take up floor space, and is a pleasure to look at besides. The curve, which is sized to hold 34 in. of material, was drawn full-size on brown paper. To make the 6-in. wide laminations, two ash planks, 2 in. thick by 12 ft. long, were resawn on the bandsaw. To achieve the final 1-in. thickness required ten strips, planed to about $\frac{1}{10}$ in. thick. We bent and clamped the laminations directly over the drawing, with no clamping form except for a short fence that ensured that the part to be screwed to the wall would be straight. Using rollers,

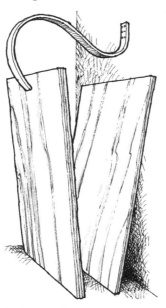

we coated each lamination with plastic resin glue. Next, three of us clamped the laminated stock first to the fence, then every 2 or 3 in. along the lines of the drawing, using 54 clamps in all. The laminations easily aligned to the curve.

One final and important note: Our choice of ash, a long-fiber, springy hardwood, came from experience. On our first attempt we used hemlock, which failed when it was loaded up with plywood. The break was fast, noisy and spectacular!

—*John Grew-Sheridan, San Francisco, Calif.*

Cabinet-hanging prop

After years of struggling to hang upper cabinets, I built this simple prop. Now I can hang the upper units by myself, regardless of their size. Make the prop from ¾-in. plywood, except for the center support beam, which is oak. Dimensions depend on the height of the jack. For this application, I believe a screw jack works better than a hydraulic jack.

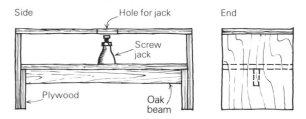

Side   Hole for jack   End

Screw jack

Plywood   Oak beam

To use, first install the lower units and set the prop on top of one (protecting the countertop with plywood). With the upper cabinet balanced on the prop, screw the jack up until the upper unit contacts the ceiling. Leveling and plumbing can be done after the top band has been anchored to the wall (I use dry-wall screws).   —*James E. Gier, Mesa, Ariz.*

Holding cabinets in place

If you make a lot of kitchen cabinets and work alone, as I do, you know that it is difficult to hold the cabinets in position while you're fastening them to the wall. This method uses pipe clamps to solve the problem. Remove the screw end from your long pipe clamps. Slide the adjustable stops up the clamps and use the clamps to wedge the cabinets in place.

—*Randy Hazlett, Ashland, Ohio*

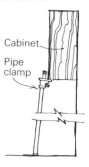

Cabinet

Pipe clamp

Reversing switch

Occasionally I find it necessary to reverse the motor on my Sears shaper and other tools. But reversing switches are expensive ($39 for the one Sears sells) so here's how I made my own for $1.59. Buy a 10 ampere, 125 volts a.c. double-pole, double-throw switch from an electronics supply house (I used Radio Shack Cat. No. 275-1533). Refer to the motor in-

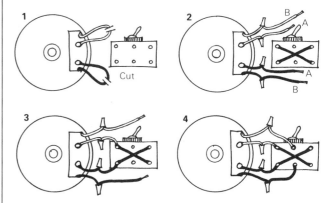

struction manual to locate the wires that can be switched to reverse the motor. You'll splice the switch into these so cut them and add 6 in. or 8 in. of #16 wire to each end. This gives you two sets of wires which are labeled set A and set B in the diagrams. Cross-connect opposite end posts on the switch. Then connect set A to one set of end contacts on the switch and set B to the center set of contacts on the switch.

The whole project takes only about 45 minutes. The 10 amp switch is really overrated—but safe.

—*Jon Gullett, Washington, Ill.*

Reversing belt-driven tools

It's easy to reverse disc sanders and other belt-driven tools if the motor is mounted perpendicular to the shaft it drives, so there's a quarter-turn in the belt, as shown. To reverse, simply loosen the belt, flip 180° (on either pulley) and tighten. The twist in the belt seems to dampen vibrations—an added advantage.

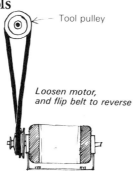

Tool pulley

Loosen motor, and flip belt to reverse

—*Roger Lynne,*
Bloomington, Minn.

Portable exhaust fan

The various home-workshop exhaust systems I'd seen either were too expensive or would simply suck all the precious heated air from the shop. The latter problem is important when you live in a northern climate and like to spend long winter nights over a lathe.

The dust-exhaust system I built solves these problems. It is inexpensive, portable and of low velocity (so as not to empty all the heat from the shop). I mounted a 70-CFM bathroom fan to a 4-ft. long maple strip notched to hang on nails adjacent to my work areas.

The fan is vented through a standard dryer vent using 3-

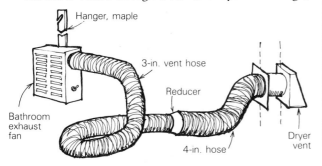

Hanger, maple

3-in. vent hose

Reducer

Bathroom exhaust fan

4-in. hose

Dryer vent

in. flexible bathroom vent hose. Since the vent hose is 3 in. in diameter and the dryer vent is 4 in. in diameter, I installed a PVC hose reducer to mate the two sizes.

For convenience and neatness, you can run the electrical wire through the hose or tape it to the outside. I installed a toggle switch to the fan box for turning the fan on and off.

The fan is handy for drawing paint fumes away, in addition to its main job of removing dust. But the darned idea works so well that even chips are drawn into the hose—I have to uncouple the hose and dump them out about once a month. —*Ronald R. Stoltz, Guelph, Ont.*

Locking up tools

A miniature padlock attached to the plug of a portable tool or a free-standing machine prevents unauthorized use in the school shop. At home it is a safety measure that keeps small children from "helping." More than one plug can be locked

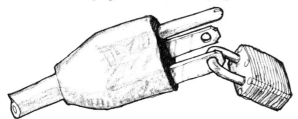

with a single padlock; the one shown here is Master Lock Co. No. 9B, available at hardware stores. Tools may be locked to a fixed object, for security.—*R. Bruce Hoadley, Amherst, Mass.*

Installing glass for easy replacement

This method for securing glass in mitered frames makes it easy to replace the glass if it's ever broken. The key to the method is a special molding that fits in a groove cut into the frame. First cut a rabbet in the inside edge of the frame stock. Then cut a groove in the frame stock offset from the rabbet's shoulder by the thickness of the glass. Next mill the molding with a tongue that slips into the groove with a snug fit. Assemble the frame and molding as shown in the sketch with two pieces on the bottom. If you have cut and fit the pieces carefully you won't need any brads or glue to lock the molding in place. —*Douglas L. Wahl, Washingtonville, N.Y.*

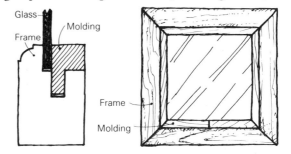

Glass

Frame

Molding

Frame

Molding

Heating the shop

Heating a woodworking shop can be a problem—sawdust and paint vapors present a fire hazard. Local heating firms suggested several approaches including a separate "heating room," a gas wall heater, infrared heating and electric baseboard heating. All these approaches were either too expensive, a fire hazard or both. Finally, I chose electric hot-water baseboard heat for my just completed 14-ft. by 22-ft. woodworking shed. I was a little worried about the operating cost, but surprisingly, costs have been only slightly higher than gas heat. The unit keeps the water at an even temperature and doesn't cycle on and off like other heating systems. Hot water baseboard units weigh less than 30 lb. and can be purchased as portable or permanently mounted models. They don't stir up the air—an ideal situation for a dusty shop or paint room. Because the units operate at a continuous low heat, they're not a fire hazard.

I chose the largest model the supplier had—a 220-volt portable unit that sells for about $150. It measures 4 in. by 9 in. by 107 in. long and produces 6,800 BTU. The supplier: Intertherm Inc., 10820 Sunset Office Drive, St. Louis, Mo. 63116. —*R. Voorhees, Ft. Wayne, Ind.*

Light stands

For temporary lighting in my new shop, I built a couple of light stands from 2x4s with 1x4 legs. Two or three inexpensive clamp-lights completed the fixtures. The poles are easy to move around and don't take a lot of room. They're versatile and inexpensive. Although I've added overhead lighting now in my shop, I haven't been able to do without my light stands.
-*A. Miller, Lakewood, Col.*

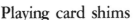

Clamp-lights

2x4 pole

1x4 legs

Playing card shims

We use playing cards for shims when making fine adjustments on setups and jigs. "Bicycle" brand cards are 0.011 in. thick—you can bet on it.

—*Edward F. Groh, Naperville, Ill.*
and Charles E. Cohn, Clarendon Hills, Ill.

Are you taking notes?

A small 3x5 pad of paper anchored to the wrist with a large rubber band is invaluable when taking measurements, sketching details or working in cramped quarters. The arrangement leaves both hands free for work yet provides an instantly available writing surface that never gets misplaced.

—James Vickery, Garrison, N.Y.

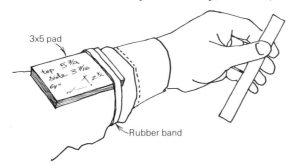

3x5 pad

Rubber band

Removing broken screws

To remove a broken screw, drill a small hole in the shank. Insert a copper wire in the hole to conduct heat, then heat the wire with a torch until the wood around the screw bubbles and smokes a bit. Quickly tap a tapered, square punch into the hole and back out the screw. The heat liquefies resins in the wood and makes removal easier. Properly done, the procedure does not damage the hole, and another screw the same size may be used.

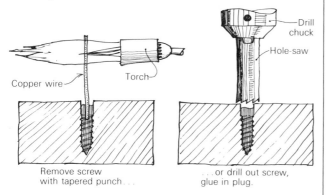

Copper wire

Torch

Drill chuck

Hole-saw

Remove screw with tapered punch...

...or drill out screw, glue in plug.

If the heat procedure doesn't work, drill out the broken screw with a tubular hole-saw just large enough to slip over the screw shank. Make the hole-saw by filing several coarse teeth in the end of a short section of thin steel tube. Drill out the broken screw, then glue in a plug to fill the hole.

—Jerry C. Blanchard, Carmel, Calif.

Sheet metal screws faster in wood

To my brother and me as builders, "time is money." We've discovered that replacing standard wood screws with Phillips-head sheet-metal screws results in a faster and stronger job in building applications. I have never felt the standard wood screw had the strength we needed. So we started using pan-head sheet-metal screws which, because of their deep thread and straight shank, had greater holding power, but couldn't use them for all applications because of their appearance.

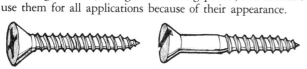

Sheet-metal screw

Wood screw

Then, by accident, one of our carpenters brought a box of flat-head Phillips sheet-metal screws on the job. Since then we've used nothing else. On an average house we use 2,000

screws. We fit a commercial-duty ⅜-in. variable-speed drill with a Phillips Yankee Screwdriver bit and start plugging away. This approach is fast, easy and gives strong results.

I don't understand why sheet-metal screws aren't a standard in woodworking procedure—perhaps it's because many lumberyards and supply houses don't carry the screws. Sheet-rock screws are similar (they have a finer thread) but are also relatively hard to find. *—Jeff Tallman, Weston, Conn.*

EDITOR'S NOTE: Screw manufacturers and fastener suppliers echo Tallman's observation. A representative of a Chicago-based company commented that sheet-metal screws are made of stronger, case-hardened, medium-carbon (1022) steel. The threads are "rolled," which results in denser, stronger work-hardened threads. Metal screws typically have one or two more threads per inch and are threaded right up to the head. On the other hand, wood screws are made of soft, low-carbon (1010) steel. Threads are "cut," which "opens the pores" of the steel and results in weaker threads. The representative felt the unthreaded shank was more of a nuisance than a benefit. His personal opinion was "wood screws are inferior—the only reason they continue to be used is ignorance."

One disadvantage of metal screws is that, in continuous use, the case-hardened heads eat up the drivers, but the case-hardening step can sometimes be skipped on special request to reduce driver wear.

Dip for screws

When you purchase a box of wood screws (brass or steel), dip them in a solution made of two tablespoons of bowling-alley wax dissolved in a pint of mineral spirits. Spread the screws out on a piece of kraft paper to dry before returning them to the box for storage. It will keep the brass bright, the steel from rusting and will make them go into the wood with half the effort, thus reducing breakage. *—Charles F. Riordan, Dansville, N.Y.*

Coating nails

Nails coated with rosin are difficult to pull out. To coat your own nails or brads, dissolve about 4 tablespoons of powdered rosin in about a half pint of denatured alcohol. Store in a tightly covered container. Pour a small amount of the solution into an old shallow pan or dish, then swirl the nails around in the solution until they are covered. Dump the nails onto old newspapers. Stir occasionally until they are almost dry, about five minutes. Then let them dry thoroughly.

—Price G. Schulte, St. Louis, Mo.

Extracting wooden plugs

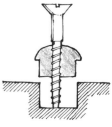

To extract a wooden plug, drill a ⅛-in. pilot hole through its center, carefully, so as not to drill into the dowel or screw beneath. Then grind the point off a #8 steel wood screw, and screw it into the hole. When the screw bottoms out, the plug will pop.
—Gerald Kaufman, Halstead, Kan.

Cleaning saw blades

Oven cleaner works well for removing pitch from bits and saw blades without harming the steel. A clean cutting surface stays sharp longer, gives better results, taxes the motor less and makes for safer use of the tool. *—Chuck Oliver, Fremont, N.H., and George Eckhart, Kenosha, Wis.*

Protecting sawblades

Plastic backbone strips (sold by office-supply stores for binding reports) make inexpensive but effective sawblade guards. Cut a strip to length with a razor blade. If a longer strip is needed, epoxy two strips together using a short portion of the strip for reinforcement at the joint. The backbone grips the blade and will not fall off easily; to remove the strip, just slide it forward. *—B.A. Cartwright, Milwaukee, Wis.*

Auxiliary shop-vac tank

For sawdust collection I use a couple of Sears shop-vacs that I connect to my tools through normal methods. But by using auxiliary dust-collection tanks, I'm able to stretch the filter-cleaning cycle considerably. To make the tank, start with a

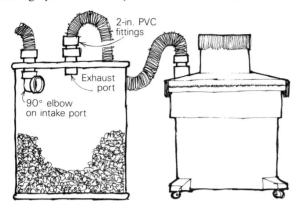

55-gal. drum or a fiber barrel (the kind with the removable clamp-on lid works well), and install 2-in. PVC pipe intake and exhaust ports as shown in the sketch. The 90° elbow on the intake port sets up a cyclone action that drops dust and chips at the perimeter and bottom of the tank. You can fill the auxiliary tank to the elbow and still have the vacuum filter open and breathing.

The 2-in. PVC pipe fittings fit the standard flexible hose ends commonly used on shop-vacs, increasing their versatility and hook-up options.   —*D.J. Greenwald, Hudson, Wis.*

Finishing

Chapter 9

Repairing trim

A piece of furniture may seem beyond repair if a large chunk of ornate trim is missing or damaged. The repairman may lack the skills to carve a new piece of wood, or the carving may cost more than the furniture itself. The answer is to make a mold from the existing trim and cast a new piece with auto body putty, better known as bondo.

Bondo comes in two parts, a resin and a catalyst. It does not dry, but rather cures, and therefore (unlike plastic wood) does not shrink. When it has cured it can be shaped and drilled like wood. It won't absorb stain, but can be painted or colored with Blendal powdered stains (from Mohawk Chemical Co., Amsterdam, N.Y.) to match the surrounding wood.

To make a mold, remove a section of undamaged trim from the furniture and drive a couple of finishing nails into the back of it, to act as handles. Fill a container with plaster of Paris, grease the front surface of the trim with any light oil, and push it firmly into the plaster. As you set the trim, wiggle it a bit to ensure a good contact and be careful not to let the plaster flow over the back of it. When the mold has hardened, use the nails to pull the trim out. The finish on it will be blushed from the moisture in the plaster, but it can be restored by using Mohawk's blender flow-out, which comes both glossy and flat.

New trim can now be made by greasing the mold and pouring bondo into it. Stir gently to get rid of air bubbles. When the bondo starts to cure, set a few nails in the back for handles so it can be pulled from the mold. After it is solid it can be pared with a knife, sanded and cut to fill the damaged area on the furniture. Attach it with epoxy glue. Bondo continues to cure for about a week and if you wait too long to trim and sand it, it will be like steel.

Bondo can also be used to repair a damaged corner or other area where it isn't practical to make a mold from existing trim. First clean the damaged area and cut away any slivers of wood. Don't be afraid to enlarge it—another half-inch won't make any difference. Drive a few finishing nails into the damaged area to anchor the bondo, but make sure the heads are below the undamaged surface. Now wrap aluminum foil around some small pieces of wood, such as tongue depressors, and tape them to the undamaged wood so they bridge the repair zone and act as a form for the bondo. Trowel in the plastic, in layers if necessary, and when it cures remove the forms. You'll have a crude representation of the undamaged area, which can then be shaped with a knife and sandpaper.

—*Glenn Rathke, Pompano Beach, Fla.*

Raising dents

To eliminate or reduce dents in wood use a soldering iron, a natural-fiber, smooth-finish cloth folded to a point, water, and discretion.

Wet the dent, allowing the crushed fibers to soak up the water. Squeeze excess water out of the cloth. Bring the iron up to the boiling point, but not to full heat. Test the wet cloth until it steams. Press the wet cloth into the dent with the hot iron for as long as steam is still produced. Repeat, if necessary, until no further rising occurs. You cannot burn the wood as long as the cloth is wet, so press the iron for brief intervals and be sure the cloth is continually wet. This should be done only on raw wood; if there is finish on the piece, remove the finish first.

Raise the dent before final planing or scraping. Otherwise, the dent may rise above the planed surface. Make one or two passes with a plane at its finest setting after raising the dent. An older method is to use a household iron. This is cumbersome and also raises the grain in the undamaged wood around the dent.

This technique works as long as the dented fibers have been crushed and not torn. —*Henry T. Kramer, Rye, N.Y.*

Bleaching walnut

Antique walnut furniture is usually a fairly even light brown color. I have had the problem of matching this color when replacing broken or lost parts with local walnut, which is dark brown and heavily streaked. My solution is to sand the entire piece rather heavily to remove scratches and discoloration. Then I cut and sand new parts to final fit, and bleach them to a cream color with Blanchit wood bleach (available from Constantine's, 2050 Eastchester Road, Bronx, N.Y. 10461), taking care to protect my hands, face and eyes. Then I boil a batch of old walnut hulls in water to cover, let them steep some time to reduce the amount of water to about ½ the original amount, cool and strain. This makes a weak stain. I apply as many liberal wetting coats as needed to match the old wood.
—*Albert J. Gnaedinger, Pocahontas, Ill.*

Natural stains

All my stains are made from natural materials—nuts, wood and plants. They are very true in color. First you must gather material for the color you desire. The dry husks of black walnut shells give a deep brown tone. Dry beechnut husks make a deep yellow tan, plug tobacco an antique yellow, red swamp cedar chips a reddish-brown. I have used other nuts and woods; I suggest experimenting with whatever is available to you. My mother, part Indian, suggested many natural materials to use for stains, and so was a great help in my search. The Indians used a homemade lye, but I found an easier answer—non-sudsing ammonia.

Place the materials to be leached in a jar, pour in the ammonia until the material is covered, and let sit. Black walnuts absorb the liquid, so it may be necessary to add more ammonia to keep the husks saturated. How long you soak the material affects the deepness of the color. Tobacco leaches out in a week. Black walnut shells still have color after a month and can sometimes be washed and used for a second batch.

After the tone is right, strain the juice off through a nylon stocking into a clean jar. (Don't use cans, because they will rust.) Leave the jar open for several days until most of the ammonia smell has dissipated. It can be used right away, but is strong-smelling! For a lighter tone, dilute with water; for a darker stain, let the liquid evaporate. Because the stain is water-based, the wood will need light rubbing after application. The stain works well under oil or varnish finishes.

Be sure to use non-sudsing ammonia. Sudsing ammonia will carry the color to the top with the suds.
—*C.H. Dimmick, Sparta, N.J.*

Staining curly maple

Curly maple—fiddleback, tiger-tail, or whatever you may call it—requires a staining technique all its own. Maple with a curl was the favorite wood for the stocks of the muzzle-loading rifles of yesteryear. The staining method described here has come down by word of mouth from the old gunsmiths.

Great-grandpa used two stains and he made both of them. For the first you must find a handful of rusty cut nails—very old and very rusty cut nails are best. Place about a dozen in a soup bowl and cover them with homemade apple-cider vinegar, the stronger the better. Do not use a metal dish and do not substitute commercial vinegars or white vinegar. Cover to prevent evaporation and let stand for two weeks.

For the second stain dissolve potassium dichromate crystals in water. It need not be a saturated solution but I use it fairly strong. You can buy these crystals, or you might try begging a few from your high-school chemistry teacher. This stain can be used immediately.

We will assume your curly maple stock is now in the white and you have it sanded dead smooth. Use a rag swab to coat the stock with the vinegar stain. When it dries it should be about the color of a slate roof—not very pretty. This stain will penetrate deeply into the soft spots, but it will only sit on the surface of the hard stripes. Allow an hour for drying, or speed it up a bit with some heat. Now with a good grade of 220 garnet paper, sand this stain off the hard stripes; you will be unable to sand it off the soft spots where it has penetrated deeply. Sand a bit more here and a bit less there to bring out all the figure. Be sure to use a sanding block. The stripes are very hard and the spaces are soft. Sanding without a block can result in a washboard effect.

Now, using a new swab, stain the stock with the potassium dichromate stain. This stain will penetrate those hard, white stripes and color them a rich orange-yellow. It will also change that slate color to a rich dark brown. When the second stain is dry, sand it off with a very fine paper. Now put several drops of boiled linseed oil in the palm of each hand and rub it in lovingly, lean back, and feast your eye. The oil is only to bring out the color. Allow plenty of drying time before you apply your favorite finish.

If you prefer to stick to grandpap's methods, give it an oil finish. An old gunsmith put it this way: ". . . three drops of boiled linseed oil and then three weeks of rub." Use as little oil as possible to cover the stock.

—*Bob Winger, Montoursville, Pa.*

Shoe-polish stain

Ordinary wax-based shoe polish makes a good stain and filler for open-grained woods such as walnut and oak. In a small jar, mix a chunk of polish with enough turpentine to liquefy, then rub the liquid in and wipe off as you would with regular stain. Several shades are available—I like the black with walnut. The coating won't interfere with subsequent finishing.

—*Carl R. Vitale, Cranston, R.I.*

Easier than pumice

Scotchbrite (an abrasive plastic wool) makes a good finishing material. It's easier to use than pumice and oil, and can be used dry so that you can see what you're doing. It's inexpensive and durable, but, being soft, is not as good as abrasive paper for taking off high spots. Scotchbrite is available in supermarkets or in various grades from welding supply houses. —*Edward S. Taylor, Lincoln, Mass.*

Shine, Mister?

When a finish is just "not quite right" I've found that a good stiff shoe brush used with fine abrasive powder can work wonders. Sprinkle a small quantity of either pumice, rottenstone or tripoli (depending on the desired effect) on the piece and brush vigorously with the grain. The sheen of a finish can be blended and evened out—light scratches and imperfections can be erased. Select finer abrasives for a glossy finish and coarser abrasives for a satin sheen. I have obtained better results faster with this method than with steel wool, oil or water hand-rubbing, and so forth. The technique can be used on oil, wax, lacquer or even French-polish finishes.

A shoe brush can also be used to embed grain accents such as red and white lead, Prussian blue, lampblack or malachite. Brush the accent in, wipe off the excess with the grain and seal—that's all that's necessary.

It's important, however, to use a natural-bristle, thick, clean brush of the highest quality. I use an old pure badger brush that I wouldn't trade for anything—well, maybe for some walnut or rosewood or. . . .

—*Christian Albrecht, Allentown, Pa.*

A replacement for rags

Before I discovered the bonded cellulose wipers I now use for oil and wax finishes, I used cloth rags. After I accumulated a pile of the dirty rags I cleaned them by first dunking in a solution of acetone and dry-cleaning fluid and then sneaking the batch through our washing machine. The cleaning solution was nasty and the whole process a headache.

Now I use Wyp-Alls, an industrial paper towel manufactured by Scott. I assume other paper companies market similar products. By the case, the 13x15 cloth-like wipers sell for a little over 4ᵗ each. The paper towels, which are designed for use with oil and solvents, work as well as, and perhaps better than, cloth. —*Bill Huggins, Issaquah, Wash.*

Cheap stain

At the picture-frame manufacturing company where I work, 12-ft. bundles of frame molding are dumped into a vat of stain and then put aside to dry. I noticed that much stain was lost as it dripped off the drying bundles and asked the owner why he let the stain drip away without any attempt to collect and reuse it. His answer was that the "stain" was actually lap cement (an asphalt-based roofing product available at building-supply stores) diluted with turpentine, so inexpensive he didn't bother to reclaim it.

Our shop mixture of 5 gal. lap cement to 50 gal. turpentine produces a medium walnut color. At home I find a half cup of cement to a half gallon of turpentine will stain pine a deep golden brown. —*George Kramer, Santa Rosa, Calif.*

Removing mill marks

In order to achieve a good finish, the tiny ridges left by milling machines must be removed. The best method my students and I have found for removing mill marks is with the cabinet scraper (we use the Stanley #80). The problem is being able to see these mill marks. By rubbing a piece of white chalk over the entire surface of a surfaced or jointed board, one can readily see these imperfections. The mill marks show up as white waves across the grain.

You can then scrape with a cabinet scraper until the chalk marks—and the mill marks—disappear. Drag the chalk across the stock again and it will hardly leave a mark. Using a cabinet scraper also reduces sanding time.

—*Dennis W. Kempf, Bellevue, Wash.*

Collapsible finish containers

Collapsible plastic bottles for photographic chemicals (available from photo supply houses) make excellent working and storage containers for tung oil and other finishing materials that skin over or polymerize in half-empty cans. As the finish is used up, the bottles can be folded like an accordian before the top is screwed on, which eliminates just about all of the air.

—*T. Carpenter, Calgary, Alta.*

Finishing clocks

I build hall and wall clocks. I use only walnut lumber. When I am finished with the case I don't fill the wood or stain it. I use only hot boiled linseed oil, nothing else. It makes a very beautiful finish. The grain seems to come to the surface in streaks of brown and some black. If there is a knot it turns black. For heating the oil I use an electric glue-pot of one quart size. I heat the oil to a point where it is too hot to put on with a rag, so I use a 1-in. nylon paintbrush. A brush also gets into the corners better than a rag. After the oil is applied, let it set until you see dry spots appear. This could take from 5 to 20 minutes, depending on room temperature and humidity. Then take a wool cloth or pad and rub the wood until the oil seems to disappear. What you are doing is forcing the oil into the wood. One or more coats can be applied. If one of my clocks is scratched or nicked, all it takes is a little sanding and a little hot oil and the scratch disappears.

—*George Eckhart, Kenosha, Wis.*

Clearing a clouded finish

It's a hot, muggy day and you've just shot a heavy coat of lacquer on a nice project. A few minutes pass and you discover the finish has clouded with moisture. Here's how to clear the finish. Shoot the clouded area with acetone. The acetone will clear the finish and bring the moisture to the surface. Quickly wipe it off. To continue, thin the lacquer and shoot sparingly. —*Robert M. Vaughan, Roanoke, Va.*

Blending veneers

Before I strip the finish from a piece of old veneered furniture, I do any necessary veneer repairs. Then when I strip, color from the old finish stains the patch and blends it into the old wood. —*Don Teach, Shreveport, La.*

Filler for knot holes

When repairing knot holes and the like, I use auto-body filler tinted with dry colors and oil colors. It sets up quick and hard, doesn't shrink, and can be shaped with woodworking tools—Surforms work particularly well, especially before the filler has cured completely. Be sure to use a filler with red catalyst, not blue. —*Pope A. Lawrence, Santa Fe, N. Mex.*

Polishing turnings

During the past fifteen years I have had considerable experience with lathe turning. I have found that after all the cutting has been completed and the turning is sanded to 200-grit and steel-wooled with 4/0, the wood is polished to a low lustre that still shows any small pits or striations remaining from sanding. Since these areas will not polish, they should again be sanded and steel-wooled. Polishing the turning with its own shavings will result in a satin lustre which can be left as is, or then lacquered, oiled, etc.

—*Paul L. McClure, Denver, Colo.*

Cleaning with shavings

Cedar shavings make an ideal cleaner for chrome or any hard finish, such as paint or varnish. They will also leave glass sparkling clean.

You can get a good supply by fine planing or by filing with a Surform, which I use. If you want to store the stuff, keep in a dust-proof container and start with a clean shingle. Or you can take a chunk about the size of a sanding block from an ordinary cedar shingle and rub a high shine on old varnish or paint that is beginning to oxidize.

In case you have some real gunk to remove, immerse a fistful of shavings in water, rub the surface clean and then finish with the dry shavings. Everything usually comes out shining. —*Robert L. Johnson, Whittier, Calif.*

Disposable foam brush

I use this homemade foam brush with its disposable insert on those little oil-finish or paint jobs where it is more work to clean a brush than to do the job.

I fold ½-in. thick foam carpet padding around the end of a ⅟₃₂-in. aluminum stiffening strip, and clamp it with a rubber band in an aluminum holder. After the job is done, you can throw away the foam and wipe off the aluminum.

—*Harry M. McCully, Allegany, N.Y.*

Decorating turned goods

To produce decorative black rings on tool handles and other lathe work, twist a dowel peg handle on each end of a 12-in. long piece of soft iron wire. Any medium-gauge wire will do.

To use, scribe a shallow starting groove in the work with the point of a skew. Then press the wire against the starting groove. In five or ten seconds friction will generate enough heat to scorch the groove. The resulting fine black ring, sparingly used, gives a tasteful decorative effect.

—*Larry Joseph, Alva, Okla.*

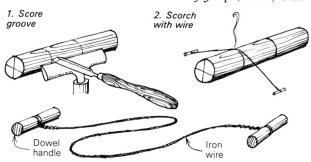

1. Score groove

2. Scorch with wire

Dowel handle

Iron wire

Keeping padauk's color

Many woods that have brilliant color when freshly cut, padauk for example, will darken and turn brown in time. Bruce Hoadley points out that the major culprit in this color change is ultraviolet light. To shield the wood from ultraviolet light and thus effectively slow the darkening process, I use a product called Armor-All, a spray-on protective liquid for auto vinyl. This product, available at auto supply stores, is quite effective—I have yet to see the color of padauk change, even after four years. To use, spray three or four coats of Armor-All on the wood before you apply the finish. I use an oil finish, which is compatible with Armor-All, but other finishes such as lacquer or varnish may not be. You'd best test the particular finish you plan to use. —*David Lewis, Phoenix, Ariz.*

Shading marquetry veneer

Sand-scorching has been used in marquetry for years to achieve the subtle shades needed to show shadows, curvature and depth. The standard procedure calls for either dipping the veneer into a hot sand bath or spooning the hot sand onto the veneer in repeated steps to gradually shade the area. Recently I discovered a direct-scorching technique that proved quite successful. I used a miniature 5-in. butane torch (available from Microflame, Inc., 3724 Oregon Ave., Minneapolis, Minn. 55246). The secret is to use unheated sand to mask the area to be scorched. I carefully line each shadow area with a layer of sand, leaving no area that I want to remain light-toned uncovered. I slowly warm and shade the exposed areas with the torch to create the appearance of gentle curves or dimples. The sand acts as a deflection shield to repel heat in proportion to the amount of sand piled up on the unexposed area. When I need to show a sharp hard-edged shadow, I cut into the veneer along the edge of the shadow, dip a thin metal heat shield into the cut and scorch the exposed veneer. Great care must be taken with open-edged pieces because they burn readily, and shrinkage is a certainty. To expand shrunken pieces I wipe on a solution of equal parts water, white glue and glycerine. This solution usually returns the piece to its original size.

—*Martin R. Zschoche, Vista, Calif.*

Inlaying with dental silver

You can inlay silver into wood using the silver amalgam that dentists use to fill teeth. Draw the design on the wood, scribe the outline, then deepen the cut to $\frac{3}{32}$ in. or so with a small chisel or a rotary bur. Undercut the edge of the design to hold the amalgam (a dentists' inverted cone bur is ideal).

Now pack silver amalgam into the groove. After the alloy has set, smooth the surface with a flat tool. After 24 hours, level and polish the inlay with wet-or-dry sandpaper, finishing with 600-grit.

The inlay won't polish to a mirror finish, but will take on a softer sheen, something like pewter. It will need a coat of finish (tung oil works) to keep it from tarnishing.

For small designs (three initials about 2 in. tall, for example) the cost is minimal, probably about $1.00.

—*Lawrence Warner, Encino, Calif.*

EDITOR'S NOTE: My own dentist's reaction was "Now why didn't I think of that." Intrigued, he showed me some premeasured plastic capsules (about the size of a cowboy's bullet), with powdered silver alloy in one end, mercury in the other, and a seal in between. A vibrating machine shakes the capsule end-to-end, and a little metal pellet inside the capsule breaks the seal and mixes the two ingredients, much like an agitator ball in a can of spray paint. He explained that different companies market different kinds of capsules with varying seal arrangements, amounts of silver, alloy mixtures and working consistencies, but none of the variables should affect the amalgam's use for inlay. The capsules he demonstrated contained silver the volume of a pea, and cost about 60¢ each.

He gave me a couple of capsules to try at home. There I found I could mix the amalgam by simply taping the capsule to the blade of a portable scroll saw and running it for 30 seconds at high speed. I also found that, in a pinch, you can mix the mercury and silver powder in a shot glass, using a rounded dowel as a pestle. Inlaying was no problem, but the silver will fill the pores of open-grained wood around the inlay, and it must be picked out later with a pin.

One cautionary note: free mercury is poisonous, as is mercury vapor. After mixing, the amalgam is non-toxic.   —*J.R.*

Cutting a dutchman

"Dutchman" is the name given to an irregularly shaped inlay that's used to repair a blemish (such as a cigarette burn) in woodwork. Typically the woodworker cuts the inlay first, traces its outline on the stock and cuts the shallow mortise to

fit. Here's an alternative approach that allows you to cut the mortise first or match an existing mortise. I'm sure the technique could be applied to marquetry work as well.

Lay a piece of paper over the mortise and shade the area around the mortise with the flat of a pencil (sketch, below). The edges of the mortise will stand out sharply. Tape the paper to the dutchman stock and transfer the pattern to the stock with a chisel and mallet. Remove the paper, cut out the dutchman and you should have a perfectly fitting inlay.

—*Donald M. Stevens, Mansfield Center, Conn.*

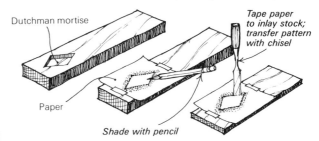

Dutchman mortise

Tape paper to inlay stock; transfer pattern with chisel

Paper

Shade with pencil

Marquetry patching

Your marquetry picture is cut, mounted, sanded and with a coat of finish, but something seems wrong. This happens often, because no matter how carefully you select veneer, you don't notice until the end that a piece doesn't look right. Some people just cut out the section to be replaced, trace the opening and insert a new piece. With my method, the section is traced before cutting.

With tracing paper taped to the picture, draw the section you wish to replace. Tape the tracing paper with carbon paper and trace the pattern onto the new piece of veneer. Then cut out the piece. Lay it on top of the picture to see how it looks; if you don't like it, cut another piece.

With the new section positioned on the picture, secure half of it with tape and score around the other half with a knife, using the veneer as a guide. Then tape the scored side, remove the tape from the first side, and finish scoring the outline. Remove the tape and the new veneer section, and cut very carefully along the marking through the veneer that is to be replaced. With a small chisel or square-bladed X-acto knife, stab this veneer in the center and pry it up, working carefully from the center to the edges. Now fit the new section into the gap. If it doesn't fit, sand or shave the edges until it does. Glue with white glue and press. Then wipe off the excess glue and sand just a little with fine sandpaper backed by a wooded block to get dust into the cracks that are filled with wet glue. Put a small board and a heavy weight atop the piece and let it dry overnight. Then sand until all is level, and finish.   —*Peter L. Rose, Saddle Brook, N.J.*

Repairing knots

As a weekend woodworker I find I cannot afford top-quality walnut, nor can I afford to waste any of the waddle walnut I buy. Many times a fine piece of well-figured waddle walnut will have a badly checked knot. I file the check out until I have about ⅛-in. vertical surface all the way around. Then I plane a scrap of similar grain and color to ⅛-in. thickness and tape it over the opening so that the grain closely matches the solid stock. I turn the entire unit over and spray a latex paint through from the back to give me the exact shape of the check, then I cut, file and sand the "plug" to a perfect fit. After gluing and filling in from the back for support, and sanding, it will be hard to spot this easy repair job.

—*Dan Quackenbush, Olathe, Kan.*

Sanding small pieces

The inlay patch for a veneered piece I was restoring was a bit too thick. Sanding it flush after gluing would have marred the surrounding finish. To hold the small piece so that it could be sanded evenly, I put coarse-grit sandpaper on the bench, then put the veneer patch on it. I could then easily sand it with a sanding block, using a finer grit. When a thin workpiece is sandwiched between two grits, it locks into the coarser grit as pressure is applied, and is thus held firmly.

—*Joseph T. Ponessa, Moorestown, N.J.*

Graining tool

To make a graining tool that works on any contour, including intricate molding, roll up a strip of inner tube and notch its end randomly on the bandsaw with cuts about ⅛ in. deep. Then using a glaze of artists' oil colors, linseed oil and varnish, you can produce a striking grain pattern...with practice.

—*J.B. Small, Newville, Pa.*

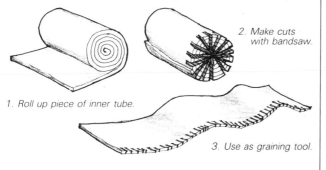

1. Roll up piece of inner tube.

2. Make cuts with bandsaw.

3. Use as graining tool.

Auto-finishing tips adapted to wood

My shop is next door to an auto paint-and-body shop. Through the association I have been able to adapt several of their methods and products to wood finishing. It seems that the technology of auto-finish suppliers is steps ahead of their wood-industry counterparts. Certainly their marketing is.

First, I use naphtha (VM&P brand) as a wetting agent for rubbing down intermediate finish coats with wet/dry sandpaper. Naphtha's advantage is that unlike oils or water, it evaporates quickly and cleanly. You can remove the sanding scum with steel wool, wipe with a naphtha-dampened rag, and the surface is clean and dry, ready for the next coat.

Second, two DuPont auto-finish products, the 3679 retarder and the 3602S acrylic lacquer thinner, work very well used with nitrocellulose and acrylic modified wood lacquers. Add the 3679 in small amounts to a cheaper utility thinner to upgrade it for use in finish-coat mixtures. The 3602S is a good damp-weather blush retarder and warm-weather thinner.

Third, I have adapted the auto shop's mist coat to produce a superior finish. After a piece has had its last finish coat and it has "flashed" or surface-dried (5-10 minutes) I recoat with a wet coat of one part lacquer to four parts thinner. This procedure seems to eliminate any overspray and overspray dust. It adds greatly to the surface uniformity. Little if any rubbing will be needed to produce a fine finish.

—*Steve Ulrich, Kingsville, Tex.*

Vacuum-aided oil finish

Here is a method for oil-finishing small articles such as gearshift knobs and knife handles in dense hardwoods like cocobolo and rosewood. Normally, these woods don't readily accept oil to any depth. First I submerge the wood article in a jar of Watco oil and put the jar in a homemade vacuum chamber. I keep the wood under vacuum for several hours until it nearly stops bubbling. Then I slowly release the vacu-

um and allow the air pressure to push oil into the pores of the wood that formerly held air. After a couple of hours I remove the wood and wipe it dry. The deep penetration slows drying time somewhat. Our vacuum pump is an old compressor. We hooked up the vacuum chamber to the inlet side. This method doesn't require a hard-vacuum—any vacuum at all achieves a better result than just rubbing in the oil.

—*Jerry Blanchard, Pebble Beach, Calif.*

Finish samples

Every woodworker and wood finisher has experienced the frustration of trying to describe the peculiar merits of a particular finish to his customers or to his fellow craftsmen. Words fail because the essence of a fine finish is sensory—one appreciates it through the fingertips and the eyes. My answer is a collection of finish samples, which I have been developing and refining for the past three years. Constant questions from my refinishing students and patrons forced me to develop it as a tangible answer; my system should work equally well for the amateur craftsman or the professional.

Start with 40 or more pieces of wood about ½ by 4½ by 9 inches, a convenient size for handling and storage, yet large enough to display the finish. Mahogany is a suitable wood because it is so often encountered in old furniture that needs refinishing. My collection includes both plain-sawed and quarter-sawed wood, and I keep a piece of raw wood as a control. It's a good idea to bleach a couple of pieces too; they will come in handy later on.

All the pieces should be carefully sanded at the same time, following your usual techniques, to ensure uniformity. I use

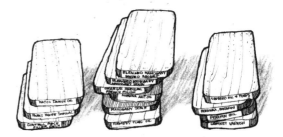

garnet paper and start with 100 grit until all the milling marks are gone, then I sand with 150 grit before filling. I apply paste wood filler to one face, edge and end of the sample to illustrate the contrasts that will appear in the finished piece, and then sand to 280 grit. When all the wood is prepared, it is ready to receive the finishes you most often work with. The samples can be set aside and worked up one at a time, or you can do intensive work to build up a nucleus of the more common finishes and add more, or play with variables, later on.

The possible variables include finishes on raw woods, finishes over various sealers, stains, fillers, and finishes over other finishes. Additives in finish materials, such as driers and stains, produce interesting results. Several blocks of wood, all finished with the same material and then rubbed out with abrasive flours to show the development of a polished surface, say more than words ever could. Finally, finish samples can be subjected to stresses such as alcohol, chemicals, water and burns to test your efforts.

It takes many hours to produce a fine set of finished specimens, but the extended exercise is worth the effort. It leads to conformity in each finished product and makes the finisher familiar with a wide range of materials and their applications. The result is a unique educational tool that can be shared with others and always expanded. It will last forever, and it saves a lot of talking. —*David Adamusko, Alexandria, Va.*

Testing finishes

After turning wooden bowls, several of my eighth-grade students asked if they could use them for eating cereal. I was surprised and intrigued by the question, so I set out to test the water resistance of various non-toxic finishes, hoping that one would be good enough for such wet food.

I tested Deft, Benjamin Moore Urethane Varnish and Constantine's Wood Bowl Seal on basswood, Philippine mahogany and pine—the woods used in our school shop. I also tested three oil finishes—Watco Danish oil, salad oil and mineral oil—on pine only.

The test pieces (which I called "concaves") were turned on the lathe from 3½-in. discs of 1¾-in. stock. The outside was merely trued, the inside cut to a bowl contour. I made a concave of each wood for each finish, plus two extras—one to test unfinished, and a control (finished but not tested). The test liquid was water; to obtain a permanent record I added a powdered red stain.

I finished the concaves according to the labels on the cans, filled each with stain, and enclosed them in plastic bags to eliminate evaporation as a variable. I arbitrarily decided to let the basswood samples soak for a week, the pine for two

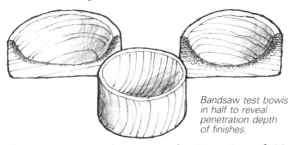

Bandsaw test bowls in half to reveal penetration depth of finishes.

weeks, the mahogany for three weeks. Since the unfinished samples quickly soaked up stain and were completely red within a day, I stopped this series after 24 hours. Every day the rest of the concaves were emptied, dried, examined and refilled with stain. At the end of the test periods I let them dry for two days before bandsawing into halves, to avoid the distortion that cutting wet wood might cause.

In every case the biggest changes occurred during the first few days. All the Deft samples stained in 24 hours—basswood the most and mahogany the least. The concaves finished with urethane and Wood Bowl Seal stained primarily on torn end grain, which had not been sanded perfectly smooth, and (in pine) along cracks in knots. The finishes themselves took on a salmon color, but penetration below the finish was minimal.

Mineral oil and salad oil were the least effective finishes, with Watco somewhat better but still not as good as Deft. The sectioned surfaces seemed to indicate that the stain traveled along the oiled surface of the wood, rather than through it. Note that two coats of the oil finishes were wiped on. Certainly the results would be different if the wood had been immersed and soaked in oil.

These tests demonstrated, first, that any finish increases the water resistance of wood, and second, that end grain must be sanded absolutely thoroughly for a finish to be effective. Knots also reduce the overall effectiveness of a finish. I concluded that two coats of urethane or Wood Bowl Seal are durable enough to resist the wetness of cereal, and that Deft and Watco are probably adequate for the usual uses of wooden bowls—salads, nuts, etc.

I don't mean to recommend these finishes or eating wet foods from them. But I do hope my testing method will be useful to others who are trying to compare the relative merits of the particular finishes they like.

—*C. Orentlicher, New York, N.Y.*

EDITOR'S NOTE: The choice of finish for wooden bowls, cups and spoons poses special problems. The finish must stand up to its intended use—dry food or wet? hot or cold? acid (vinegar)? alcohol?—and, even more important, it must be nontoxic. Clear finishes used safely on walls and furniture may contain compounds that are toxic if ingested.

Metals or metal compounds are added to drying oils and varnishes to speed polymerization and thus to cut drying time. Foods and liquids can leach these compounds out of the finish so they are consumed with the meal. Although the amount of metal ingested at one sitting may be minute, these compounds can build up in the body; no amount of any metal is considered absolutely safe. Linseed oil, polymerized tung oil, urethane varnish and alkyd varnish call contain metallic driers.

Finishing materials that do not contain metallic compounds include clear woodfinishing lacquers (both spraying and brushing types) and water-based (latex) varnishes. Most mail-order woodworking supply firms carry a latex varnish specifically labeled for salad bowls. Some penetrating oils, Watco in particular, should not be used with food for 30 days after application to ensure complete polymerization; after that, they are nontoxic. Two-part epoxy-resin paints and varnishes will resist acids, detergent and alcohol. Peterson Chemical's No. 100 Clear Epoxy satisfies federal standards for use with foods; check the label or the manufacturer for other brands.

Sharpening & Grinding

Chapter 10

Enlarging flute bores

Recently I used a spade bit in a bit extender to enlarge the bore of a wooden flute I was making from ¾ in. to ⅞ in. The method worked so fast and left the bore so smooth I'll use it from now on, even to work the hole size up from the ⅜-in. shell auger I start with. A major advantage of the thin shank is that you don't have to stop so often to remove chips. The secret is to regrind the cutting edge of the spade bit so it will enlarge and follow a pre-drilled hole.

Grind away and taper the corners of the bit so it can enter the smaller hole. Then sharpen one edge (I used a polishing belt on a Dremel sander, followed by a hard Arkansas stone) and relieve the other edge of the bit so that the sharpened edge can cut. The more you relieve it, the deeper the bit will bite. To avoid scoring the inside of the bore as you remove the bit, round the back corners.
—Vasco Pini, Woodstock, N.Y.

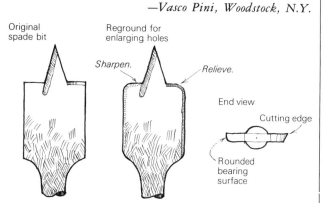

Original spade bit

Reground for enlarging holes

Sharpen.

Relieve.

End view

Cutting edge

Rounded bearing surface

Enlarging flute bores revisited

Here's my variation on the method Vasco Pini uses to enlarge the bores of flutes. First drill a pilot hole through the flute blank with a ¼-in. shell auger. Then construct a follower bit by cutting a slot in a short length of ¼-in. rod and slipping it over the tip of a spade bit. The rod will follow the pilot hole and the spade bit will self-center.
—Bob Vernon, Keuka Park, N.Y.

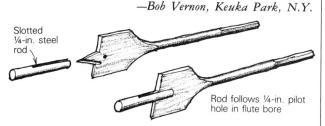

Slotted ¼-in. steel rod

Rod follows ¼-in. pilot hole in flute bore

Sharpening a wire wheel

If you use a wire wheel to remove rust from old tools, you know how soon the bristles bend over and lose effectiveness.

Reversing the wheel helps, but just before you do this, run the wheel against a coarse grindstone. This puts a chisel edge on the wires that really cuts fast.
—Mark A. Latour, Saint John, N.B., Canada

Improved spade bit

You can improve the performance of the common spade bit by regrinding it to the shape below. The reground bit will cut a smoother hole and won't tear out the grain as much when it comes out the other side. *—Ray Yohe, Altoona, Pa.*

Grind away areas indicated.

Modifying twist drills for wood

A worn-out twist drill can be modified to perform much better in wood. First grind the tip flat. Then, using a cone-shaped stone in a hobby grinder or the rounded-over corner of an abrasive wheel, grind two hollows—one on each side of the center. The hollows form a center spur and two outer spurs. Be sure to bevel the hollows so that the back side of the flutes will clear the wood.

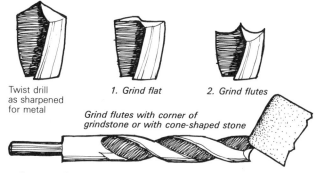

Twist drill as sharpened for metal

1. Grind flat

2. Grind flutes

Grind flutes with corner of grindstone or with cone-shaped stone

In use, the center spur holds the bit stable and keeps it from wandering. The outer spurs cut the wood's fibers in advance of the cutting edge to give straight, clean holes.
—Stanley F. Kayes, Richmond, Va.

Reground hole cutter

You can use an adjustable hole cutter and a drill press to make smooth toy wheels and small wooden discs. Simply regrind the cutter so that its inboard side enters the material first. Regrind the tip slowly on a bench grinder, pausing frequently to dip the metal in water so that it doesn't overheat. Be sure to maintain the proper front-to-back bevel on the cutter. *—Bob Raiselis, White River Junction, Vt.*

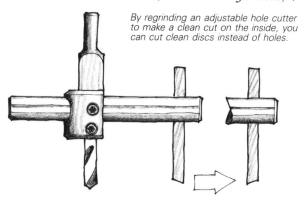

By regrinding an adjustable hole cutter to make a clean cut on the inside, you can cut clean discs instead of holes.

Adjustable tool rest

Here is an adjustable bench-grinder tool rest that's accurate, easy to use and cheap to build. Cut a 1½-in. thick pine hinge-block at the angles shown and mount it to the base with screws from underneath. Cut down two Stanley 10-in. lid supports to make the table-adjusting hardware. Drill out the center rivets and replace with screws into the 1x1 hardwood block. Pin the ⅜-in. threaded rod in a mortise in the pine hinge-block. Now mount the plywood or Formica-covered, composition-board

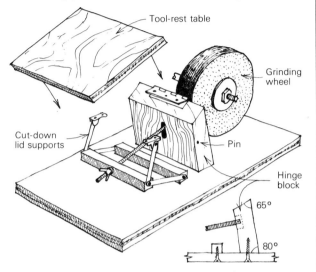

Tool-rest table

Grinding wheel

Cut-down lid supports

Pin

Hinge block

65°

80°

table as close to the grinding wheel as possible. Recess the hinge into the bottom of the table if necessary.
—*Mike Perrin, Knoxville, Tenn.*

Bicycle-tire sharpening wheel

During my seventy-two years, mainly through trial and error I've found certain methods that work well for me. One example is this sharpening setup made from a bicycle wheel.

Start with the complete front wheel and fork. I used a 26-in. by 2.125-in. tire. Mount the wheel assembly on a base so that its tire contacts the pulley (1½-in.) of a ¼-HP, 1725-RPM motor. Your wheel should revolve at about 100 RPM, with a surface speed of 650 ft. per minute. Now glue a strip of abrasive cloth to the tire surface, and you have a very efficient, low-cost grinding wheel. Use it so the sparks fly away from the tool. Because the speed is slow and the wheel is large, there is little heat buildup

to burn a tool and ruin the temper. If you place the whole assembly on a bench, the work area will be at eye level.

As a companion tool I use a belt-driven mandrel fitted with five side-by-side, 6-in. muslin buffing wheels. I charge this thick buffing sandwich with 1000-grit abrasive, which gunsmiths use to polish gun barrels prior to bluing. I then polish all edge tools to a mirror-sheen, razor-sharp edge. The whole system is inexpensive and can be mastered by any flub-dub.
—*Ray "Pappy" Holt, Tampa, Fla.*

Lineshaft sharpening

This inexpensive sharpening setup puts a keen edge on tools in seconds without the usual heat build-up problems of powered abrasive wheels. To construct the setup, laminate four 7-in. wheel blanks from plywood or particleboard. Epoxy the blanks to shaft collars, which are set-screwed to the ½-in. lineshaft. The shaft turns in pillow blocks mounted on an oak frame. If a lathe is not available, the wheel blanks can be trued right on the lineshaft with a chisel and a temporary tool rest.

Cement emery-cloth strips (80 grit and 320 grit) to two of the wheels, lining the wheels first with burlap-backed cork (from a linoleum dealer). Cement leather to the other two wheels. Mount the leather flesh side out to one wheel and hair side out to the other. Charge the "flesh" wheel with

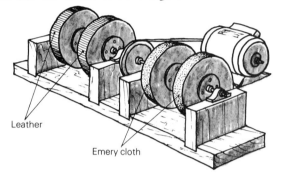

Leather

Emery cloth

emery, the "hair" wheel with rouge. Using rubber cement for all mountings will make replacement easier later on.

An old ¼-HP appliance motor will provide sufficient power. Size the motor and lineshaft pulleys so the wheels turn at 500 to 600 RPM up and away from the operator.

Dull tools may need treatment on all four wheels. But most tools can be sharpened on only the finer two or three wheels.
—*Robert L. Koch, Tarlsio, Mo.*

Maintaining sharp carving tools

I ran across this tool-sharpening trick on a trip to Mexico. There I watched a carver working on mahogany chairs frequently plunge his gouge into a pine bowl full of some waxy substance. Upon inquiry he said the bowl contained a mixture of beeswax and fine carborundum abrasive powder. The plunging kept a keen edge on his sharpened carving tools. When I returned home I tried the trick and found it to work fine—especially on a warm day or near a stove so the wax stays soft.

To make the concoction, warm up ½ lb. of beeswax and knead in two or three tablespoons of 400-grit or 600-grit carborundum powder. The grit is available at any lapidary shop. To protect your carving tools, keep the mixture in a softwood box or bowl.   —*Jim Thomas, Cerrillos, N.M.*

Stones and strops from the attic

There have been several good articles on sharpening and honing devices lately, but I haven't seen anybody comment on the old-time water stones that folks used to sharpen their straight razors on. You can sharpen up smaller edged tools with one right smart. They're cheap and available at flea markets, etc., or better yet from older family members or friends. Get ahold of a razor strop too; they work well.
—*David Blackley, Matthews, N.C.*

Sharpening knives with care

EDITOR'S NOTE: To add a point of caution to all these methods based on the table saw and drill press, Carl Henry of Houston, Texas, writes: "At a wooden-boat school I attended last summer we used a grinding wheel mounted in a table saw to remove a lot of metal from a set of large planer knives. An hour later smoke began to pour from the sawdust in the saw's base. The hot embers from the grinding had been smoldering there in the sawdust. I recommend cleaning out the saw completely before and after sharpening."

John Gibbons of Madison, Wis., adds another cautionary note: "Grinding operations on the table saw spray a stream of abrasive dust all over the saw's gears, trunnions, bearings and other working parts. This grit will cling to these parts and grind away at their machined surfaces. Those who expect continued smooth operation of their machinery would be well advised to avoid such abusive practices."

For those who will take the necessary precautions, here are several ways to sharpen jointer and planer knives.
—*Jim Richey*

Table-saw sharpening

Here's a simple jig I use on my table saw to sharpen the knives of my 16-in. thickness planer. The jig is nothing more than a block of hardwood with an angled shoulder to give the right sharpening angle. The knives on my planer are slotted so I use screws and washers through the slots to fasten the knife in place.

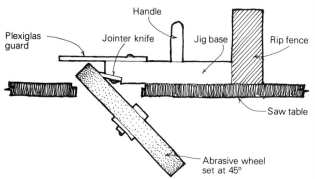

To use the jig I put a fine-grit 6-in. abrasive wheel on the table-saw arbor and tilt the arbor to 45°. I use the rip fence for rough adjustment and the blade-height crank for fine adjustment. —*John Kolkman, Thornhill, Ont., Canada*

Sharpening jointer knives

Here's how I sharpen jointer or thickness-planer knives on the table saw. Mount a 6-in. medium-grit emery wheel on the saw's arbor. Then clamp a straight-edged guide board across the table in front of the wheel. Fit the knife in a block that has been grooved along one edge. Be sure the groove is uniformly deep and parallel to the opposite edge of the block, and that the knife is firmly seated at the bottom of the groove.

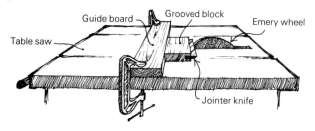

Adjust the height of the emery wheel to touch the center of the knife's bevel. Keeping the block flat against the table, pass the knife slowly back and forth across the wheel. Take the lightest of cuts. Duplicate this on the other knives. Slowly raise the wheel until each knife is ground to a feather edge. Honing the knives on an oilstone completes the sharpening.
—*Charlie K. Thorne, San Luis Obispo, Calif.*

Jig for knife sharpening

I sharpen jointer and planer knives on the table saw using the miter gauge. The approach offers several advantages: The knife edges are stronger (because they're straight-ground rather than hollow-ground), the grinding angle adjusts easily and the fixture handles long knives (up to 24 in.).

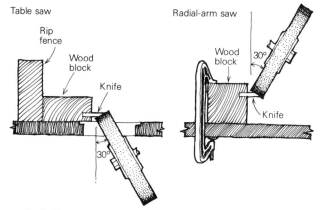

To make the fixture, drill and tap two holes in the slide of your miter gauge and fasten the plywood base of the fixture to the slide with machine screws. Now screw the top part of the fixture to the base so that the blade is sandwiched and clamped snugly in place. Install two adjuster bolts from the back edge of the fixture into nuts that have been mortised and epoxied into the base. Turn these bolts to adjust the first knife into perfect position. The bolts provide a reference for the last two knives so they will be ground exactly like the first. —*Jack Down, Maseru, Lesotho*

More jointer-knife sharpening jigs

The sketch below shows my method for grinding jointer-knife blades on the table saw. The blades are ground on the circumference of the grinding wheel, not the side.

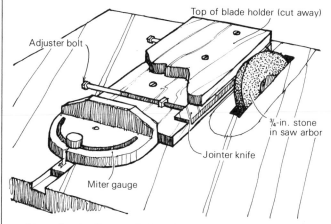

A similar setup allows blade grinding on the radial-arm saw. Clamp the blade holder to the table parallel to the saw arm. Mount the stone in the saw arbor and run the arbor/stone unit back and forth on the radial-arm to grind the knives. Feed the stone by lowering the arm.
—*Mark Palmquist, Lilburn, Ga.*

Drill jig for knives

Here is a jointer-knife sharpening jig that saves money, eliminates frustrating at-the-sharpening-shop delays and gives the woodworker a bit more independence. The jig, used with a drill press and cup stone, consists of a ¾-in. plywood or particle-board base and a sliding knife-holder. The holder, slotted to accept the jointer knife at the right sharpening angle, slides in an accurately sized channel in the base. Several thumbscrews, tightened in threaded holes, threaded inserts or T-nuts, lock the knife in the holder slot during grinding. (To tap wood, drill pilot holes, use a tapered tap and back the tap out often; maple and other hardwoods tap about like hard brass, and hold as well.)

To use the fixture, chuck a medium-grit 1½-in. cup stone (contact Norton Co., 1 New Bond St., Worcester, Mass. 01606 for distributors) in the drill press. True the stone if necessary (I use an old masonry blade). Then clamp the base in position on the drill-press table so the knife and stone are aligned as shown in the sketch. Lower the quill until the stone barely touches the knife, lock the quill and grind the knife by sliding the holder under the stone. Lower the quill a bit and grind again. Repeat this operation until all nicks have disappeared. When the final depth is reached on the first knife, set the drill-press stop to preserve the setting for sharpening the second and third knives.

To avoid warping the knife by heating unevenly, take light cuts, move the holder smoothly and use plenty of thumb-

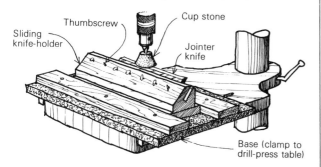

Sliding knife-holder
Thumbscrew
Cup stone
Jointer knife
Base (clamp to drill-press table)

screws to lock the knife in the holder. Long knives are especially prone to warping, so mist them or let them cool between passes. —*James E. Gier, Mesa, Ariz.*

Modified knife-holder block

I built several variations of the cup-stone-in-drill-press jointer-knife sharpening jigs (as described by James Gier, above, and Tom Moore, in the next column). All proved unsatisfactory because they either distorted the blade or didn't hold it securely. However, I've modified the design of the knife-holder block and have had good success.

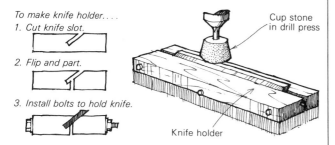

To make knife holder....
1. Cut knife slot.
2. Flip and part.
3. Install bolts to hold knife.
Cup stone in drill press
Knife holder

Start with a maple 1x3 a couple of inches longer than the jointer knives. Drill a ¼-in. hole at each end across the width of the block. The distance between holes should be about 1 in. greater than the knife length. Drill an additional hole midway across the block well below the centerline. Now cut a

groove in the block at the sharpening angle (I used 36°), but don't cut into the hole you drilled midway across the block. Flip the board over and cut the board so that it looks like the sketch. Insert ¼-in. carriage bolts in the holes, insert the blade in the slot and tighten the nuts. Don't over-tighten, or you'll distort the blade.

The knife holder can be fastened to a base so you can slide it freehand under the cup stone mounted in your drill press. Be sure to glue only one part of the holder to the base so you can install and remove the knives easily. Or you can devise a two-part jig with a sliding track in the base as shown with Gier's and Moore's devices.

—*George Pfeiffer, Seward, Neb.*

Improved knife-sharpening fixture

When I tried to adapt James Gier's drill-press jointer-knife sharpening fixture to the small knives in my 8-in. jointer, I ran into several problems. The biggest problem was positioning a row of thumbscrews of sufficient size to hold the narrow knife so they wouldn't interfere with the cupstone. To solve the problems I modified Gier's design as shown below.

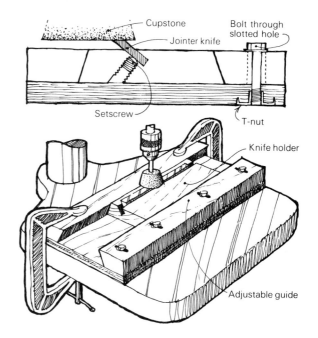

Cupstone
Bolt through slotted hole
Jointer knife
Setscrew
T-nut
Knife holder
Adjustable guide

First, I replaced the top-side thumbscrews with hex-head setscrews tightened from the bottom side of the sliding knife-holder block. Second, I beveled the edges of the block and the guide channel for a dovetail arrangement, so the block won't tip as it runs under the cupstone. I fastened the rear guide with bolts through slotted holes to T-nuts in the base, so the guide can be adjusted. If you want a really first-class fixture don't tap the wood. Rather use Rosann inserts (available from Constantine and others) to hold the setscrews.

As Gier suggests, take extremely light cuts and preserve the setting of the first knife with the quill-stop. Take light cuts with the second and third knives until you hit the stop depth. —*Tom E. Moore, Springfield, Va.*

Regrinding plane irons

To grind an accurate bevel on a plane iron, remove the cap iron and replace it on the beveled side of the iron at 90° to its usual position, as shown in the sketch. The cap iron will work as a stop against the tool rest, maintaining a perfect bevel angle while allowing you to slide the plane iron to and fro. Vary the bevel angle by positioning the chip breaker closer to or farther from the cutting edge.

—Drew Woodmansee, Fairbanks, Alaska

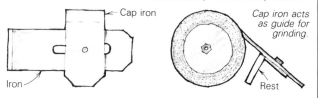

Cap iron

Iron

Cap iron acts as guide for grinding.

Rest

Plane-iron honing tool

Here's a simple, inexpensive jig for honing slotted plane irons. Just attach a 4-in. long, ⅜-in. or ⁷⁄₁₆-in. carriage bolt to the iron, as shown in the sketch below. The round head of the bolt slides easily on the bench, maintaining a constant honing angle. For fine adjustment or for honing microbevels, you can shim the stone, or twist the bolt up or down a hair.

—Paul Weissman, Centerville, Ohio

Constant-angle honing

Most of us know an old-timer who has demonstrated a method of work so effective and simple you wonder why it never occurred to you before. This happened to me recently while honing my plane iron. I was struggling to maintain a constant angle against the stone, lamenting that I did not have one of those fancy roller tools that locks the plane iron at a constant angle while rolling it across the abrasive. Here's the simple solution presented to me.

Slide the chip breaker back from the cutting edge about ¾ in. Then lock the double iron in the plane with the blade extending through the throat about ½ in. Now with the heel on the bench top and the plane iron on the stone, slide the plane back and forth. The setup holds the iron at a constant

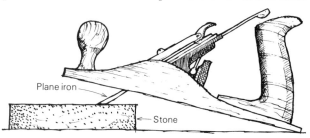

Plane iron

Stone

angle to the stone to grind a perfect secondary bevel.

You may have to adjust the setup slightly to fit different-size plane bodies, stones and bevel angles, but the basic idea seems to work with any plane.

—James Vasi, Cheektowaga, N.Y.

Stick helps regrind irons

With a simple stick jig you can quickly, easily and accurately regrind plane irons on a bench grinder, and it's more fun than you can imagine. Select a good, stiff hardwood stick—mine is 44 in. long. Add a short wooden spine (to fit the iron's screw slot) and a stove-bolt/washer arrangement to hold the iron in place. Now, keeping the stick in line with the wheel, brace the stick against the inside of your left foot and lightly arc the iron across the wheel. The stick can be picked up to check the progress of the grind, then—as long as you don't move your foot—returned to the same spot against your shoe.

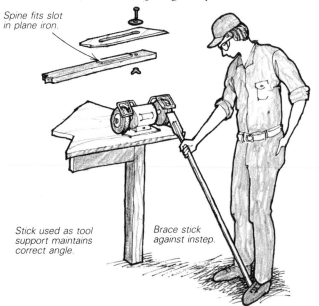

Spine fits slot in plane iron.

Stick used as tool support maintains correct angle.

Brace stick against instep.

The resulting blade grind won't be perfectly straight but crowned ever so slightly. This convex profile will prove superior to a straight profile for most hand-planing applications, and is tricky to achieve any other way.

—Paul D. Frank, Fond du Lac, Wis.

Hazardless honing

Here is a simple combination storage box and jig that will enable you to use your oilstones more effectively and safely. What makes the box unique is a wide tongue cut into the bottom. In use, the tongue is secured in a woodworking vise, ensuring a stable, firm foundation for the oilstone.

To make the box, cut blocks for the base and cover from any hardwood. Use a drill press with a multispur or Forstner bit to remove most of the waste. The cavity in the base should be about half as deep as the stone. The cavity in the cover should be ¹⁄₁₆ in. or so deeper to provide clearance. Chop out the remaining waste with a chisel, making sure the stone fits snug in the base and doesn't rock. To complete the box, saw away the bottom corners of the base to leave the tongue.

—Al Ching, Fullerton, Calif.

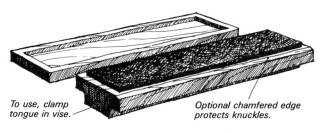

To use, clamp tongue in vise.

Optional chamfered edge protects knuckles.

Grit-slurry sharpening

Here's yet another sharpening method to add a bit more lore to the subject many craftsmen approach with almost mystic reverence. The method uses a slurry of loose grit on a flat glass plate. It is the same method laboratories use to sharpen the microtome, an instrument that slices tissue into thin sections for microscopic examination. The method is effective for sharpening woodworking tools, particularly plane irons. Start by dumping a half-teaspoon of #400 grit on an 8x8 pane of glass, adding several drops of light machine oil to make a slurry. Hone the plane iron as though you were using a bench stone. When you obtain a good bevel, wipe the glass clean and repeat the process using #600 grit to obtain the final cutting edge. For optimum results, polish with a polishing compound or give the blade a few strokes on a leather strop.

This method is superior in several ways to sharpening on a stone. The glass is flat and wears little even with much use, and the large surface area allows for a more comfortable hand motion. The large surface is particularly suitable for the use of a roller device to hone the iron at a constant angle. Finally, you can buy a wide range of abrasive powders at hobby shops that deal in lapidary supplies (one source is Grieger's Inc., 900 S. Arroyo Parkway, Pasadena, Calif. 91109). A small investment in materials will allow you to perform work that would otherwise require several different grades of stones.

—*George Mustoe, Bellingham, Wash.*

Fixing new saws

As a general rule, new crosscut hand saws are not sharpened properly. The trouble appears to be the result of forming and sharpening the teeth by machine, after which the teeth are set. As these saws are sold, they feel sharp enough but they don't cut as well as they should and they tend to wander. One can tell about this by looking along the teeth. They should look like *A*, but they almost always look like *B*.

Sharpening a new saw to correct this is easy. It is well worth the trouble. Any set of accepted directions will do, just ignore those for leveling the teeth and resetting them. Neither is necessary. The only trick is to make sure the teeth are at equal depth. Even, the saw cuts straight with no problem. Uneven, it wanders and cannot be held true. Count the file strokes for each tooth and don't try to make each tooth perfect the first time. Give each, say, five firm but not heavy strokes. Then, when all the teeth are done, check the saw. If one needs more, they'll all need it. Carry on with the same number of strokes per tooth, maybe two or three if you're close, until they're all alike.

You need a thinner file than you think. But you don't need a saw vise or some other special tool. A couple of pieces of heavy wood or plywood on both sides of the blade, the edges just below the teeth, and the whole put in any vise, will do, and you'll never again have to say you can't saw a straight line. Amazing how much time you can save using a hand saw, especially if you have a good setup table to use for the purpose instead of your fancy cabinetmaker's bench, one with an overhanging top so you can clamp a piece along the side of the table if you need to.

—*Henry T. Kramer, Somerville, N.J.*

Jointing circular-saw blades

For a circular saw to cut with all of its teeth, it must first be jointed and thereafter mounted the same way every time.

To joint, mount the blade with the trademark up. Then tighten so that all the slack between the arbor and the saw-hole stays opposite the trademark at top. It is a good idea to mark the arbor too, so you can also keep it always in the same position when mounting. With the saw running, slowly raise the blade into a grindstone lying flat on the table surface. When you've gotten a shine on all teeth, carefully sharpen each tooth (file or grind) until the shine disappears. When you return the blade to the machine, always mount it with the trademark up. The blade mounted in any other way will run in an orbital pattern; only a few teeth will cut.

I always joint and file even new blades—they need it as much as used blades.   —*Norman Brooks, Greenville, Pa.*

Knife profile patterns

Because shaper knives and hand planes cut at an angle, a molding profile cannot be directly traced onto a blank and ground to shape. This method will help you make a blade that will reproduce a desired molding pattern. First, determine the angle *a* of the knife as it cuts (either in a shaper or a hand plane). Then draw a cross section of the molding shape.

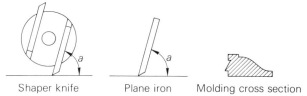

Shaper knife   Plane iron   Molding cross section

To this sketch add the outline of the knife as it cuts the wood. Then draw a folding line and a side view of the knife at angle *a* and at its true length. Now add another folding line parallel to the knife length, and beyond it draw a knife blank. Extend construction lines from several points on the

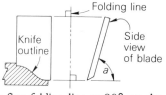

molding profile, through the first folding line at 90°, to the edge of the knife length. It is possible to construct a template the actual shape and size of the knife you want to make by measuring with dividers from the first folding line back to the construction line intersection points on the molding outline, then transferring these measurements from the second folding line to the knife blank. All construction lines must pass through the folding lines at 90°.

—*Ron Davidson, Port Angeles, Wash.*

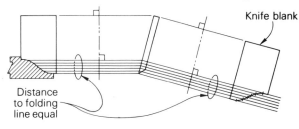

Pulls, Latches & Hardware

Chapter 11

Wooden pull/catch

This cabinet door pull serves a double function—it's also a locking catch. The material cost is negligible but you'll spend about an hour making and installing the pull. The catch is designed for doors hung flush with the framing, so a separate door-stop must be incorporated.

First, square a line from the edge of the cabinet door at the position you want the pull. Bore a ⅝-in. hole through the cabinet door 1 in. from the door's edge and centered on the line. Then cut a 1-in. deep, ¼-in. wide mortise into the door edge. Start the mortise ⅛ in. below the position line and stop the mortise 1 in. above the line. Cut a corresponding ⅜-in. deep mortise in the frame.

After the mortises are completed, lathe-turn the pull handle with a knob on the front and a round tenon on the back. The tenon should slip-fit in the ⅝-in. hole and be as long as the door is thick. Dry-fit the pull in the hole and, while holding the knob at the locked position, reach through the mortise

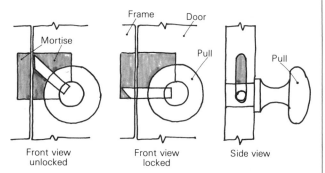

Front view unlocked | Front view locked | Side view

and drill a ¼-in. hole in the tenon to receive the latch-dowel.

To complete the pull/catch, coat the tenon with beeswax, put a drop of glue in the latch-dowel hole and set the pull in place. Insert the latch-dowel through the mortise into the hole. Then, with the handle turned to the unlocked position, cut the latch-dowel flush with the door edge.

—*Michael Lynch, San Francisco, Calif.*

Aligning hinged box tops

To assure that the tops of small hinged boxes will align perfectly with the bottoms, seat the hinges first with "5-minute" epoxy and install the screws later. Smear a thin coat of the epoxy on the hinges, place them in position (separating the leaves slightly with a wedge if necessary) and put the top on the box, aligning all around. To be safe, give the epoxy a full half-hour to set, open the box top, drill pilot holes and install the screws. —*H.W. Reid, Cincinnati, Ohio*

Wooden bullet catch

This wooden bullet catch takes a little more time to make and install than its store-bought metal cousin. But the sound alone is worth the effort. The catch consists of a turned (or whittled) maple bullet, a small compression spring and a brass retainer pin. First turn the bullet with a retainer notch in its middle and a spring-sized finger on its tail. To complete the bullet, shape the head to a rounded point.

Next, drill a hole in the door edge just deep enough to accept the entire bullet under spring pressure. Pencil the outline of the hole on the inside face of the door to aid in locating the retainer-pin hole. Hold the bullet on the outline of the hole (with the bullet tip protruding) and mark the retainer notch location. Drill the retainer-pin hole so that the pin fits in the notch and lets the bullet protrude just enough to catch in the jamb. The pin hole can be drilled from the inside, blind to the door's outside. But if the pin hole is drilled through to the face, the pin can be knocked out later to replace the bullet when worn.

To complete the catch, drill a dimple in the jamb to fit the bullet tip, or install a wooden striker plate in a shallow mortise. If desired, a striker plate and doorstop can be combined in one unit. —*Michael Lynch, San Francisco, Calif.*

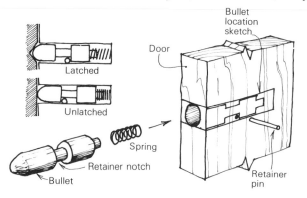

Latched

Unlatched

Bullet location sketch

Door

Spring

Retainer notch

Bullet

Retainer pin

Wooden box hinge

This box hinge is easy to make and provides a built-in lid stop. First fit the hinge pieces to the lid. A short sliding dovetail is probably the best joint. Set the lid on the box and scribe the outline of the hinge pieces on the back. Cut the

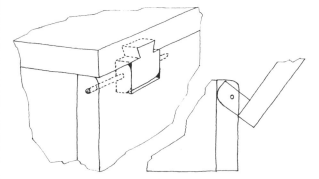

slots in the back. After measuring pin location drill pinholes in from the side of the box with the lid in place. Redrill the holes through the hinge pieces for easier operation. Install the pins. An ordinary nail works well. The hinge and the back edge of the box should be slightly rounded off.

—*Jim Richey*

Segmented hinge column

This segmented joint works like a hinge for pivoting panels or doors, but also is a structural member capable of supporting loads like any other column. The hinge is composed of three basic elements: a pin, bushings and wooden joint segments. For the pin I use an ordinary threaded rod. The bushings are washers cut from brass shim stock. Wooden joint segments are made from a large dowel. The design of the joint segments may vary depending on strength requirements, panel thickness and aesthetic preferences.

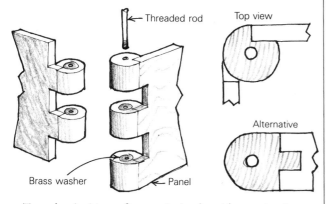

To make the hinge, first notch the dowel by passing it over a router mounted in a table. To keep the dowel from turning, tack a thin board to it. Cut the shaped dowel into segment lengths, keeping in mind that their length shouldn't exceed that of your drill bit. Next, drill the bushing hole in each segment. Proper alignment is important, so clamp a locating block to the drill-press table so that the bushing hole will be straight and centered. Assemble the segments on the threaded rod with brass bushings between, then glue the segments in place, one panel at a time.

—*Peter Kaphammel, Jr., Abbotsford, B.C.*

Laminated leather hinge

This hardware-free leather hinge is laminated into the wood to be revealed later by routing. Faced with designing some wooden book covers, I decided to use thin, home-laminated plywood for strength. To allow the covers to flex when the book opened, I embedded a 1-in. wide strip of thin leather in

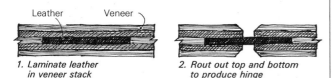

1. Laminate leather in veneer stack *2. Rout out top and bottom to produce hinge*

the center of the 5-ply veneer stack. After the plywood glue cured, I used a ⅛-in. straight router bit to rout away the two plies of wood on the top and on the bottom of the leather hinge. To achieve precise depth control I used paper shims between router base and book cover, removing one sheet at a time until the depth was exactly right. Although I chamfered the edges of the routed groove by hand, it is possible to chamfer with a *V*-groove bit. The width of the routed groove depends on the thickness of the plies and the required travel of the flexing pieces.

I would not use this hinge for a vertical cabinet door but it would work fine in many horizontal applications such as the top of a lap desk. There is no crack for dust to get through. The general principle might be useful in making tambours as well. Just keep in mind that the leather hinge must be routed out of the surrounding stock if it ever wears out.

—*James D. Thomson, Toronto, Ontario*

Cam hinge reveals hidden compartment

The sketch below shows how I used a modified hinged lid to construct a hidden compartment in the top of a bookshelf I was building. When the compartment is closed, there are no seams. The dowels lock down the front, making the top snug and tight. The pivoted cam rolls the top forward so it will clear the wall.

—*James B. Eaton, Houston, Tex.*

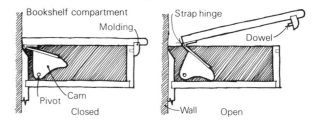

Wooden high-chair mechanism

This high-chair tray adjustment mechanism is simple, won't pinch, rust or jam and is sturdy enough to survive several rowdy babies.

Turn the high-chair arms in a series of rings and flats, then

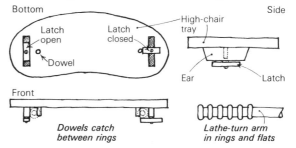

mount them on the chair level and parallel. Install two dowels on the underside of the tray to engage the inside of the arms. This gives the needed in-out adjustment. Two pivoting latch-dowels mounted on ears hold the tray down.

—*J.B. Small, Newville, Pa.*

Flush hanger plug

This wooden hanger plug, when fitted to a mirror or picture frame, allows the frame to be hung flush against the wall with the hanging screw concealed.

To make the hanger, cut a 1-in. diameter, ½-in. thick plug, counterbored with a ¾-in. bit to a depth of ¼ in. Cut a keyhole slot through the face of the plug (drill a ⅜-in. hole and a 3/16-in. hole and saw out the slot between the two). In the back of the frame, bore a blind hole 1 in. in diameter and

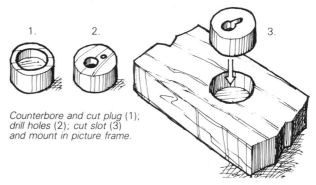

Counterbore and cut plug (1); drill holes (2); cut slot (3) and mount in picture frame.

½ in. deep. Glue the plug in the hole with the narrow end of the keyhole slot up. The frame may then be hooked over a roundhead screw driven into the wall so that its head is just over ¼ in. out. On heavy frames, you'd best use two.

—*Edward Groh, Naperville, Ill., and Charles Cohn, Clarendon Hills, Ill.*

Drawer "push"

I have seen several small boxes whose beautiful forms are interrupted by a knob. Indentations for the fingers to pull the drawer out may also work against the design of the box. My father taught me an alternative to these "pulls" and that is to push the drawer out. First drill a hole about two-thirds the stock thickness into the back of the box. If the rear wall is ¾ in. thick, I drill down ½ in. Now drill a small hole the remaining distance through the wall of the box, then countersink the small hole on the inside of the box. Make a plug ¼ in. thick and fasten it from the inside with a screw that will move freely through the small hole. Pushing the plug in causes the screwhead to push the drawer out enough so that one can get hold of the drawer in front to pull it out the rest of the way. —*John Roccanova, Bronx, N.Y.*

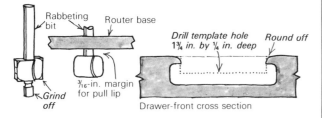

Side view of box

Plug Drawer

To open drawer, push plug.

Routed drawer pull

Here's a simple and versatile drawer or door pull made with a modified router bit. Start with a small rabbeting bit (I used Stanley 82 150, which rabbets ¼ in. wide and ⁷⁄₁₆ in. deep). Grind off the pilot and round the corners, taking care not to lose the correct bevel. Chuck the bit in the router with the cutter about ³⁄₁₆ in. below the base.

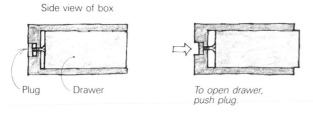

Rabbeting bit Router base

Grind off

³⁄₁₆-in. margin for pull lip

Drill template hole 1¾ in. by ¼ in. deep Round off

Drawer-front cross section

Next drill or rout a template hole in the drawer front. I use a 1¾-in. multi-spur bit, boring to a depth of only ¼ in. so the bit's pilot hole will later be removed. A flat-bottomed Forstner bit would be better because it leaves no pilot hole. If you use a straight router bit, you can cut any shape template hole.

Now plunge the router with the modified bit into the center of the template hole and work it out to the edge, using the bit's shank to guide (apply paraffin) against the side of the template hole. Finish the pull by rounding the top with a reverse-curve spoon gouge.

—*Miles Karpilow, Emeryville, Calif.*

Door bumpers from cue tips

Replacement leather tips for pool cues make excellent bumpers for sliding and swinging doors on projects. They do a fine job of quieting and cushioning the doors when they are slammed, and they are certainly better looking than the black rubber bumpers that are commonly available. The tips,

which can be bought at sporting goods suppliers, have a threaded brass shank for fastening to the cue. To install the tips on a project, drill a slightly undersize hole and use a hammer to tap the threaded shank into the hole. The threads hold like ring nails, and all that shows is leather.

—*C.W. Moran, Larchmont, N.Y.*

Integral drawer pull

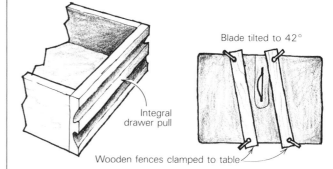

Blade tilted to 42°

Integral drawer pull

Wooden fences clamped to table

This flush, integral drawer pull can be made on the tablesaw. The profile seems to mirror gripping fingers, making it well suited to its task.

To make the grip, tilt the blade to 42° and undercut the stock, running it 10° off line with the blade. Make several passes, raising the blade ⅛ in. or so each time, until you reach the final depth. As with all undercutting operations, the stock must remain flat on the table. To keep the board in place, I use two fences (straight pieces of wood clamped to the tabletop on either side of the workpiece) and a hold-down.

—*Ronald Neurath, Louisville, Ky.*

Adjustable table feet

If the floor is not even, a small table will rock despite your efforts to have cut all four legs to the same length. These adjustable feet solve the problem better than cardboard or wooden shims, the usual solution. To make the feet, tap the head of a #10 or #12 wood screw to accept a #4-40 machine screw. Drill ½-in. holes in each table leg, then assemble the dowel-plug feet as shown below. Loosen or tighten the screw to adjust the foot. —*J.A. Hiltebeitel, S. Burlington, Vt.*

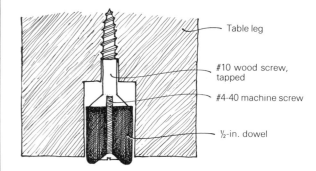

Table leg

#10 wood screw, tapped

#4-40 machine screw

½-in. dowel

Cabinet latch

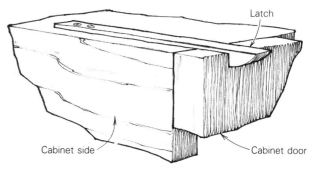

Latch

Cabinet side Cabinet door

To make this handy latch for tool-cabinet doors, bandsaw the shape shown from a 6-in. long, ¾-in. thick piece of springy hardwood, such as ash. Screw the latch to either the top or the side of the cabinet. —*James F. Dupler, Jamestown, N.Y.*

Chest lid stop

Here is a sketch of a chest lid stop that has worked well for me. It is simple to make and is completely out of the way when the lid is closed. The stop consists of two brass or aluminum plates, a short length of ball chain and a 30-caliber hollow-point bullet for weight. Drill a hole for the bullet in the side of the box and inlet the two plates to complete the construction. Be sure to position the top plate right over the bottom plate. Other construction details are shown in the sketch.   —*John Warren, Eastham, Mass.*

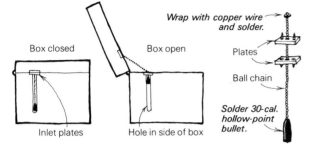

Box closed

Box open

Inlet plates

Hole in side of box

Wrap with copper wire and solder.

Plates

Ball chain

Solder 30-cal. hollow-point bullet.

Homemade Handtools

Chapter 12

Mortising plane

Here is a very old design for a plane to cut the mortises when inlaying hardware. It works like a router plane, but is more flexible as it can reach places the router cannot go, such as when inlaying hinges in door jambs. Because the two side pieces are raised from the sole, the corners of the blade can cut right up to the shoulders and molding. I have found the 14-in. plane most useful because it gives a sure surface for any hardware up to 7 in. long. Of course for a special job the plane can be made longer or shorter.

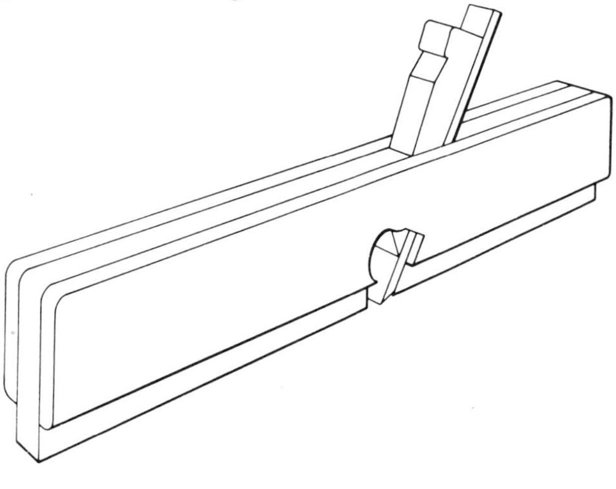

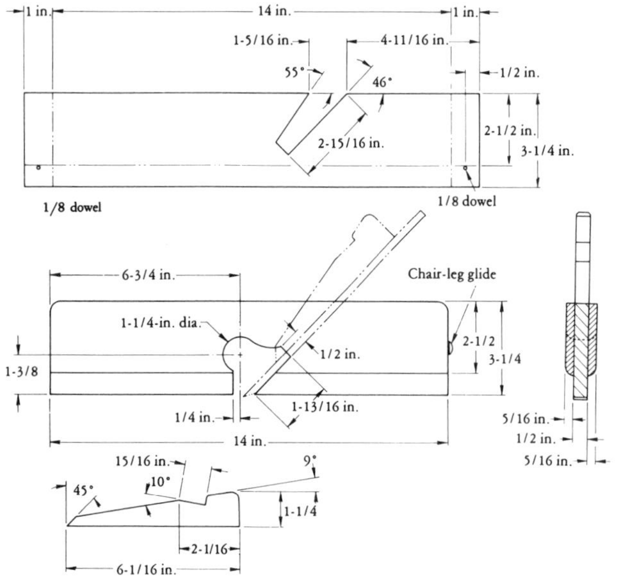

1 in.
14 in.
1 in.
1-5/16 in.
4-11/16 in.
55°
46°
1/2 in.
2-1/2 in.
3-1/4 in.
2-15/16 in.
1/8 dowel
1/8 dowel
6-3/4 in.
Chair-leg glide
1-1/4-in. dia.
1/2 in.
2-1/2
3-1/4
1-3/8
1-13/16 in.
1/4 in.
14 in.
5/16 in.
1/2 in.
5/16 in.
15/16 in.
10°
9°
45°
1-1/4
2-1/16
6-1/16 in.

You need one piece ⅝ in. x 3½ in. x 16 in. of maple or some other dense wood; two pieces ⅜ in. x 3 in. x 16 in. that may be in a contrasting wood if you like; one piece ⅝ in. x 1½ in. x 6½ in. for the wedge; and one piece of steel ¼ in. x ½ in. x 9 in. Oil-hardening steel, which comes in 18-in. lengths, is well-suited and that is why the iron is 9 in. long. After the steel is cut and ground, send it out to be hardened or do it yourself.

First make the centerpiece, which is notched and finished to ½ in. thick. Drill two ⅛-in. holes as shown in the drawing and insert two dowels, to locate the side pieces during glue-up. Plane the side pieces to 5/16 in. thick and clamp the assembly together, using cauls for straightness because the sides are so thin. Be sure to clean out the glue where the wedge and iron will fit, and clean it off the bottoms of the side pieces. When the glue has set, cut the plane to length, locate and drill the 1¼-in. hole and complete the cut-out shape. Round the edges of the upper part of the cut-out, so the shavings will slide off easily.

Now make the wedge and fit the iron. Move the iron back a quarter inch from the bottom and tap the wedge home, and then correct the sole for straightness. If you true the plane without the iron and wedge in place, it may change when they are pressing against the wood. To lower the iron, tap it at the top. To move it up, tap on the back of the plane. To protect the wood, you might want to hammer in a chair glide, or inset a hardwood striking button. If you wish to remove the iron completely, tap against the notch in the wedge. *—Tage Frid, Foster, R.I.*

Refurbishing wooden-soled planes

There are hundreds of old wooden-soled Bailey and Sargent planes that, because they're missing blades, chip breakers or cap irons, can be bought for next to nothing. These planes are excellent tools that can be refurbished for a fraction of the price of a new plane, if one doesn't mind a bit of puttering. The planes come in four widths: 1¾ in., 2⅛ in., 2⅜ in., and 2⅝ in. Replacing the blades and cap irons for the 1¾-in. and the 2⅜-in. planes is no problem as both sizes are still made by Stanley and Record. Blades and cap irons for the 2⅝-in. plane are made only by Record now, but some Stanley blades and caps in this size are available from tool specialists. The 2⅛-in. blade is a problem because no one makes them anymore. Your best bet is to grind the edges off a 2⅜-in. blade. A 2-in. cap iron works fine on the 2⅛-in. plane.

The major problem, however, is the chip breaker. Both Bailey and Sargent use a "high-hole" breaker, but modern

Blade width A	High-hole placement B	C	Cap-iron size
1¾	⅜	4	1¾
2⅛	½	4¼	2
2⅜	⅝	4½	2⅜
2⅝	¾	4⅝	2⅝

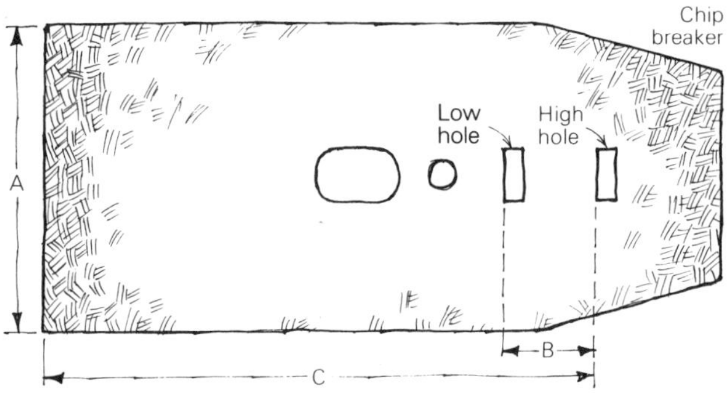

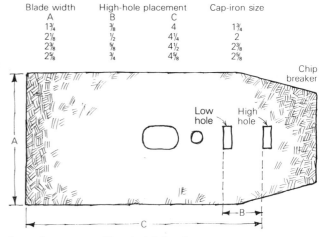

Chip breaker
Low hole
High hole
A
B
C

iron planes use a "low-hole" breaker. The two types won't interchange. The answer is to cut a new ½-in. by 3/16-in. slot in a modern "low-hole" breaker to fit the "high-hole" mechanism. The accompanying table shows where to cut the slot. *—Jim McGill, Seattle, Wash.*

Homemade scraper plane

The cabinet scraper sets the standard of excellence for smoothing wood, but it has some drawbacks: tired, blistered fingers (these things get hot!) and uneven surfaces. Scraper planes are available, but the most common one (which resembles a large iron spokeshave) has such a short sole that it is difficult to control and often chatters.

With these thoughts in mind I decided to make a simple wooden scraper plane. It went together in only a couple of hours and proved to be quite successful.

The body of the plane is laminated from three pieces of wood as shown in the illustration. The block against which the blade bears must be dished slightly to spring the blade into a curve. The back of the wedge must be correspondingly convex. This curve should be roughly 1/32 in. across a 2½-in. wide throat. The wedge must fit accurately and should extend through the body nearly to the sole. The support provided by the wedge, the curve of the blade and the length of the plane combine to prevent chattering.

A scraper plane is useless unless the blade is properly sharpened. To sharpen, joint the edge with a file, then bevel the edge on a stone to a 45° angle. Hone the edge just as you would a plane iron. Then with a burnisher or hard steel rod, rub back and forth. At first hold the burnisher parallel to the bevel, then gradually tilt it until it is perpendicular to the blade. This technique produces a razor-sharp curl every time.

—*Bradley C. Blake, Redwood, Miss.*

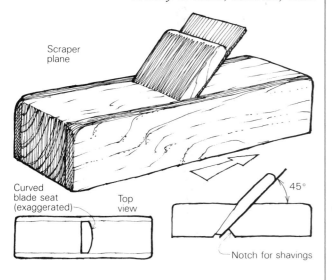

Scraper plane

Curved blade seat (exaggerated)

Top view

45°

Notch for shavings

Ball plane

I was recently asked to make a double-curved "ball plane" with which to smooth a laminated cherry sphere 5 ft. in diameter.

The wooden sole of the plane is curved throughout its length and width, combining the traditional sole design of the wheelwright's compass plane and the joiner's hollow molding plane. I followed traditional plane-making methods to make the basic plane, which is 10 in. long, by 2⅞ in. wide and

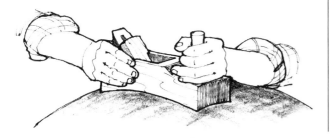

high. The blade angle is 47° and the iron is a 51-mm (2 in.) Record tungsten-vanadium iron and cap set.

After making the block, I used a template to trace a section of a 5-ft. diameter circle on the sole. The sole was then chiseled to within 1/16 in. of true, and a flat scraper was used to finally reach the true line. This operation formed the curve throughout the sole's length. The plane bottom was scraped slightly hollow so it would function like a Japanese smoothing plane, hitting the work at three points only: front, back and cutting iron. This helped level the ball in every direction. A spokeshave and another scraper, ground and shaped to the same 5-ft. arc, were used to curve the sole across its width.

The iron was then roughly ground to the same curved line and finally brought to the exact curve with a sequence of increasingly fine sharpening slips.

I used white beech for the sole and the main part of the block, oak for the top plate and wedge, walnut for the front horn and cherry for the rear palm handle. The handles were shaped to fit the hand whether pulling or pushing. The entire plane weighs only two pounds, an important consideration since many days were spent bringing the sphere to within ¼ in. of a 5-ft. diameter.

—*Eduardo A. Rumayor, Bronx, N.Y.*

English plane

There are thousands of old Stanley wood-bottom planes to be had at antique shows, flea markets and garage sales—usually for under $10. With a little work, most of these can be put back into service. I usually cut ¼ in. from the bottom of the plane, then epoxy a new sole of lignum vitae or rosewood in place, and then recut the mouth.

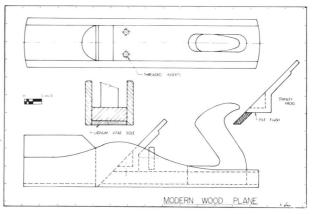

THREADED INSERTS

STANLEY FROG

FILE FLUSH

LIGNUM VITAE SOLE

MODERN WOOD PLANE

Last year I saw a beautiful English plane that was not available here, so I made one like it. The heart of the plane is a modified Bailey frog mechanism, which provides the standard metal plane adjusting features. The frog could be removed from an old metal plane or purchased as a replacement part. It was modified by filing away the two tongues at the base, then mounted in the wooden body by setting two threaded inserts for bolts.

Depending on the thickness of the sole, it might be necessary to modify the cap iron by retapping the screw hole and adding a second square hole for the depth-adjusting lever. I wanted the plane to be as colorful as possible so I used lignum vitae and walnut for the sole, purple heart for the sides, rosewood for the front and beech for the handle.

—*Allen Weiss, Queens, N.Y.*

A router plane

You can build your own routing plane that will work as well as a commercial one for the cost of a cheap offset screwdriver and a U-bolt. The cutting irons are ground from the screwdriver bits, a blade about ¼ in. wide at one end, and a

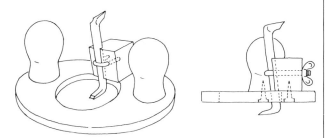

narrow plow at the other. The blades sit almost flat to the work, like paring chisels. Relief under the heel of the blade is obtained by making the blade holder with a tilted face.

Dimensions and shape can be suited to the builder's fancy and to the materials at hand. The illustrated design is simple enough to be produced in a single evening at the workbench.

—*Van Caldwell, Cincinnati, Ohio*

Guide blocks for accurate hand-planing

Because I don't own a jointer, I rely on my bench planes for truing up my lumber. To maintain a consistent angle, I cut guide blocks from scrap pieces of hardwood and clamp them to the plane.

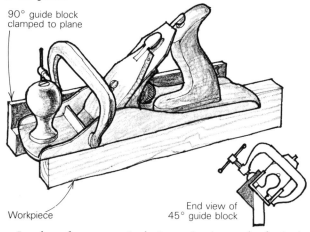

90° guide block clamped to plane

Workpiece

End view of 45° guide block

I make a few passes, check the angle, then make final adjustments using the plane's lever arm to tilt the blade.

—*Jack Gabon, Missoula, Mont.*

Chisel rabbet plane

The rabbet plane is not needed often in a modern electric shop. But when it is, nothing else will quite do the job. This

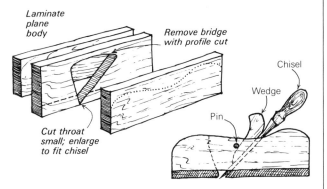

Laminate plane body

Remove bridge with profile cut

Chisel

Wedge

Pin

Cut throat small; enlarge to fit chisel

design, using a standard ½-in. chisel for the plane iron, requires a minimum of both cash and intricate work. For the body, laminate three pieces of hardwood, as shown in the sketch. A ⅞-in. step from the outside laminations to the middle one should be adequate to handle most rabbet depths. The middle lamination should be just slightly thicker than the chisel is wide, then dressed down with a rasp after assembly. Bandsaw the laminated blank to the desired shape, install a ¼-in. steel pin across the throat, then fit a wedge to hold the chisel in place. Saw the initial throat opening small, then enlarge it a little at a time with a file until the clearance is right. If shavings clog in the throat, drill a 1-in. hole above the throat to give room to push the shavings out.

—*Robert M. Vaughan, Roanoke, Va.*

Making chisels

One source of steel for making special tools is the local junkyard. High-carbon steel can be found in auto leaf springs, spring-tooth harrows, bed rails and many other things. You can determine the type of steel, or at least its relative hardness, by trial and error with a file or a hacksaw: If you can cut it or mark it with relative ease, then it is not what you want.

I needed several mortising chisels, and old bed rails lent themselves to this type of tool. Bed rails are usually ⅛ in. thick and 1½ in. across the right-angle flats. The rails can be cut with a hacksaw, but you will use a lot of blades. They are easy to cut if you first remove the temper by heating with a propane torch wherever you wish to cut.

First I laid out the design for the tang and sides of the blade, then I roughly cut out the blank with a hacksaw. I

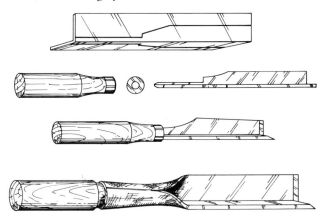

finished shaping the tool with bastard and second-cut files, leaving the cutting edge until after the handle was driven onto the tang. The handle can be bought or turned on a lathe, or shaped by hand. To keep the wood from splitting, I used ½-in. thin-walled electrical conduit for the ferrules, and a common washer on the shoulders of the tang. I predrilled the hole and drove the handle onto the tang. Then I filed the cutting edge to shape and tempered it.

My method of tempering the cutting edge is adapted from a technique I learned from an old blacksmith. First heat the metal to cherry red, place the tip in cold water for a few seconds, then file across the beveled cutting edge until a straw color appears. Then immediately and completely immerse the metal in cold water. You will have to use trial and error to get the right hardness. The propane torch is not hot enough to temper a complete cross section of bed rail.

When a furnace or an acetylene torch is available, you can make larger tools such as socket chisels and mortising chisels from bed rails and auto leaf springs. I use a tapered pin in a machinist's vise as a form for the socket. By hammering and reheating it is possible to form the socket around the pin.

Then I turn handles of hickory wood to fit the socket. First drive the handle into the socket, then shape the cutting edge on a grinder and with files. Finish by tempering and polishing.
—*Lester E. Rishel, Bellefonte, Pa.*

Veneer strip thicknesser

For decorative inlay and border work, it is often an advantage to have all the strips of uniform thickness, or to alter the thickness for a special design. A simple scraper thicknesser assembled from scrap hardwood will do a quick and accurate job. A trued-up 2-in. square about 14 in. long forms the body of the jig, while two identical rotating arms (say 1 in. by 2 in. by 5 in.) support the scraper and adjust the cut and thickness by means of a common pivot bolt (say ⅜ in.). The scraper is clamped to the arms with two small C-clamps.

To use the thicknesser, clamp one end of the body in the vise and loosely position the arms at an appropriate scraper angle. Clamp the scraper to the arms as shown, using shims on the body to determine thickness and to orient the edge parallel. Tighten the pivot nut and make fine adjustments by tapping with a hammer. Feed the strips under the scraper in

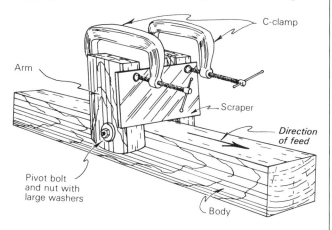

the direction shown and pull them through. Sometimes it helps to angle the strip to the blade. If the strips pull hard, rotate the arms and take a lighter cut. When sharpening the scraper, file straight across only about three-quarters of its length, then taper away at the end. This will permit starting the strips under the scraper near one arm, then sliding them over under the straight-cutting section for thicknessing.
—*William D. Woods, Phoenix, Ariz.*

Triangular scraper

This graunching tool (that's what we called it in the old days back in New England) is used for deburring metal, enlarging holes, scraping paint or glue from hard-to-reach places and many other jobs where a sharp, hard tool is necessary. Break off an old triangular file, hollow-grind it to the shape shown and mount in a handle.
—*H. Norman Capen, Granada Hills, Calif.*

Shake shingles for dollhouses

To make realistic shake shingles for dollhouses, I constructed a guillotine splitter using a plane iron attached to a wood fixture. The fixture consists of a vertical board screwed to a horizontal base. Loose round-head wood screws guide the plane iron and hold it in place. The end-grain shingle stock

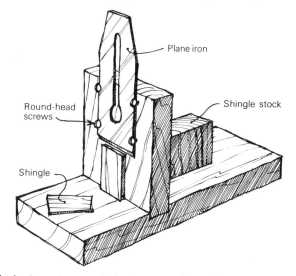

feeds through a notch in the vertical board. One sharp tap from a mallet will produce a perfect miniature shake shingle.
—*Gene Balzer, Flagstaff, Ariz.*

Tool holders

This tool holder is simple to build from scrap lumber and Masonite. The hole spacing can be varied for different tools. A mounting hole on each end allows the rack to be hung from the wall, the workbench or even a door.
—*Jay Wallace, Gilbert, Ariz.*

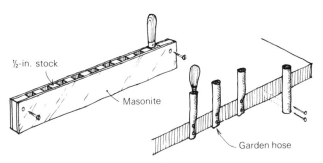

Hose holds tools

Six-inch lengths of garden hose fastened to the wall or bench with two nails at the bottom make excellent tool holders for screwdrivers, awls, etc. Tools are easy to remove, and the soft, flexible hose won't damage sharp edges.
—*Carl R. Vitale, Cranston, R.I.*

Restoring old tools

To restore old tools the process I generally follow is: Use Murphy's oil soap with very little water to wash off excess dirt and grit, and let it dry thoroughly; sand with 6/0 wet-dry sandpaper or 4/0 steel wool; treat the wood with two coats of Minwax antique oil, which does a better job than linseed oil; apply paste wax and buff; soak all metal parts in a rust remover and then buff them on a wire wheel; coat the blades with clear lacquer to keep them from rusting again.
—*R.K. Brunner, South Charleston, W.Va.*

Poor boy's scriber

Perhaps my poor boy's scriber might suggest a useful project. The point is a nipped-off 6d nail in a hole drilled undersize

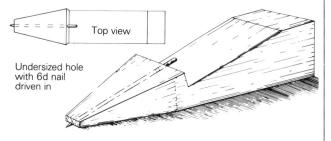

Top view

Undersized hole
with 6d nail
driven in

for a drive fit. This gadget eliminates error that a round-pointed tool might make because of the angle at which it is held.   —*Earl Solomon, Orchard Park, N.Y.*

Socket reamers

Here are two spur-of-the-moment, large-diameter reamers that work well for tapering candlestick sockets and the like. Since a candlestick reamer won't be used often, practically any scrap of steel will do for the cutter on the "deluxe" version. Install the sharpened cutter in a saw kerf with a screw. Use two screws or pin the blade through the dowel body if the cutter shifts in use.

You don't need a lathe for the sandpaper version—it can be whittled and filed sufficiently round by hand. Install one end of a sandpaper strip in a slot in the head. Then wrap the

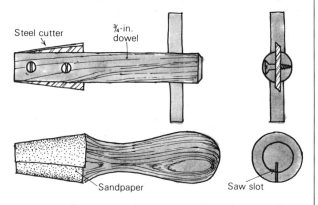

Steel cutter

¾-in. dowel

Sandpaper

Saw slot

strip around the reamer; there's no need to fasten the other end of the strip.   —*Van Caldwell, Cincinnati, Ohio*

Tool for scraping beads

This homemade lathe tool is handy for making scraping cuts on beads. Start with a ⅜-in. square bar of tool steel and grind a 30° bevel from one corner back, as shown below. By rotating the chisel 90°, you get two angled cutting edges, one for each side of a bead.   —*James F. Dupler, Jamestown, N.Y.*

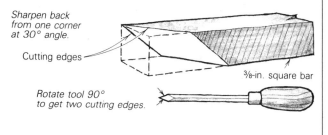

Sharpen back
from one corner
at 30° angle.

Cutting edges

⅜-in. square bar

Rotate tool 90°
to get two cutting edges.

Wooden mallet

At least one wooden carpenter's mallet belongs in every woodworker's tool chest. The advantages of wood over steel are obvious—less damage to tools, work, thumbs and eyes. For the price of one steel hammer, you can make a dozen mallets, each tailored to a particular job.

The traditional mallet has a solid-wood head mortised through for the wedge-shaped handle. My laminated head design is just as strong and much easier to make. Begin by cutting the handle and two center laminations for the head from the same 1-in. thick board (this saves a lot of fitting later). Copy the handle's wedge angle (no more than ½ in. of taper) onto one of the side laminations. Then glue up the head block, carefully aligning the center laminations with the wedge-angle pencil lines. When the glue has cured, bandsaw

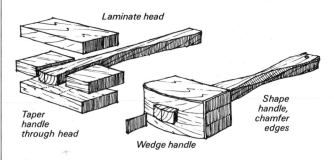

Laminate head

Taper
handle
through head

Wedge handle

Shape
handle,
chamfer
edges

the head to shape. Then chamfer all the edges to reduce the chances of splitting, and insert and wedge the handle.
                    —*Daniel Arnold, Viroqua, Wis.*

Poor man's mallet

If you have an old baseball or softball bat stashed in the attic, then you also have a first-class hickory or ash mallet. Cut a tapered section about 15 in. long from the middle of the bat, such that the smaller end fits your grip comfortably. My own mallet tapers from 1⅛ in. at the handle tip to 2 in. at the head. This long mallet is shock-resistant and will replace the usual assortment of carver's mallets, since by regulating the position of your grip on the handle, you can in effect vary the hitting weight of the head.

The head of any mallet, including the bat mallet, can be saved from inevitable flaking and checking. Cut a piece of thick, stiff, unoiled leather large enough to wrap around the entire head. Dampen the leather until pliable, then finish the fitting on the head, stretching the leather and making a reasonably good joint where the edges meet. Glue the leather on the head with water-based glue, using tacks to hold the joint (leave the heads proud). After complete drying, remove the tacks and trim the leather down to the head. A mallet treated in this manner should never need replacing—the leather is incredibly tough and will not lift away.
                    —*William D. Woods, Phoeniz, Ariz.*

Reground parting tool

I've found that when reground to the shape below, a parting tool cuts cleaner and faster—and is easier to handle, too.
                    —*Howard W. Escher, Seattle, Wash.*

Cutting Plexiglas

You can quickly and easily cut Plexiglas with these two tools. To make the scribing table, start with a sturdy bench and add two lengths of angle iron for a vise as shown in the sketch. Set the bottom angle iron into the bench so it's flush with the bench top. Weld two short sections of ⅜-in. threaded rod to the bottom iron so you can tighten the top iron on the Plexiglas with wing nuts. The scribing tool is a piece of hacksaw blade fit to a handle and ground as shown.

To cut the Plexiglas, tighten it in place on the scribing table. Then drag the scribing tool across the Plexiglas using the top iron as a guide. The tool should produce a thin, continuous curl on each pass. After several passes, whack the projecting Plexiglas with your hand. It will break clean and square. —*Jay Wallace, Ashland, Ore.*

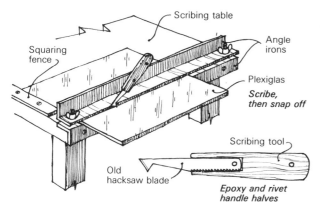

Scribing table

Angle irons

Squaring fence

Plexiglas

Scribe, then snap off

Scribing tool

Old hacksaw blade

Epoxy and rivet handle halves

Recycling sawblades into knives

If one of your old circular-saw blades has seen better days, you may want to use it to try your hand at knife-making. Most sawblades are made of excellent high-carbon steel and are about the right thickness for a beefy camping knife or a custom-fitted woodcarving tool.

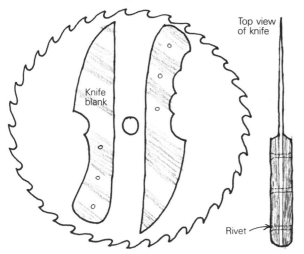

Top view of knife

Knife blank

Rivet

First, cut the blade into manageable pieces with an abrasive cut-off wheel. Then anneal the knife blanks using charcoal in a barbeque—play a hair dryer on the coals if you need more heat. Heat the blanks until they glow red (as seen in dim light), then allow them to cool very slowly in the fire as the charcoal burns itself out. Grind the annealed blank to shape and drill holes through the tang for the rivets that will attach the handle's "scales." Taper the blade's thickness from heel to point, and bevel the cutting edge with a belt sander, a file, or even sandpaper wrapped around a stick.

Now you're ready to harden the blade with the barbeque forge. Heat it cherry red, then plunge it into a pail of water. Next, polish the blade with sandpaper, and reheat it in a 550° kitchen oven for about twenty minutes, until the surface turns bronze, verging on purple. When the color is right, you can quench the blade in water or just let it air-cool.

Finally, attach the hardwood scales to the tang with epoxy glue and rivets. You can make your own rivets with heavy brazing rod or copper ground wire. This is not only a good use for old sawblades, but also a good use for those small pieces of fine hardwood that you just couldn't throw away: they make beautiful handles. —*Jim Stuart, Covina, Calif.*

Ferrules from end caps

Over the years I have seen all kinds of homemade tool handles ranging from an old corncob jammed on the tang of a rasp (a surprisingly comfortable improvisation) to ornate, French-polished creations. For most of us whose efforts fall between these extremes, locating a suitable ferrule is a larger problem than turning the handle. Plumbing stores stock an attractive, inexpensive solution—copper-tubing end caps. The end caps, available in several sizes, are tough enough to

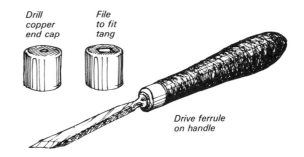

Drill copper end cap

File to fit tang

Drive ferrule on handle

hold up to mallet blows. To make a ferrule, drill a hole for the tool's tang through the soft metal. Shape the hole, if necessary, with a needle file. Drive the ferrule onto the wood handle, which has been sized to give a tight friction-fit. Rubbing the copper with fine steel wool produces a beautiful satin finish and reddish-gold color that complements all woods. An occasional coat of paste wax will protect the copper from tarnish. —*George Mustoe, Bellingham, Wash.*

Hand drill

I made this tool ten years ago for holding cut-off Allen wrenches. Since then I've found several other uses for it and I use it often in my workshop. I haven't seen a hand drill this size available commercially, but it is easy to make. Smaller versions are available as pin vises. Some uses are:

—a holder for sharpening small drill bits.
—a handle for needle files.
—a leather or scratch awl (chuck a sharpened nail).
—a handle for hex screwdriver bits.
—deburring wood or metal holes (chuck a countersink).

And, in its primary use as a hand drill, for a few shallow holes it is easier to use than a power drill.

—*Robert J. Harrigan, Cincinnati, Ohio*

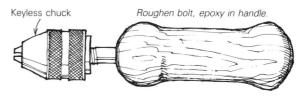

Keyless chuck

Roughen bolt, epoxy in handle.

Recycling tool handles

One way I beat inflation is by making my own tool handles from old mop, broom and shovel handles, usually made of ash, hickory or beech, that the average homeowner pitches in the garbage.

Here's how I make octagonal handles for new carving-tool blades (which I buy unhandled). First, clamp a beech mop-stick in the vise, leaving about 6 or 8 in. protruding diagonally at the top. Mark the handle length and taper the sides from this line to the ferrule end with a drawknife. Take shallow cuts at first, turning the stick frequently for uniformity.

For the ferrule, use the metal end of a spent 20-ga. shotgun shell. If you're not a hunter, look for empty shells at a skeet shooting area. To separate the ferrule from the shell, drill through the center bottom (where the shotgun hammer hits the shell) with a ¼-in. bit. This releases the hull and inner packing, which can then be pulled out with pliers. The hole that's left is usually the right size to receive the carving tool's tang. To mount the ferrule, mark its length on the handle,

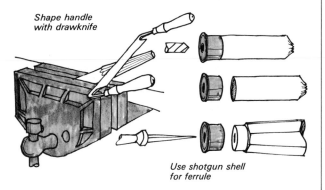

Shape handle with drawknife

Use shotgun shell for ferrule

and with a second-cut wood file, remove enough wood to seat the ferrule snugly.

Beech works well for carving-tool handles, but other woods are more suited to striking-tool handles. Old shovel handles (usually hickory) are best for replacement hammer handles; I work them down also with a drawknife. Broken ash baseball bats (check the local high school's practice field) are excellent for hammer, hatchet and lathe-tool handles. I finish all these handles with a couple of coats of tung or linseed oil.

—*Rob Russell, Joliet, Ill.*

Fitting a froe handle

In splitting out billets, the froe is used for wedging, levering and sometimes even chopping. The handle must be fitted very securely to withstand the different strains caused by these varied functions. A traditional froe has a tapered eye, and the

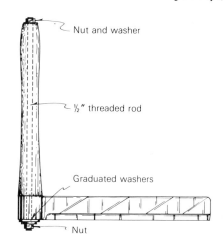

Nut and washer

½″ threaded rod

Graduated washers

Nut

blade was slid over the handle like an adze or mattock. Froes sold by modern suppliers have cylindrical eyes, and the handle is usually held on by a wedge, as on a hammer. I've had trouble keeping the handle on using both these methods.

I solved this problem by passing a ½-in. threaded rod through a hole bored lengthwise through the handle. Nuts on both ends of the rod pull the eye of the froe firmly against the shoulder of the handle. I use hornbeam for my froe handles but oak, ash or hickory would do as well. Before turning a handle to shape, I bore it using a ½-in. shell auger on the lathe. Boring may also be done by hand using a long electrician's auger, which will chew right through end grain if the spurs are ground off. The handle is then chucked in the lathe centered on the bore, and turned to shape. The tenon is turned to a snug fit in the froe eye, and its length trimmed short of the bottom of the eye. The handle may be tapered back from the shoulder to make a comfortable grip, but avoid a sudden taper that would weaken the shoulder's ability to resist the tension of the threaded rod. A stack of graduated washers is needed to cover the end of the froe socket on the bottom end of the threaded rod.

—*Richard Starr, Thetford Center, Vt.*

Homemade froe

The froe is a traditional tool for cleaving green wood that's enjoying a revival due to a renewed interest in "country" woodcraft. But the tool is rarely found through antique tool sources (I've never seen one) and new froes cost up to $30. Fortunately, for those of us with more time than cash, an excellent froe can be forged from a discarded auto spring.

Old leaf springs are easy to find behind auto garages and in junkyards. The springs are about the right thickness and width for a froe and are excellent steel. The bottom leaf of the spring cluster has an eye on each end. This is the leaf you're looking for—the eye serves as a ready-made handle socket.

To make the froe, cut a 10-in. to 12-in. section off one end of the leaf, straighten the curve or grind in a knifelike bevel on one edge. Lacking blacksmithing tools, I cut the spring with an oxyacetylene cutting torch (an abrasive cut-off wheel would have worked as well). Then, with a helper to hold the torch, I heat the blade red hot, forge a bevel on one edge and straighten the curve on a makeshift anvil. The bevel is completed on a grinder. Next, I harden the blade in oil and temper to light blue. A 14-in. black locust handle driven in the handle socket completes the froe.

1   2   3

Cut 12-in. section from leaf spring

Forge and grind bevel

Install 14-in. handle

A more skillful blacksmith probably would have enlarged the smallish socket and bent it to be in line with the blade. These operations seemed beyond my skill and equipment. But, in using the froe, the socket size seems adequate and the offset increases splitting leverage in one direction.

—*Larry Joseph, Alva, Okla.*

Cleaning file teeth

A blind sharpening-shop operator showed me this simple file-cleaning tool—it works better than a file brush. Hammer flat the pointed end of a 16d or 20d nail and grind the front edge straight. Remove the head of the nail and fit into a drilled dowel handle. Now push the straight edge of the tool along the grooves of file teeth. Soon tiny teeth will form in the edge of the tool which push metal, grease and rust out of the file. Turn the tool on edge to remove stubborn particles in one or two file grooves. —*John Foote, Clarksville, Tenn.*

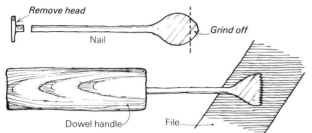

Edging with a leathercraft tool

To break the sharp, hard corners on straight or curved boards I use a simple tool that leather workers will find familiar. It's called a leather edger and is available in several sizes wherever leatherworking tools are sold.

If you're not near a source of leatherworking tools the edger is easy to make at home. Start by inserting one end of a 4-in. length of drill rod in a handle. Shape the other end of the rod into a curved fork with two tines about ⅜ in. long. Use the edge of a small rectangular file to cut the slot from the top and to form the appropriate cutting angle. Sharpen the cutting edge between the tines from underneath with a thin, rounded slipstone.

To use, push the tool along an edge with the grain. It should remove a thin, curled shaving and leave a delicately rounded edge in one pass.

—*Norman Odell, Quathiaski Cove, B.C., Canada*

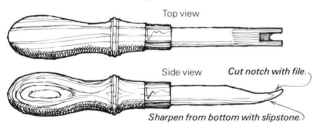

Brad-setting tool for tight places

Here is a simple tool to set brads or escutcheon pins in tight places. It consists of a 16d nail and a 3-in. brass tube that slides over the nail. Grind the point of the nail flat, dimple the end with a center punch, then drill a small cup with a

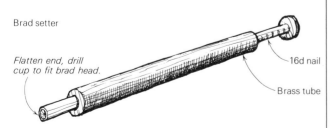

No. 32 drill bit. To use, set the brad in its pilot hole, drop the tube over the brad to the work surface and tap the brad home with a small hammer. —*Malcolm Murlless, Staunton, Va.*

Mini-drawknife

This mini-drawknife is as small and handy as a spokeshave but can slice away a good deal of wood on each draw. It is great for getting in close to the bench and for use in tight quarters where neither of its brothers could perform.

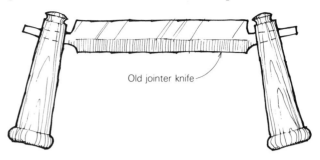

To make the tool, start with an old 6-in. jointer knife and slowly grind the handle tangs as shown in the illustration. Grind the tangs at a slight angle back from the cutting edge so that the handles wedge on the tangs and stay tight when the tool is pulled. Turn the handles to any comfortable shape, and fit the tangs. For a perfect fit, glue up the handle blanks with paper between. Turn, split apart, and groove each half to fit the tang. Then glue the halves together.

—*Jim Clark, Jr., Bridgeville, Penn.*

Sliding dovetail saw

To make a sliding dovetail saw you will need a piece of hardwood (maple, beech or fruitwood) 1 x 5½ x 13 in. and two flat-head ³⁄₁₆ x 1-in. bolts with tee-nuts. The blade can be an

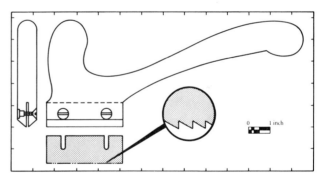

old band saw or bow saw blade. It should have 10 points to the inch, although 8 will do. I use a ripsaw blade, which I find cuts better and faster than a crosscut. The slots allow the blade to be set to the desired depth.—*Tage Frid, Foster, R.I.*

Radial-Arm Saw Jigs & Fixtures

Chapter 13

Pin-router adaptation for radial-arm saw

You can easily convert a radial-arm saw to a pin router. This tool will open up a whole new world of operations, and make many familiar tasks—such as rabbeting for book shelves or cutting mortises and slots—much easier.

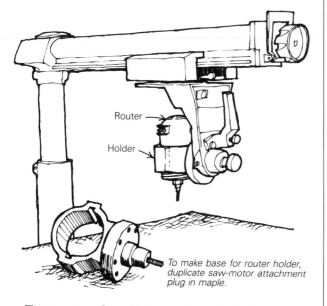

Router

Holder

To make base for router holder, duplicate saw-motor attachment plug in maple.

To convert my Sears 10-in. saw, I merely duplicated on the lathe, in rock maple, the saw-motor attachment plug where it fits the motor support arm. I laminated the ring assembly that holds the router from plywood. Then I glued and bolted together the laminated rings and the maple plug to form a single unit. Details of this fixture would vary to suit the saw/router combination. Also, if the setup is combined with a machinists' dual-feed rotary table, to hold and move the work, very precise work is possible.

The router is normally used in the vertical position, but it can be rotated to any orientation (just like the saw) for special routing cuts. —*Donald Wigfield, Moneta, Va.*

Square cuts

Most table-saw and radial-arm-saw blades that I've worked with have a tendency to climb and squirm when crosscutting. The result is an out-of-square cut. I've found, quite by accident, that if the crosscut is very thin, say one half the kerf, the saw cuts amazingly true. This approach does require that you make two cuts—one to rough length (leaving a half-kerf extra) and the second to final length. Of course if the machine is out of square to begin with, all bets are off.
—*Pat Warner, Escondido, Calif.*

Fluting columns

On the clock I am building now are four fluted half-round columns, each 1 in. high and 1¾ in. wide, two of them 41 in. long and two of them 16 in. long. Each has five flutes. To make these columns I took pieces of walnut 1¹⁄₁₆ in. by 1¾ in. and marked the ends to the half-round I wanted. I then took

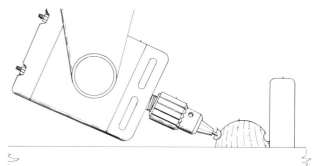

off some of the waste on the jointer and the rest with a hand plane. To get them perfectly half-round I took a 6-in. length of tubing with an inside diameter of 1¾ in. and cut it in half lengthwise. Inside of this I put a piece of 60-grit sandpaper to shape the wood, followed by finer grits until it was smooth. To make the flutes I put a drill chuck with a router bit on my radial arm saw. I set the saw to the proper angle for the first flute, with the wood against the rip fence, and ran both edges of all four pieces through. I adjusted the saw setting for the succeeding flutes. —*George Eckhart, Kenosha, Wis.*

Slot-mortising table

I cut slot mortises on my radial arm saw using this two-way sliding table. The table consists of three separate ¾-in. thick plywood or particle-board sections. Cut the middle and top sections wider than the bottom to leave room for clamping stop blocks. To get the two-way sliding action, cut tracks and set rails in the parts, as shown in the sketch. I used ¾-in. square, waxed hardwood rails glued into grooves cut just less than ⅜ in. deep. The shallow grooves will separate the sections a little so the surfaces won't rub. Notch the back corners of the top section (so you have a place to clamp stop blocks) and add fences, handles and work hold-downs as needed.

To use the table, mount an end-mill cutter in a chuck on the saw's spindle and set the height and depth of cut with the saw's adjustments. Clamp the stop blocks in place to control side-to-side movement. Now you're ready to mortise. Secure the work in position, turn on the saw and move the table from side to side as you slowly push the work into the cutter.
—*Bill Horton, Chino, Calif.*

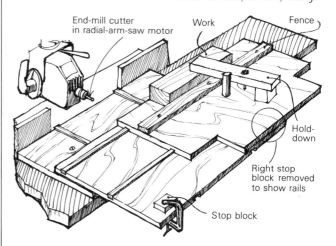

End-mill cutter in radial-arm-saw motor

Work

Fence

Hold-down

Right stop block removed to show rails

Stop block

Cutting angled rabbets

This simple radial-arm saw method makes it easy to cut mir-ror-image angled rabbets on the ends of a workpiece, as re-quired for the skirt of a splay-legged table for instance. This

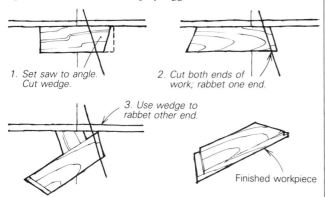

1. Set saw to angle. Cut wedge.

2. Cut both ends of work; rabbet one end.

3. Use wedge to rabbet other end.

Finished workpiece

approach makes it unnecessary to reset the saw to the same angle on the other side for the second cut.

Set the saw to the necessary angle and cut a wedge from a wide piece of waste stock. Don't cut the wedge to a point—the blunt end allows a little overhang, which will be needed. Leaving the arm at the original angle, cut one end of the workpiece, then turn the work over and cut the matching angle on the other end. Next, raise the saw and cut the first rabbet. Finally, place the wedge against the fence and cut the second rabbet, as shown, taking precautions that the work-piece doesn't pivot. The angle is bound to come out right. Be aware that this method is dangerous with short stock.

—*Wendell Davis, Hampton, Conn.*

Miter jig

With this fixture I can make tight, clean production-run miter cuts on my radial arm saw. Those of us who can't always take time to readjust and tune our saws realize they work out of true. The miter jig overcomes this because any error on one piece is compensated by matching error on the other.

To make the jig, glue and screw two 1x2s to a sheet of ¼-in. plywood about the size of the saw table. The 1x2s are fast-

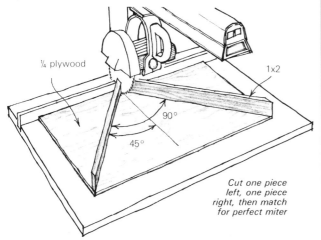

¼ plywood

1x2

90°

45°

Cut one piece left, one piece right, then match for perfect miter

ened 45° from the line of the saw cut. Care with the orienta-tion of the miter fences improves the device—a 45° plastic drafting triangle will be helpful. The fixture can be clamped to the saw table or made as part of a permanent fence.

To use, clamp the fixture on the table (or in the fence channel if the fixture has a permanent fence). Cut one piece left and one piece right. Match these cuts and a perfect fit will result.

—*C.H. Dimmick, Sparta, N.J.*

Improved miter fixture

C.H. Dimmick's miter fixture for the radial arm saw is very useful as described. But by leaving a 4-in. gap between the fence and the 45° guides, boards can be cut to length, then shifted to the 45° guides for mitering. Without the gap, the boards can be cut to length only by using another saw or by removing the jig.

—*M.B. Williams, Potomac, Md.*

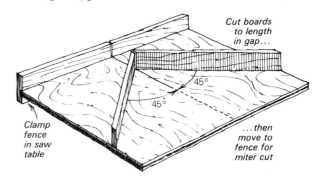

Cut boards to length in gap...

45°

45°

Clamp fence in saw table

...then move to fence for miter cut

Portable-saw guide

Surely I am not the only small-shop woodworker who has spent an inordinate amount of time trying to cut up large sheets of plywood or trim the ends off long, heavy boards on a table saw. I have been happy with my small table saw, but I'm delighted to find my portable circular saw will do equally precise work on unwieldy pieces with the help of a guide that takes just minutes to make. The beauty of the guide is that it positions the blade right on the cut-line in one step.

The main components of the guide are a ¾-in. wood straightedge nailed to a thin base of ¼-in. plywood or Mason-ite. The saw rides on the base and is pressed against the straightedge. A long guide for cutting large sheets of plywood is best held with two C-clamps—one at each end. Be sure to make the straightedge wide enough so that the saw's motor housing will clear the C-clamps. After nailing the straightedge to a base piece slightly wider than needed, just run the

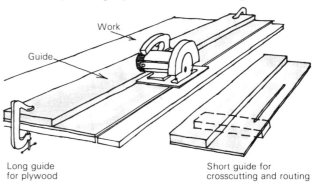

Work

Guide

Long guide for plywood

Short guide for crosscutting and routing

saw (with the blade you intend to use) along the base to trim off the excess. The guide is now ready to use.

A shorter variation of the guide is useful for cutting off long boards. Nail a strip of wood to the bottom of the short guide at right angles to the straightedge. Sandpaper glued to the underside will keep the guide from slipping when held at the far end with one C-clamp.

The short guide can also be used for cutting dadoes with a router. Just rout a slot into the base of the guide, carefully pressing the router base against the straightedge. Start the router cut over the right-angle strip on the bottom (remember to remove a bit of the sandpaper first). It's easy to clamp the guide at the right position on the workpiece by eyeballing the layout lines for the dado through the slot in the base.

—*Rich Baldinger, Schenectady, N.Y.*

Space-saving saw setup

Here's one solution to the problem of squeezing both a table-saw with long extension rails and a radial-arm saw with long extension tables into a narrow shop. My shop is 10 ft. by 25 ft. and until recently these machines took up most of my

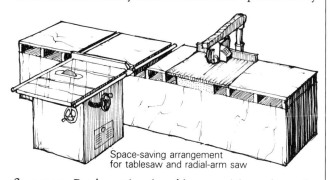

Space-saving arrangement
for tablesaw and radial-arm saw

floor space. But by setting the tablesaw at right angles to the radial-arm saw and combining the extension table space of the two machines I was able to recover much of this lost area.

To combine the machines the two tables must be the same height. I chose to block up my radial-arm saw to the height of my tablesaw. Cut two troughs in the radial-arm table to accommodate the tablesaw's rails. Cut the front trough wide enough for the rip-fence lock. Position the rails so that the rip fence rides just a fraction of an inch above the radial-arm saw's table.   —*Andrew A. Ruotsala, Seattle, Wash.*

"Poor boy" radial-arm saw

For crosscutting long boards and making miter cuts, this shopmade saw guide is accurate, portable, easy to use and economical to build.

The guide is simply an angle-iron and plywood track sized to fit the base of a portable circular saw. The guide is perched atop legs at each end. Each leg is made from a pair of 3½-in. pipe flanges connected by a ¾-in. by 1½-in. pipe nipple. The legs provide clearance for the work and allow the track to pivot for making angle cuts.

To use, clamp the guide at the proper angle in relation to the fence on the plywood base. Before cutting, secure the saw's blade guard up out of the way with a screw threaded through a hole in the blade housing. Make sure you remove the screw before the saw is used in the conventional manner.

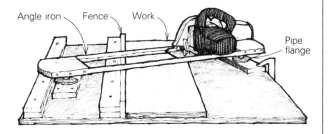

Angle iron   Fence   Work

Pipe
flange

Another note of caution: The direction of blade rotation tends to lift the work from the table, so make sure the work is tight against the fence and can't shift. Otherwise, the work might pinch the sawblade and cause the saw to lift out of the guide rails.

On my 7¼-in. saw, the depth of cut is limited to 1¾ in., but this covers most of the crosscutting work I do.
—*Jack Fisher, Dayton, Ohio*

Jointing on the radial-arm saw

Lacking a jointer here's an improvised radial-arm-saw setup I devised to joint the thick oak boards I used in two butcher-block tabletops. First rip a thin board the exact thickness of the saw kerf of the blade you're using. Tack the thin board to the saw fence behind the blade. Bring the blade up against the fence and adjust so that the blade and the piece you've added to the rear fence are flush. If your setup is accurate, your fence is long and straight, and your blade has 60 or more carbide teeth, you should get perfectly jointed edges ready to be glued up. Using variations on this fence, you can joint on the table saw and router table as well.
—*Dale Snyder, Duluth, Minn.*

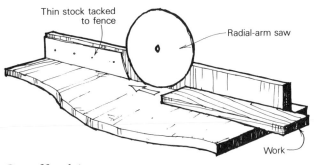

Thin stock tacked
to fence

Radial-arm saw

Work

Cutoff table

Back in the days before I had a radial arm saw in my shop, I worked out a cutoff table to use with my portable circular saw. The fixture consists of a 2x12 table, a 2x4 fence and a guide bridge. The rabbets on the two bridge pieces should face each other and be spaced just wide enough to fit the base of your portable circular saw. If desired, a stop block can be *C*-clamped to the fence for accurate duplicate cutoff work.
—*C.G. Fader, Ketchikan, Alaska*

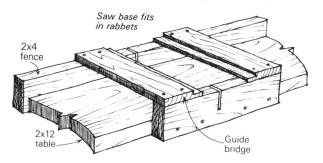

Saw base fits
in rabbets

2x4
fence

2x12
table

Guide
bridge

Reversible jig for the radial-arm saw

This reversible jig is useful when you need to cut a number of identical pieces with angled dadoes on opposite sides. The two dowels and the saw fence locate the work. Two stops clamped to the fence define the width of the dado. Once you have cut all pieces on their top sides, flip the jig end-for-end, push the dowels through to the opposite side of the jig, relocate the stops and proceed to cut the bottom dadoes.
—*J.A. Hiltebeitel, S. Burlington, Vt.*

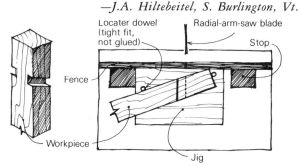

Locater dowel
(tight fit,
not glued)

Radial-arm-saw blade

Stop

Fence

Workpiece

Jig

Cutting round tenons on slats

With a metal pipe, a simple jig and my radial-arm saw, I solved the problem of cutting round tenons on the ends of slats for the sides of a cradle. Find a 6-in. length of pipe that slips snugly over the slats (my slats are ¾ in. wide by ⅜ in. thick). Add masking tape to the slats to tighten up the fit if they're loose. Build the simple jig shown in the sketch below and clamp it and the stop block to the saw's fence. Carefully adjust the stop block so that the tenons will be the right length. Mount a sharp plywood blade in the saw and center

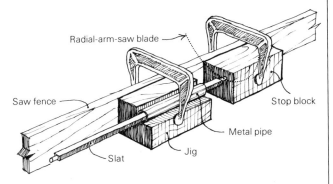

Radial-arm-saw blade

Saw fence

Stop block

Metal pipe

Jig

Slat

the blade over the slat location. Now push a slat into the pipe and place the pipe in the jig with the slat up against the stop. Lower the blade until it just touches the flat side of the slat (this will result in a slightly undersize ⅜-in. tenon). Rotate the pipe to cut a clean shoulder on the slat. Work the slat back and forth under the blade, slowly rotating the pipe. A round tenon will result. This process leaves the tenon a little bit rough, but so much the better for gluing. After you're set up, you can cut the tenons on 20 or 30 slats in an hour.

—George Eckhart, Kenosha, Wis.

Tablesaw Jigs & Fixtures

Chapter 14

Table-saw sliding crosscut fixture

Crosscutting wide panels using the table saw's miter gauge is awkward at best. Faced with a project requiring accurate crosscuts on 2-ft. wide, 6-ft. long panels, I investigated commercial sliding-table crosscut setups. Finding these too expensive for the flexibility and accuracy delivered, I designed and built an inexpensive all-wood sliding crosscut fixture. It's quite accurate and, depending on how it's mounted, has the capacity to crosscut pieces over 4 ft. wide.

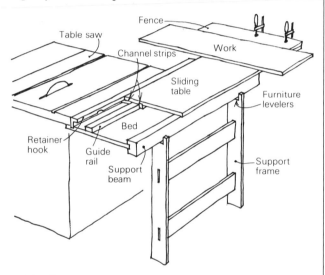

The fixture consists of three parts: a sliding table, a guide bed and a support stand. For stability, I selected mahogany for the solid-wood pieces and ¾-in., 14-ply aircraft plywood for the table and guide bed; any good-quality hardwood and hardwood plywood could be substituted. You'll need a 4x4 sheet of plywood and several 4-ft. lengths of hardwood in various dimensions for the sliding table and guide bed. Make the support stand from pine or whatever is available.

The guide bed attaches to the left side of the table saw (in place of the left extension wing) using existing mounting holes and hardware. The mounting bracket for the bed also doubles as a retainer hook to keep the sliding table from tipping with long, heavy pieces. A guide rail on the bed keeps the sliding table parallel to the sawblade.

The sliding table is a plywood panel with two strips on its bottom to form a channel for the guide rail. One of the channel strips doubles as a lip to fit under the bed's retainer hook.

The support stand is an H-frame dimensioned to support the bed. I used mortise-and-tenon construction. Furniture levelers in the top give needed adjustment capability.

To construct the fixture, first rip the bed, table and retainer hook strips from the plywood. Glue up the retainer hook and glue and screw it in a dado cut in the bed. Cut a groove in the support beam and install it on the left edge of the bed

with glue and screws. Cut the guide rail to size but save the installation for later.

Next, cut a dado in the bottom of the sliding table and mount the left-hand channel strip in the dado, screwing from the bottom without glue so the strip can be replaced when worn. Now, to set the channel gap accurately, place the guide rail temporarily against the left-hand channel strip and glue the right-hand channel strip in place on the table bottom.

Complete the support stand, mount the bed to the saw and level it, using the furniture levelers between the stand and the support beam. Set the sliding table in place and shim out ¹⁄₁₆ in. or so from the retainer hook. Now slide the guide rail into its channel and carefully fasten in place with screws through the bottom of the bed. To complete the fixture, paraffin all contact surfaces to cut down friction.

You can mount a permanent fence to the sliding table top. (Be sure to shim it off the table slightly so it won't catch on the front of the saw table.) I've found it convenient, however, to use temporary fences clamped to the sliding table. The gap between the bed and the table leaves plenty of room for C-clamps or sliding clampette heads. To square a temporary fence, push a scrap of wood of the right thickness into the miter gauge channel and use a framing square.

I mounted the fixture so that the back of the base lines up with the back of my saw. Although this gives maximum capacity, it is slightly inconvenient because the fixture projects about a foot in front of the saw. Others may want to consider shortening the fixture (thus lessening capacity) or mounting differently to minimize inconvenience.

—*Roger Deatherage, Houston, Tex.*

Table saw tenoner

This jig, designed to cut tenons and bridle joints on the table saw, performs as well as expensive, commercial versions.

It consists of a base, which travels in the miter gauge slot, and a fence assembly. Dadoes in the fence assembly slide on rails in the top of the base to allow the blade-to-fence distance to be varied. The two pieces are locked at the right position by a nut mortised in a block of wood. Make the other jig parts of high-quality ¾-in. aircraft or hardwood plywood; don't waste your time with fir plywood.

To use the jig, clamp the work to the fence with a C-clamp, or a hold-down clamp mounted on the fence. Align the jig for the cut and push through the saw.

—*Larry Humes, Everson, Wash.*

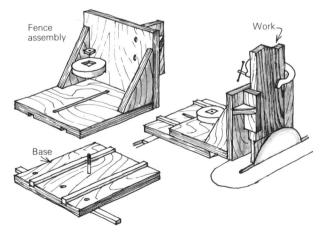

Table saw tenons

This method for cutting tenons on the table saw uses two blades with spacers between. The beauty of this system is that the tenon thickness is "locked in" and does not depend on variables such as stock thickness or pressure against the fence.

I keep a pair of special hollow-ground blades for tenon work. They are jointed as a pair and filed for ripping. Since the hub and tooth thickness are the same, cutting a $\frac{5}{16}$-in.

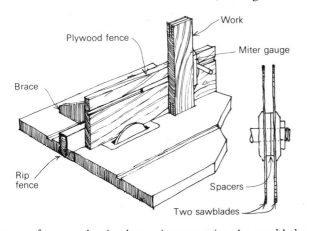

Work
Plywood fence
Miter gauge
Brace
Rip fence
Spacers
Two sawblades

tenon, for example, simply requires mounting the two blades with a $\frac{1}{4}$-in. and a $\frac{1}{16}$-in. spacer between. My set of custom-machined spacers are $2\frac{1}{2}$-in. discs drilled to slip over the saw arbor. Spacer thicknesses range from $\frac{1}{4}$ in. to 0.005 in. To pass the work through the blades, I use a standard miter gauge tracked in a plywood fence as shown above. This approach eliminates vertical rocking and thus is safer and more accurate than other methods.

—Mac Campbell, Harvey Station, N.B., Canada

Space-age saw guard

This table-saw guard, developed for cutting space-shuttle insulation, holds several advantages over conventional guards. Because it is counterbalanced, the guard makes lighter contact and is easier to operate, especially with thick materials. By sliding the counterweight up or down the arm, the operator can adjust the downward force of the clear plastic enclosure.

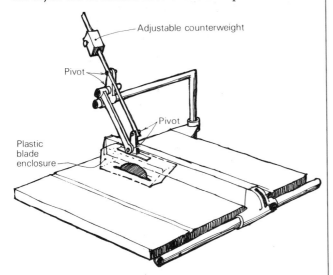

Adjustable counterweight
Pivot
Pivot
Plastic blade enclosure

The guard doesn't preclude dadoing and grooving operations, which are impossible with some other types of guards. The design was developed by Benjamin R. Dunn and Paul P. Zebus of Rockwell International.

—NASA Tech Briefs, Johnson Space Center, Tex.

Shopmade tablesaw guard

During an evening's discussion with several other mechanics, I found that each of us came up with a good reason or two for not using the guards that came with our tablesaws. My long-tested shopmade guard, however, seemed just the sort of thing people would actually use. While it won't control kickback, and won't protect against outright carelessness, it is a real help in my shop.

The guard is a piece of Lexan plastic suspended on a parallelogram arm fixture that keeps the guard parallel to the table at any height. The guard can be lifted for upright work and

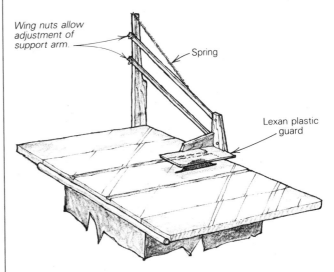

Wing nuts allow adjustment of support arm.
Spring
Lexan plastic guard

blade changes, then quickly lowered for ripping and crosscutting. It keeps knots out of your face and sawdust from cascading behind your safety glasses. The plastic, if cleaned once a day, allows full view of the work without distortion, and its width keeps fingers well away from the blade.

The support post should be set back far enough to clear normal crosscut widths, and the entire post should be easily removable for cutting long work.

—Rod Goettelmann, Vincentown, N.J.

Crosscutting wide panels

Here is an accurate and simple way to crosscut plywood panels or boards that are too wide to cut using the saw's miter gauge. Start with a straight 1x2 longer than the panel is wide. Clamp the 1x2 underneath the panel so that it becomes a

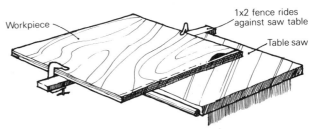

Workpiece
1x2 fence rides against saw table
Table saw

fence that runs against the saw table's edge. Carefully measure and position the fence using a framing square. Then clamp the new fence to the panel with C-clamps. The method can be adapted to ripping plywood and wall paneling by lengthening the fence. By clamping the fence to wide panels at an angle, you can make miter cuts that are virtually impossible any other way.   —Steve DeLay, Hollister, Calif.

Raising arched panels

The shaper is the correct tool for making a raised panel door with an arched top. I don't have a shaper, so I do the job with the table saw and a chisel, the hard way.

Make the rails and stiles, with tenons and mortises, in the usual way and cut the panel to shape. Set up the table saw to cut the bevel, with the blade angled to the correct slope, the height set for the width of the bevel, and the fence placed to the edge thickness of the panel. The straight sides are no problem, just run them through. On the arched top, run the piece through resting on the top of the arch, then again rest-

ing on the top and one corner, and again resting on the top and the other corner.

Now set the table saw to cut the shallow shoulders on the bevels, thus removing the waste from the work. This com-

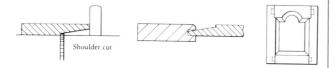

pletes the straight sides, except for cleanup with a rabbet plane, and removes most of the wood from the arched top.

Mark the shoulder line on the arched top and the 45° lines at the changes of direction. Use a wide, sharp chisel to carve the bevel down, making a neat, sharp juncture at the 45° line. Marking the correct thickness on the panel edge and carving back to the shoulder line is one way to do it.

The grooves that accept the panel in the straight sides are easily made with a dado blade in the table saw. To make the groove in the top rail, drill holes somewhat smaller than the desired thickness of the groove, then chisel out the groove to the line. Don't worry about the sloppy bottom of the groove, just make the sides nice and even.

Assemble the door dry, pin through the tenons with dowels, and fit it to its opening. Then take it apart and reassemble without the panel to round over the inside edge of the frame with a router. The panel should be finished before glue-up to prevent an unfinished edge from showing through as the door expands and contracts over the years. Make sure the panel is slightly loose on final assembly; that's the whole idea, allowing a little room for expansion and contraction.

—*Cary Hall, Hampton, Ga.*

Duplicating wood parts

You can produce exact duplicates from a master pattern using this overhanging jig on your table saw. To make the jig, glue the pieces of ½-in. plywood in an *L*, reinforcing the joint with braces and screws. Clamp the smaller side of the jig to the saw's rip fence with two *C*-clamps. Allow ⅛-in. clearance between the underside of the jig and the stock to be cut. Now, by moving the rip fence, set the guide edge of the jig directly over the outside of the blade.

Cut a master pattern from ½-in. plywood to the exact size and shape of the part to be duplicated. Fasten the pattern to oversize precut blanks with tacks or double-sided tape. Now you are ready to cut the duplicate part. Press the master pattern against the guide edge of the jig and push through the

blade. For safety's sake remove scraps from under the jig as you cut and stand to one side of the line of cut. Otherwise you'll be dodging projectiles of scrap that pile up under the jig and eventually get fired out by the blade.

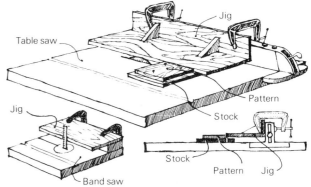

The table-saw jig is limited to duplicating straight-edged parts in plywood and thin, solid stock. To reproduce thicker parts, and those with curved edges, set up a similar jig on the band saw.   —*Ed Stevenson, Hammonton, N.J.*

Ogee molding

Ogee molding is easy to make using the table saw with a jointer or hand plane. By setting up a diagonal fence on the table saw, the boards, usually 3 in. to 5 in. wide, are hollowed, leaving a flat section along each edge, one narrow and

one wider. For 4-in. molding of the type usually used for bracket feet on case pieces, I usually leave a ¾-in. flat along one edge, which will remain flat. Along the other edge is a wider plane, which I joint or hand-plane into the graceful curve that makes this molding so useful. For safety, always use a push-stick and make several passes over the table-saw blade, raising it perhaps ⅛ in. at each pass. The fence is simply a board with a straight edge, clamped to the saw table at about 30° to the line of the blade. Other moldings, chair seats and even raised panels with beautiful curves forming the rise may be made using variations of this method.

—*James B. Small, Jr., Newville, Pa.*

Recessed tabletops

Wasting the central area of a top to form a lip on a bedside table or bureau is attractive and functional. Recessing emphasizes the grain, shows that solid wood has been used and prevents pencils and spills from falling to the floor. I cut the recess on the table saw using a dado head with all the chippers to get the widest cut. The circumference of the dado head leaves a pleasant curve at the inner edge of the tabletop.

To cut the recess, first clamp blocks of wood to the saw's rip fence to serve as stops. Then set the dado head to the right depth (¼ in. suits my taste). Holding the wood against the back stop, carefully lower the tabletop into the dado head. Do not cut across to the near edge, as it's liable to split out. Instead, cut halfway across, reverse the tabletop and cut halfway again from the outer edge. Waste the bulk of the materi-

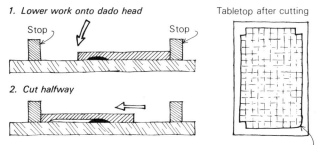

1. Lower work onto dado head — Stop, Stop — Tabletop after cutting
2. Cut halfway
3. Reverse work, cut from other edge — Hand-carve corners

al by cutting crossgrain, repeat passes along the grain, then carve out the corners by hand. Finish the surface by scraping and sanding. —*Pendleton Tompkins, San Mateo, Calif.*

Making dowels with the tablesaw

I prefer to make my own dowels for several good reasons. I can make any size dowel in any length from any wood. My system is simpler and certainly less expensive than the commercial dowel-making tools that are limited to only a few sizes. The drawings show the complete tooling required: a hardwood block and your tablesaw. The block size isn't critical, but it should be thick enough to clamp easily to the saw's rip fence and long enough to cover the sawblade in use. This last point is important because you'll need to reach across the saw to withdraw the finished dowel.

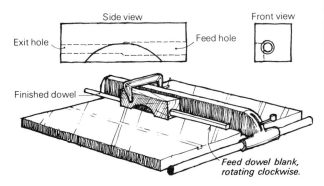

Side view — Front view
Exit hole — Feed hole
Finished dowel
Feed dowel blank, rotating clockwise.

To construct the fixture, first drill a dowel-sized exit hole through the length of the block. Enlarge this hole from the front, halfway through the block, to produce a feed hole. The diameter of the feed hole should be the same as the diagonal of the square dowel blanks you use. As a guide, the radius of the feed hole shouldn't exceed that of the exit hole by ¼ in. Now clamp the block to the saw's rip fence. Center the block over the blade. In a succession of cove cuts (made by raising the sawblade into the block) cut a channel from the edge to just into the wall of the exit hole. The best blade to use to

channel the block and make dowels is a heavy, small-diameter carbide-toothed blade. Next rip the dowel blanks so they will turn easily in the feed hole. With the block clamped and the fence locked, start the saw and insert the blank. Rotate the blank clockwise and feed slowly until the blade starts cutting. Adjust the block's position with the rip fence until the dowel fits snugly in the exit hole. It's a good idea to withdraw the dowel and check the size of the first few inches.

In smaller sizes, which are difficult to rotate by hand, I cut a short dowel on one end. Then I chuck the short dowel in my portable drill. A slow feed and a slow rotation yield the smoothest dowels. —*Larry Churchill, Mayville, Wis.*

Making louvers

This simple jig cuts the pins on the ends of the individual louvers in homemade louvered doors. It consists of a V-notched base, which slides in the tablesaw's miter-gauge track, and a cylindrical louver holder. A slot in the cylinder holds the louvers in the correct cutting position, using adjustment and stop screws as shown in the sketch. To use the jig, load a louver blank into the cylinder, then tighten a hose clamp around the cylinder to lock the louver in place. Place the cylinder in the base, push the jig into the blade and rotate the cylinder to cut a pin on one end of the louver. Remove the louver, reverse it in the cylinder and repeat to cut the other end's pin. —*R.F. Paakkonen, Stafford Springs, Conn.*

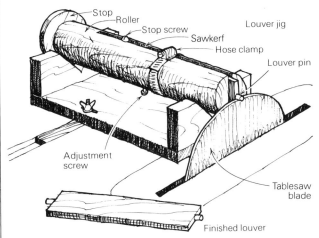

Stop, Roller — Stop screw — Sawkerf — Louver jig — Hose clamp — Louver pin
Adjustment screw
Tablesaw blade
Finished louver

Non-skid finger pressure boards

A small board cut 45° across the grain and kerfed to form fingers is quite useful for holding work against the fence in shaping and ripping operations. But the fingers jam unless you shim the board off the table. Also, the board tends to move under the clamps and lose tension. I solved both these problems by ironing on twill, iron-on patches sold for repairing work clothes. —*R.P. Sykes, Thousand Oaks, Calif.*

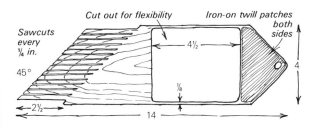

Cut out for flexibility — Iron-on twill patches both sides
Sawcuts every ¼ in.
45°
4½
⅛
2½
14
4

Cutting wide panels

A simple wooden strip tacked to the bottom of the workpiece will let you rip panels that are too wide for the rip fence on your table saw. Size the wooden strip to run in the miter-

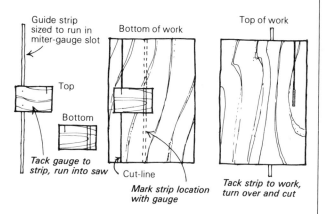

Guide strip sized to run in miter-gauge slot

Bottom of work

Top of work

Top

Bottom

Tack gauge to strip, run into saw

Cut-line

Mark strip location with gauge

Tack strip to work, turn over and cut

gauge slot (generally ¾ in. by ⅜ in.), and cut it slightly longer than the cut to be made. To lay out the strip's location on the workpiece, I used a small piece of ⅛-in. thick birch plywood as a distance gauge. Tack the plywood to the strip, then run the assembly into the saw for about an inch. Turn the assembly over and mark on the plywood the strip's location with a pencil line on both sides of the strip. Remove the plywood and you have a gauge that shows the exact relation of table slot to saw kerf.

To use the strip, draw an accurate cut-line on the back of the work. Now use the distance gauge to lay out the strip location, and brad the strip to the bottom of the work. Remember to position the strip so that the saw kerf is to the waste side of the cut-line. Turn the assembly over, feed the strip into the table slot and make the cut. If you have done the layout carefully, the cut will be right on. I use a thin-rim plywood blade, which, since the finished side of the work is up, produces a smooth, clean cut.

The procedure is not practical for the first cut on a 4x8 sheet of plywood or for quantity cutting. But it works fine for those 30-in. and 36-in. panels that are so awkward to cut on a small saw.   —*William Langdon, Lake Forest, Ill.*

Miter jig with holding block

I use a table-saw miter jig that includes a holding block in a channel, shown below, to press the work against the fence. Be

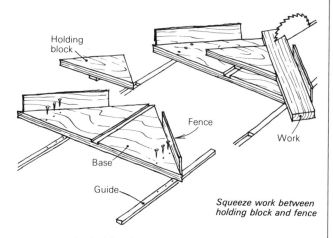

Holding block

Fence

Work

Base

Guide

Squeeze work between holding block and fence

sure to cut the holding block large enough to secure the stock against the fence and to keep your fingers away from the blade.   —*John C. Ort, Portsmouth, R.I.*

Cutoff box

This easy-to-build box is superior to the miter gauge for simple 90° cutoff work on the table saw. Right-angle accuracy is built into the fixture; there's no adjustment necessary. Also, because the work is supported on both sides of the cut, there is none of the creeping that plagues cutoff work with the miter gauge.

Although the size of the fixture is discretionary, I suggest you make it just a little smaller than the table-saw top. For a typical saw this will give you room to handle work that's 18 in. to 24 in. wide. Make the bed from ⅜-in. plywood and the fences from 2x4s. Glue and screw the fences to the bed

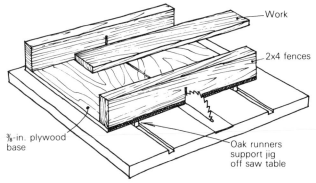

Work

2x4 fences

⅜-in. plywood base

Oak runners support jig off saw table

(avoid putting a screw in the path of the blade). Cut the oak runners so that they slide easily in the miter gauge tracks and support the bed about ¼ in. off the table. Be very accurate in attaching the runners and you'll always get a square cut.
—*Jon Gullett, Washington, Ill.*

Enhanced table-saw miter gauge

For five years I have looked unsuccessfully for a 10-in. table saw with a "rolling table" facility for crosscuts and miters. The one I'm familiar with is a big, old Oliver. The new Rockwell and Powermatic sliding table attachments are similar in concept and are fine if you have $2,000 to spend on the saw and rig. They take up room on the left of the saw and are really designed for the large stock requirements of a cabinet shop. There are plywood jigs that sit atop the saw and serve the purpose, but I've found them to be inaccurate. My solution is simple, inexpensive and as effective as the expensive attachments if you are not cutting whole sheets of plywood.

Simply take your miter gauge apart and insert a piece of Formica between the miter-gauge bar and the protractor fence. Cut the Formica the same size as the left half of the table and fasten the smooth side down. When using the fixture you can press down on the piece of wood being crosscut without causing the wood to bind as it slides on the table. The Formica spreads the pressure over a wider area. The addition of a backboard faced with abrasive paper practically eliminates creep.   —*Michael J. Hanley, Cedarburg, Wis.*

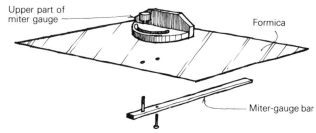

Upper part of miter gauge

Formica

Miter-gauge bar

Accurate miter jig

This table-saw jig, below, has helped me to cut accurate miters for 25 years. To make it cut two table-length rails from well-seasoned oak or hickory and sand to a sliding fit in the miter-gauge channels. With the rails in place in the channels, set the ½-in. plywood base (cut a little smaller than the saw table) on the rails so that the midpoint of the forward edge is aligned with the sawblade. Fasten the base to the rails

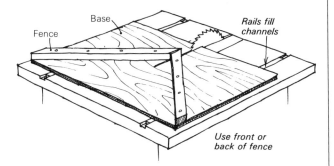

Base

Fence

Rails fill channels

Use front or back of fence

with ¾-in. flathead screws. Now slide the jig back, raise the sawblade and saw into the jig 3 in. or so. From the center of the kerf, extend the saw-line to the back side of the jig. Mark two lines 45° from the saw-line with a draftsman's triangle and fasten the two 1-in. wide fences on the lines with screws.

Ordinarily, I use the front edges of the fences to hold the pieces to be cut. But to cut, say, the four pieces for a picture frame, cut the pieces square to length plus twice the thickness of the saw kerf and use the back edges of the jig fences. One fence aligns the work, the other serves as a stop.

—*Bayard M. Cole, Marietta, Ga.*

Trig jig for accurate angles

With this simple jig and a little trigonometry, you can cut odd angles on the tablesaw more accurately than with the saw's miter gauge. First, construct a sliding table using two maple rails and a piece of ¾-in. plywood. To ensure perfect alignment, lay the rails in the saw table's grooves and tack the plywood to them temporarily, then flop the plywood over and screw the rails down. Next, raise the sawblade and fit the rails in the grooves to cut halfway across the jig.

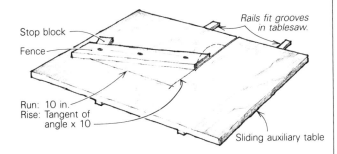

Stop block

Fence

Rails fit grooves in tablesaw.

Run: 10 in.
Rise: Tangent of angle x 10

Sliding auxiliary table

Trigonometry provides an easy and accurate method for laying out the angled fence. Find the tangent of the desired angle from a trigonometry table or with a pocket scientific calculator. The tangent gives you the ratio of the angle's vertical rise to its horizontal run. If your angle is 11.25°, for example, the tangent is 0.19891 (rounded to 0.2). Therefore, for each inch of horizontal run, the vertical rise is 0.2 in. To make layout easier, scale up the measurements by multiplying by 10. This results in a base horizontal line of 10 in. and a vertical rise of 2 in. Mark these measurements on the jig as shown in the sketch and draw a line between the two points to locate the fence. —*Eric Schramm, Los Gatos, Calif.*

Cutting circles on the table saw

Round tabletops, lazy-susan shelves and other large circles can be cut on the table saw with a simple jig. Cut a dado in the underside of a ¾-in. high-density particle-board base and glue in a hardwood key, sized for a sliding fit in the saw's left-hand miter slot. Wax the jig bottom and key to reduce friction. Measuring from the blade, accurately locate and paste sheets of ¼-in. graph paper to the jig top to aid in layout.

To use, first cut the circle blank somewhat oversize and locate its center. Next mark the radius of the finished circle on the graph paper and pin the center of the circle blank at this mark. Make sure the blank will rotate freely but is firmly pinned to the jig. Start by lopping off the corners of the blank. Hold the blank and jig firmly while sliding them past the blade. If hand-holding the work appears unsafe, mount a hold-down clamp on the base to lock the blank while cutting. Continue cutting off the corners of the blank until it is almost round. Then, with the work just touching the blade, rotate the blank to trim off all the high spots. The smoothest circles are produced using high-quality, sharp carbide blades.

—*Philip Margraff, Coeur d'Alene, Idaho*

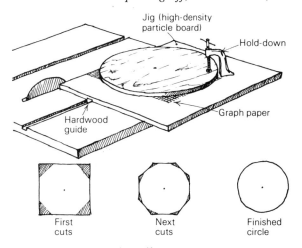

Jig (high-density particle board)

Hold-down

Hardwood guide

Graph paper

First cuts

Next cuts

Finished circle

Miter-gauge setting jig

Some tablesaw miter-gauge settings are the result of tedious trial-and-error, cut-and-fit procedures. Here's how to preserve that hard-won setting for future use. Cut two 1x2 strips about 1 ft. long. Clamp one to the bar and one to the gauge face. Glue and clamp the strips where they overlap. Reinforce this joint with a couple of screws or dowel pins. When the glue has cured, you can reproduce the setting anytime you like simply by pushing the jig against the gauge.

—*Tim Rodeghier, Highland, Ind.*

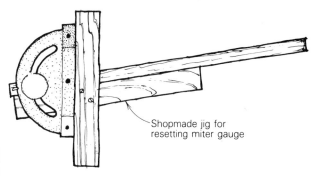

Shopmade jig for resetting miter gauge

Adjustable miter-gauge stop

Here is a jig that's easy and fast to make and to use. It's basically a stick with a dowel through it, clamped to the table-saw miter gauge to give precise production-run cutoffs. It works at any angle.   —*Alan Miller, Lakewood, Colo.*

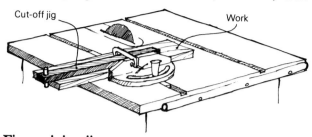

Finger-joint jig

Here is a box or finger-joint jig that uses the table-saw rip fence rather than the miter gauge—a sturdier, easier-to-adjust arrangement. It consists of a guide rail bolted to the saw's rip fence, and a sliding-fence assembly that holds the work. Make the guide rail from particle board or hardwood plywood and cover both sides with plastic laminate to reduce sliding friction. Bolt the rail to the rip fence with four ¼-in. bolts. Countersink the bolt heads on the inboard side.

As with the rail, the sliding-fence assembly is made from particle board or plywood with plastic laminate glued to the bearing surfaces. An essential part of the jig is the hardwood tongue installed in the rail that slides in a groove in the fence assembly. Tack nylon furniture glides to the bottom of the fence assembly to allow the jig to ride freely along the table.

Set-up time is fast—a good-fitting joint can usually be achieved in two test runs. The first step is to install a dado blade for the desired finger size, say ⅜ in. Raise the dado blade about 1/32 in. above the thickness of the stock to be cut. Now screw a scrap of ¾-in. material to the front of the sliding fence assembly to serve as a disposable fence. Drill a ⅜-in. hole in the center of the scrap fence about ½ in. from the saw table. Insert a short ⅜-in. dowel in the hole to act as a guide pin. Now adjust the rip fence/rail so that the distance between the guide pin and the dado blade is equal to the size of the dado—⅜ in. in our example.

Using a piece of scrap, start a test pass. While holding the stock vertically against the fence assembly and against the guide pin, pass the stock over the dado blade. After each cut, shift the stock to the right so that the previous cut registers

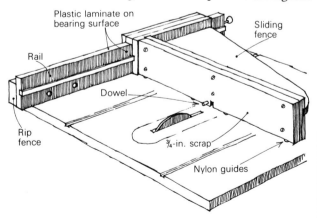

over the guide pin. Start the cut in the second test piece by lining it up with the sawcut in the fence (rather than the guide pin). The joint should be snug but loose enough to allow gluing. If the joint is too tight, move the rip fence to the left. If it's too loose, move the fence to the right.
    —*Tom Burwell, St. Paul, Minn.*

Rubber tire hold-in

The simple lawnmower-wheel fixture sketched here has made featherboard hold-ins obsolete in my shop. I have two: one as shown and the other a mirror image of the first. I use them on both the table saw and the router table for ripping, cutting grooves, shaping, and other operations.

The advantages of this fixture over featherboards are significant: Feed friction is greatly reduced, hold-down pressure is adjustable and consistent (even when the stock is uneven) and set up is quicker and easier. Since fore/aft friction is all but eliminated, there is little tendency for the fixture to squirm and turn under the clamp. Only one clamp will keep it in place, even on a waxed saw table. The disadvantage is that there is no kickback resistance as with featherboards. But kickback can be all but eliminated by using sharp, clean blades and carefully setting up for each cut.

The idea for rubber-tire pressure wheels is not mine—similar fixtures are used on large power-feed industrial woodworking machines. I suppose the wheel could be cut from plywood to save the extra few dollars for the ball-bearing lawn-mower wheel and special axle bolt. But I find it comforting to see the rubber tire flatten a bit as it pushes the work against the saw fence. —*Bob DeFrances, Delray Beach, Fla.*

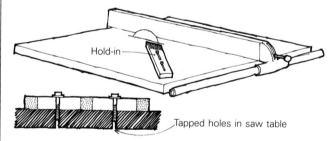

Improved hold-in

Fingerboards perform much more effectively if you screw them to tapped holes in the saw table rather than clamping them. Clamped fingerboards don't lie flat, and they can slip and lose pressure against the work.

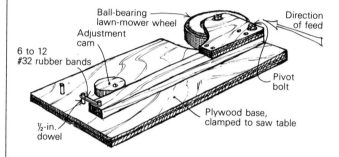

To make the fingerboard, saw kerfs ⅛ in. or so apart in the end of an angled 1x3. Rout two ¼-in. slots down the centerline of the fingerboard—one at the head, one at the tail. Now set the fingerboard in position on the saw, so it will exert pressure just ahead of the blade, and mark the center of each slot on the saw table with a punch. Drill and tap holes into the table at these points. Lock the unit in place with cap screws or bolts threaded into the tapped holes.
    —*Ben Erickson, Eutaw, Ala.*

Molding head hold-in

The molding head for the tablesaw is a valuable tool. But without the proper hold-ins it is practically impossible to shape thin stock without chattering. The hold-in fixtures I use to overcome this handicap consist of an auxiliary fence and a horizontal hold-in. The auxiliary fence is a maple 1x3 that screws to the saw's rip fence. Since this fence may cover part of the rotating cutterhead, it's a good idea to cut a recess into the fence beforehand by raising the cutterhead into the fence. The top of the fence is fitted with an adjustable pressure shoe that holds the work to the saw table.

Make the pressure shoe from a stick of maple by sawing two (or more) sawkerfs from opposite ends. This gives the shoe some spring, allowing it to adjust to minor variations in thickness and to damp out any chattering.

The horizontal hold-in is simply a slotted arm fitted with another pressure shoe. It holds the work firmly against the fence. The arm locks in place with cap screws that fit tapped holes in the table.

Design the fence and hold-in so you can reverse them and use them on either side of the saw's rip fence. This will allow you to take full advantage of both left-hand and right-hand cutter designs. —*Walter O. Menning, LaSalle, Ill.*

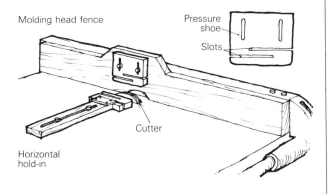

Molding head fence

Pressure shoe

Slots

Cutter

Horizontal hold-in

Shaper hold-in

I wouldn't use this gadget for ripping, because it would tend to close the kerf, but it's a solution to the problem of holding the feedstock against the fence on a shaper, or when using a molding head on the tablesaw. Start with a 1½-in. square

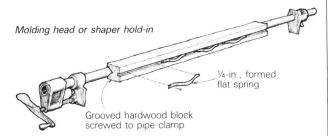

Molding head or shaper hold-in

¼-in., formed flat spring

Grooved hardwood block screwed to pipe clamp

length of hardwood. Cut a V-groove in one side (to fit the pipe of a pipe clamp) and rip a ¼-in. slot in the other side. Screw the hardwood to a pipe clamp long enough to fit your saw table or shaper table.

Now install several ¼-in. flat steel springs in the groove. These springs, available at hardware stores, are used to repair old double-hung windows with broken weight ropes. Clamp the hold-in across the machine table in a position so that the springs flatten as the work is pushed through. To prevent the work from moving upward, it's a good idea to use this pipe-clamp hold-in in conjunction with a fingerboard that will press the work to the table.—*Raymond Yohe, Altoona, Pa.*

Straightening curved lumber

Here's a trick for straightening a bowed board. Tape a piece of angle iron to the concave edge of the board to serve as a guide, as shown below. If the board is thin, block up the angle iron so it won't drag on the table. Pass the board through the saw with the flat edge of the angle iron against the rip fence. Remove the iron, flip the board and pass through the saw again. The result is a straight board with parallel sides. —*Charles F. Riordan, Dansville, N.Y.*

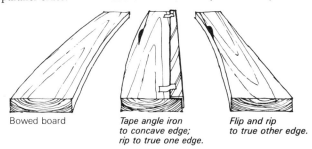

Bowed board

Tape angle iron to concave edge; rip to true one edge.

Flip and rip to true other edge.

Tablesaw jointing fixture

I wouldn't try this setup on a board shorter than 10 ft., but one of the handiest jigs in my shop is a tablesaw setup for straightening the edges of 1-in. hardwood boards. It does the

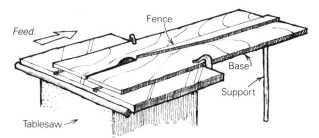

Feed.

Fence

Base

Support

Tablesaw

same job as the jointer, but it is faster and more convenient for the 18-ft. boards I use in my boat shop.

To build the jig, joint a 7-ft. long 1x2 and cut a long tapering point on one end. Glue the 1x2 to a ¾-in. plywood base, about 8 ft. long. Cut a slot in the base in front of the fence for the tablesaw blade.

To use, clamp the fixture to the saw table with the 1x2 fence flush with the left-hand face of the sawblade at its rear edge. Support the tail of the fixture so that it's level. As you pass a board over the sawblade, the waste edge is split away by the long bevel. Press the board tight to the 1x2 fence to get a straight edge.

You do have to freehand the first 6 in. or 7 in. of the cut, as the board must pass the sawblade before it picks up the fence. Freehand cuts can easily kick back, so be careful. —*Colin Pittendrigh, Bozeman, Mont.*

Setting a saw fence

I have always found it awkward to set the rip-fence of a table saw parallel to the blade using a ruler or tape measure, because I have to crane my neck over the saw table to read the measurement at the back of the blade. Also, using both edges of the tape or ruler, which may not have the same unit of measurement, can cause confusion. I now use a large set of inside calipers with a maximum extension of 12 in. for cuts within that range. I have ground the tips of these calipers to give a minimum reading of ¼ in. The calipers are set to the desired width of cut, and by alternately placing them between the fence and the front and rear of the blade, I can not only see any necessary adjustment but also feel it. —*Kent McDonnell, Newcastle, Ontario*

Spacing dadoes

Recently, while building a cabinet for cassette tapes, I experimented with several methods for spacing the numerous dadoes needed. Using an auxiliary miter-gauge fence gave the measure of accuracy and easy use I sought.

Bolt a piece of wood the length of the saw table and about 1 in. wide to the miter gauge. This auxiliary fence becomes an extension of the gauge, stabilizing long pieces of work and preventing twisting on the saw. The auxiliary fence should be the same thickness as the workpiece. After the dado width

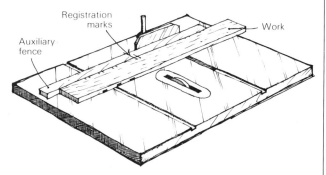

Registration marks

Auxiliary fence

Work

is set and tested on scrap, make a cut into the auxiliary fence. Mark the right and left edges of the cut on the top of the fence. The workpiece, marked for spacing, is moved along the auxiliary fence. When the lines meet, slide the gauge into the dado blade, making the cut.

—Paul Saffron, Rockville Centre, N.Y.
EDITOR'S NOTE: A variation of Saffron's method is common practice in many cabinet shops. Screw a new auxiliary fence to the miter gauge and trim off the excess by pushing the fence through the saw. Since the end of the fence now coincides exactly with the saw kerf, it can be used for accurate cut-off work. Just slide the mark on the workpiece up to the end of the fence and push through the saw.

Improved tablesaw push stick

The notched push sticks used in many shops seemed unsafe and unwieldy to me. So I designed a push stick that lets me concentrate on sawing boards instead of fingers. First I traced the handle from a comfortable handsaw onto a piece of scrap, 10 in. by 18 in., positioning the handle at an angle that

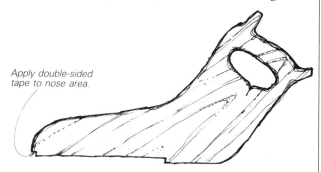

Apply double-sided tape to nose area.

keeps my fingers away from a fully raised blade. I made a notch and ended it well ahead of the heel. This positioning contributes to the push stick's safety: if you carelessly lower your hand, the end of the stick will bottom out on the saw table, pivoting the notch up and releasing its grip on the end of the board. It will still hold the work, but it's a reminder that you're courting trouble. Two push sticks are better than one. With a second small notch at the end of both, either can be used to hold stock against the rip fence while you push with the other. I applied stair tape to the end notch to improve the grip on the work.

—David L. Wiseley, Waters, Mich.

Accessible saw switch

I recently bought a nearly new tablesaw, and soon decided that I could not get used to the location of the motor starting switch, which seemed too far away for comfort and safety. To correct the problem, I attached an extension rod to the switch so that I could shut the saw off instantly without contortions.

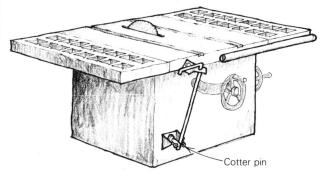

Cotter pin

The rod is supported by an aluminum plate that I twisted in a vise to the correct angle and attached to the saw table in an existing bolt hole. *—Alfred Gorski, Stratford, Conn.*

Roller support for ripping

Here's an inexpensive, adjustable roller support for long stock as it leaves the table saw or jointer. The support is made from an old rolling pin and a sturdy frame. The hand grips of the rolling pin are each supported by notched blocks which are adjustable for height by means of a bolt and a wing nut.

—Rogier De Weever, Kelowna, B.C., Canada

Rolling pin

Refinements on the roller support

The heart of my roller horse for supporting long stock off the table saw, radial saw or jointer is a worn-out typewriter platen. These are available, often just for the asking, from typewriter service shops, and they stay truer than wooden rollers, an advantage particularly for jointer-feed support. The wedges between the roller carriage and the horse allow for fine height adjustment. *—D. Kerman, Swampscott, Mass.*

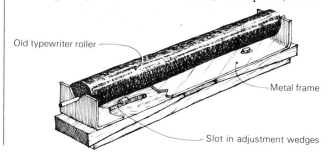

Old typewriter roller

Metal frame

Slot in adjustment wedges

And another supporting idea

The key to an efficient table saw ripping support or panel crosscut support is a smooth-working, friction-free roller. I've found nothing that fills this requirement better or cheaper than ball-bearing furniture casters.

Fasten several of the casters in a close-spaced pattern on top of a home-made, adjustable stand. Or, for an instant support, fasten eight or ten casters to the end of a 2-ft. long 2x12. Then clamp the 2x12 in a Workmate vise at the right height. Since the casters roll easily in any direction just put the support where it's needed. There's no need to fuss with the orientation of the support as there is with other types.

—*Larry Joseph, Alva, Okla.*

Tape tricks for little sticks

I find myself making lots of little things—small boxes, wooden jewelry and the like. Until I discovered a couple of tricks using double-faced tape, I had a devil of a time sawing the little hunks of wood needed for this kind of work.

To make a straight cut on an odd-shaped, thin slice of wood, run a scrap board through the saw using the rip fence. Stick down a length of double-faced tape to the top of the scrap, peel off the protective paper and mount the odd-

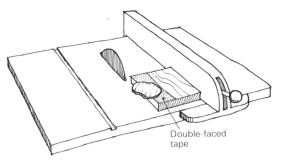

Double-faced tape

shaped slice on the tape for cutting. Don't rely totally on the tape's holding power—hold the piece down with a finger or stick while cutting.

Double-faced tape can also be used effectively in cutting thin strips from the edge of a board. Cut a scrap board with a built-in stop as shown and mount the tape along the inside

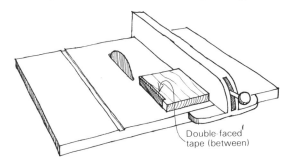

Double-faced tape (between)

edge. The tape holds the slice away from the blade after it is cut. Use the same care in making the cut as if the tape were not there. —*H.N. Capen, Granada Hills, Calif.*

Sawblade disc sander

To make a really good disc sander, glue coarse and fine discs to an old flat-sided, fine-tooth sawblade and mount it on the tablesaw's arbor. For safety, use a bench grinder to remove the teeth, then true-up on the arbor.

—*Stan Haywood, Sylvan Lake, Alta., Canada*

Waxing saw tables

On all machine platens, such as saw tables and jointers, bottoms of planes and such: Use a good car wax such as Simonize, and you will be surprised how much better they perform. Wood will slide and not stick; rust will not form in wet weather. I use it on all of my chisels and any tool that comes in contact with the wood.—*Ellis Thaxton, Arlington, Tex.*

Drafting triangle sets saw

An inexpensive but accurate plastic drafting triangle gives a perfect 45° setting on the table saw. A long wood face on the fence with sandpaper attached prevents slippage and further

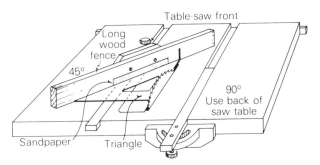

Table-saw front

Long wood fence

45°

90° Use back of saw table

Sandpaper   Triangle

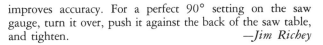

improves accuracy. For a perfect 90° setting on the saw gauge, turn it over, push it against the back of the saw table, and tighten. —*Jim Richey*

Bandsaw Jigs & Fixtures

Chapter 15

Roller hold-in for resawing

Before I built this roller hold-in, I found myself using one hand to hold the work against the bandsaw fence and the other to steer and feed the stock. I didn't feel balanced and comfortable, and my hands were too close to the blade at the end of the cut. The roller fixture that solved these problems cost me $2.50, two hours of work and two trips to the hardware store.

The fixture consists of a base, two roller brackets and a roller. I made the base from plywood and glued and screwed it together for strength. Be sure to make the base large enough so you can clamp it easily to both the back and side of the saw table. I cut the roller brackets and turned the roller from maple. My version of the roller is about 1¼ in. in diameter and 5½ in. long, an ideal size for my 8-in. resaw-capacity bandsaw. I turned the roller and the ½-in. axles as a single unit. An enhancement that I didn't include on my roller fixture would be to point the axle ends to provide a low-friction bearing where the axle runs in the brackets. Attach the roller brackets and roller to the base with bolts, washers, nuts, and a small but stiff compression spring, as shown in the drawing. Be sure to use bolts with a smooth shank where they pass through the brackets, else the brackets will bind on the bolt.

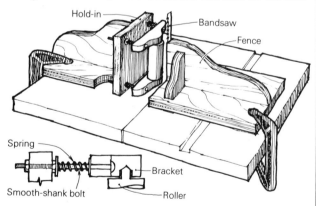

To use the hold-in, set the fence in position for the proper thickness of cut. Now bring the roller fixture into position and clamp so the roller exerts the proper pressure and touches the work just forward of the blade. If you use the narrow-faced fence shown in the sketch it is important to plane the stock between each resaw, because the narrow contact tends to duplicate any waviness or imperfection in the face of the stock. Re-set the roller hold-in after each cut to regain the proper hold-in pressure.

—*Dennis LaBelle, Traverse City, Mich.*

Vee-block for resawing

I have had only mixed results using a rip fence on a band saw for resawing wood. Unless the blade teeth are perfectly set and sharpened, the blade tends to drift even though the

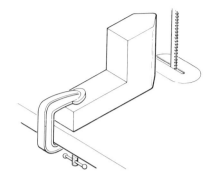

board is firmly held against the fence. This drifting can cause the wood to bind and will leave a wavy surface.

The blade's tendency to drift can be sidestepped by using a vee-edged block attached to the band saw table, as in the drawing. The block is located so that its rounded point is even with the toothed edge of the blade, and at the desired thickness of board from the blade. The block must be carefully made so that the radius at the vee is square to the face of the blade.

To use this approach the board to be resawed is scribed along its edge at the desired thickness. The vee-block provides a guide to hold the side of the board parallel to the blade. The board is fed into the blade with the operator free to swing the unsawed end to counter the drift. The surface will still need to be planed before it is of furniture quality, but this setup is much easier, faster and more accurate than using a rip fence. —*M.G. Rekoff, Jr., Minneapolis, Minn.*

Bandsaw rip fence adjusts for drift

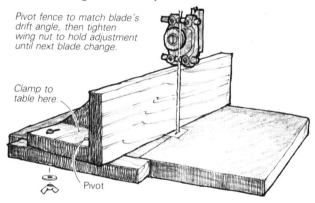

Pivot fence to match blade's drift angle, then tighten wing nut to hold adjustment until next blade change.

Clamp to table here.

Pivot

Those who use the bandsaw for ripping and resawing know that each blade has its own line of cut, which is rarely parallel to the fence. This shopmade rip fence reduces the time-consuming chore of redetermining the drift angle every time you move the fence. The base clamps to the front of the table, and the fence itself pivots and locks as shown in the sketch, allowing you to set the drift angle into the fence.

To set the guide, first determine the drift angle by freehand ripping a piece of waste stock. Feed the board, angling it until the blade tracks straight down its center. Transfer the drift angle from the board to the adjustable rip fence with a T-bevel. Tighten the guide at the angle, and the drift is set into the fence until the next blade change.

—*Richard Farwell, San Luis Obispo, Calif.*

Cutting finger joints on the bandsaw

Here's how to cut finger joints on the bandsaw. In addition to being simpler and faster than the tablesaw approach, this method may be used with long boards (impossible on the tablesaw), and it allows you to lay out uneven spacing of tails and pins for decoration if desired.

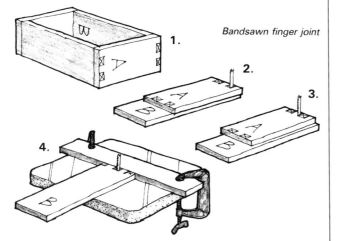

Bandsawn finger joint

First lay out the spacing of the pins on the ends of the box members as shown in step **1**, above. Strike an X through the areas to be sawn out. Now select one end and clamp it on top of its adjoining side member, offsetting the edge by one sawkerf as shown in **2**.

Clamp a stop to the saw table behind the blade, extending the full width of the table. Position the stop so that the stock will be cut to the proper depth (just a shade deeper than the stock thickness). Make sure the stop is perpendicular to the blade's actual line of cut, which may drift to right or left.

To cut the joint, feed the clamped workpiece into the saw to the stop. On the first pass cut only the *left* side of the pins, splitting the line to the waste side. Now unclamp the two workpieces, shift the top workpiece (the box end) two sawkerfs to the left, reclamp and saw the right side of the pins (**3**).

Next unclamp the two boards and, working with one workpiece at a time, nibble out the waste between fingers by sawing kerfs as close together as possible. Dress the bottom of the notch by feeding the stock sideways across the face of the blade (**4**). Repeat the waste-nibbling process on the other workpiece. The two should fit together perfectly. If the joint proves too tight, don't shift the two boards quite as much for the second set of cuts.

—*Walter D. Sweet, Hazardville, Conn.*

Squaring bandsaw cuts

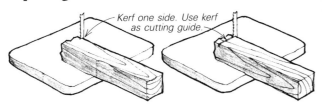

Kerf one side. Use kerf as cutting guide.

Here's a bandsaw trick that lets you true the end of a turning square without pausing to use a try-square. All you have to do is begin a crosscut on one side of the blank, then turn that side up and use the mark as your cutting line. As long as your bandsaw blade is at 90° to the table, you can't miss.

—*Jim Ryerson, Guelph, Ont.*

Chair-rung tenons on the bandsaw

Here is an easy method of using the bandsaw to make tenons on round pieces such as chair rungs. Take out the saw's miter gauge, put it in backwards (with the face toward you) and clamp it to the table with a C-clamp. Position the gauge so that its face is the same distance from the cutting edge as the depth of the desired shoulder on the tenon. Deep shoulders

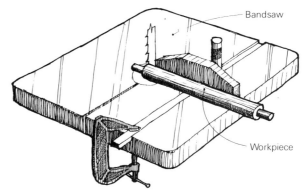

Bandsaw

Workpiece

may require two or three passes. With the saw on, rotate the workpiece against the face of the miter gauge. Done properly, the result is a smooth, properly sized tenon.

—*George Kramer, Santa Rosa, Calif.*

Bandsawn drawer bottom

By carefully bandsawing the center section from a solid-wood drawer at an angle, you can use a slice of the interior plug for the drawer bottom. If you intend to use the top face of the plug for a prescribed thickness of drawer bottom, carefully determine the cut angle using mathematics, a scale cross-section drawing or trial-and-error test-cuts on a piece of scrap. The proper angle varies depending on the thickness of the drawer blank, the thickness of the desired bottom and the width of the bandsaw blade's kerf.

—*J.A. Hiltebeitel, S. Burlington, Vt.*

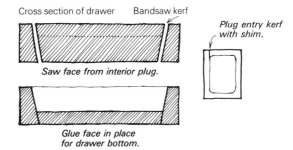

Cross section of drawer   Bandsaw kerf

Plug entry kerf with shim.

Saw face from interior plug.

Glue face in place for drawer bottom.

Bandsawing duplicate parts

To bandsaw multiples of intricate wooden-toy parts, I stack several blanks together with double-sided tape between. The tape holds firm during bandsawing, drilling and edge-sanding operations Double-sided tape eliminates nail holes, replaces awkward clamps and reduces layout time (lines need be drawn only once). Parts are easily separated by inserting a chisel into the tape joint and tapping lightly.

—*Larry D. Sawyer, Ridgecrest, Calif.*

Solder balances wheels

I balanced my bandsaw's wheels the same way I balance motorcycle wheels, by wrapping solder around the spokes where needed.

—*Jim Hassberger, Richland, Wash.*

Curved edge joint

A simple system exists for making close-fitting edge joints along a curving line. This quick and reliable method works equally well for major design pieces and for rough work.

The idea is to cut both of the pieces to be joined simultaneously, as in marquetry, one above the other. The desired design is laid out on the upper one, and the boards overlapped a distance appropriate to the line. They need to be firmly but temporarily fixed in this position, by means of nails, glue, clamps, double-stick tape, etc. The assembly is then cut on the band saw with a bold and sure stroke, since any stopping and wiggling will result in a hole along the glue line. Frequently the two pieces can be held during cutting just with one's hands, doing away even with the fastening.

When the waste parts are removed, the major pieces should fit together very well. Even if the sawing went off the line, at least they match. There may be a small gap evident along the glue line where the curve is sharp. This results from the radius differential between the two sides of the saw kerf.

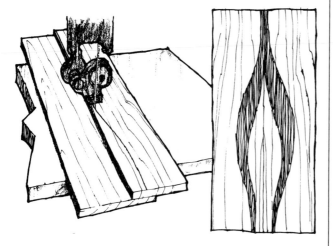

In practice this is not a problem, however, because it usually can be pulled up in gluing without undue stress. A little judicious shaving at the ends would also solve this problem.

When wide boards are cut by this technique, the upper one sometimes droops out of parallel with the band-saw table. This is prevented by tacking a filler piece along its outer edge to hold it up. Joining thick wood brings out new possibilities—the lamination can then be resawn and bookmatched.

This method is good for relatively unimportant edge-joining such as in jigs, mockups and secondary pieces. Here a strong, acceptable joint can be accomplished in a few seconds, with no concern for straightening edges, planing, etc.
—*Sam Bush, Pottstown, Pa.*

Hot-melt holds parts

When I am bandsawing complex shapes where material must be removed from two or three sides, I use hot-melt glue to temporarily reattach the discards to stabilize the piece during further sawing. The hot-melt glue is superior to tacks or tape in this application. It's very fast and it just takes a couple of dabs here and there to hold the discard in place. Later you can easily pry or strike the waste piece off.
—*J.A. Spratt, Smithville, Ont.*

Cutting circles

A good method for cutting perfect circles on a band saw: Take a strip of plywood or chipboard about a foot wide and several feet long. Divide it lengthwise with a line. Lay it on the band-saw table and cut a slot from one edge to the center

line. Along the line from the slot, mark off the radii of the circles you wish to cut and drill pilot holes. Countersink these holes on the back of the board and insert a wood screw in any hole. Mark the screw, remove it and grind it so only a point protrudes. Now you can put the screw in the appropriate

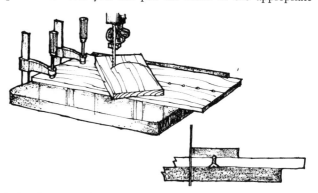

hole, clamp the board to the band-saw table, and pivot the blank you wish to cut on the protruding point. You can finish the edge of the circle with a similar setup on a disc or belt sander.
—*Larry Green, Bethel, Conn.*

Cutting circles—revisited

I made Larry Green's band saw circle-cutting jig as described above. I found it was difficult to set blanks on the jig in the desired center. So, I built a pivoting jig that solves this problem and has other advantages.

The jig, made of plywood, has a base, a pivot board and a stop glued to the base. To use, clamp the base to the saw table so that the pivot pin and the circle holes are lined up with the front of the saw blade. Pull the pivot board off the base, install a pin in the desired circle hole and center a blank on the pin. Fit the pivot board back on the base, swinging it back clear of the saw blade. Now start up the saw and swing the pivot board into the saw blade, which will cut a reverse circle in the scrap area of the blank. When the pivot board hits the stop, rotate the blank to cut the circle.

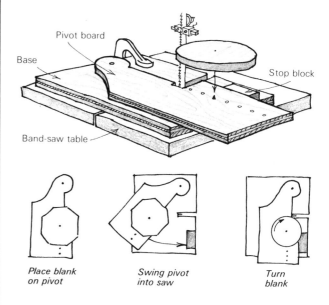

Place blank on pivot   Swing pivot into saw   Turn blank

An advantage of the jig is the ease of changing circle diameters. Just pull off the pivot board and reposition the circle center pin—there's no need to remove the whole unit.
—*Jerry Elvin, Nezperce, Idaho*

Cutting circles on the bandsaw

The circle-cutting jig I use in my shop offers several advantages over other circle-cutting jigs you've published. First, because the jig uses the miter-gauge slot in the saw's table, no clamps are necessary. This not only saves time but also guarantees perfect size duplication even if the jig is removed from the saw. Second, since the jig's base stays in a fixed position relative to the blade, you can put marks on the base to calibrate circle sizes. Third, you can reverse the sliding-dovetail center guide to cut large circles. And last, an adjustable stop can easily be added on the front of the jig so it can be used with a variety of blades. The stop ensures that cutting always takes place at the true tangent of the circle.

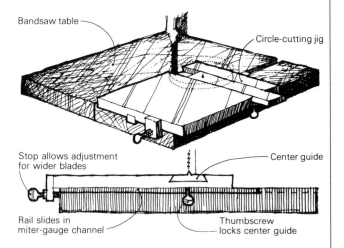

Bandsaw table

Circle-cutting jig

Stop allows adjustment for wider blades

Center guide

Rail slides in miter-gauge channel

Thumbscrew locks center guide

To use, set the center guide to the desired radius, lock it in place with the setscrew and place the circle blank on the center pin. If the blank cannot have a center hole in it, then cut a dummy disc from plywood and secure the blank to the dummy disc with double-sided tape. With the jig's rail riding in the saw's miter-gauge slot, ease the jig straight into the blade until the stop contacts the front of the saw table. Then turn the blank until the circle is completed.

Although you can make the jig from solid stock, it is easier to make the dovetail slot if you laminate the base. My jig (shown above) is made of acrylic plastic, which is threaded for the two thumbscrews. If you use wood, let in square nuts for the thumbscrews and secure them with epoxy.

—*Thomas G. Marston, Mill Creek, W. Va.*

Increasing the bandsaw's throat capacity

To increase the throat capacity of my bandsaw, I designed two blade guides to replace those provided with the saw. The new guides twist the blade outward 25°, as is done on a

metal cutoff saw. The guides were made from maple and fitted with three ⅝-in. ball bearings held in place with screws. Two of the bearings act as the side guides and the third is the back-up bearing for the blade. Of course the guides had to be designed within the limitations and characteristics of the bandsaw.

The results were gratifying; I can now crosscut a 10-in. board without the board hitting the bandsaw's column.

—*Ralph Luman, Virginia Beach, Va.*

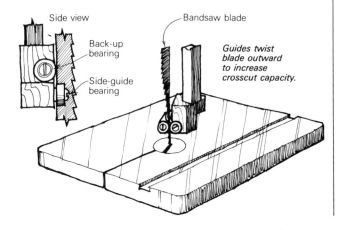

Side view

Back-up bearing

Bandsaw blade

Guides twist blade outward to increase crosscut capacity.

Side-guide bearing

Drill Press Jigs & Fixtures

Chapter 16

Center-drilling dowels

Here's a procedure for accurately center-drilling dowels. Clamp a piece of scrap to the drill-press table and drill a through hole the diameter of the hole to be bored. Without moving the block, change to a dowel-sized bit and drill a shallow seating hole. This completes the cap.

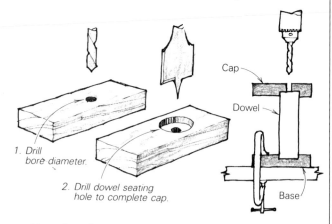

1. Drill bore diameter.

2. Drill dowel seating hole to complete cap.

Cap

Dowel

Base

To make a base, clamp another piece of scrap to the drill-press table and drill a seating hole in it. Place the dowel in the base hole, and cap the top end so that the boring bit is centered. For long dowels, drill first from one side, flip, and complete from the other side.

—*Robert J. Harrigan, Cincinnati, Ohio*

Reducing the diameter of dowels

The sketch below shows an old patternmaker's trick to reduce the diameter of a dowel. Simply chuck a router bit in a drill press and clamp down a couple of scrap blocks to guide the dowel and to serve as a length stop. Lower the quill to take a light cut, lock the quill in place and rotate the dowel under the bit. Continue taking light cuts until you're at the desired diameter. —*Wallace C. Auger, Fairfield, Conn.*

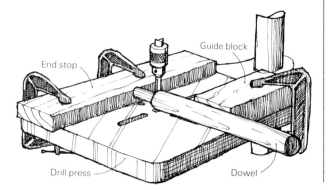

End stop

Guide block

Drill press

Dowel

Low-tech horizontal boring machine

My home-built horizontal boring machine isn't sophisticated, but it's simple in design and sturdy enough to do an outstanding job. Its simplicity comes from a sliding table that moves the stock into the bit rather than vice versa.

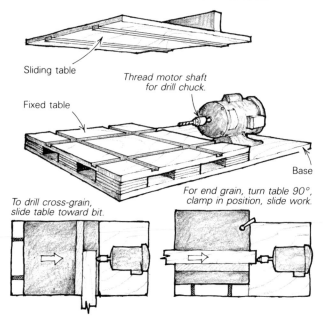

Sliding table

Thread motor shaft for drill chuck.

Fixed table

Base

To drill cross-grain, slide table toward bit.

For end grain, turn table 90°, clamp in position, slide work.

To begin, you'll need a ¼-HP to ½-HP, 1750-RPM motor, with its shaft threaded to accept a ½-in. drill chuck. I made the base, the fixed table and the sliding table out of ¾-in. Baltic birch plywood.

Cut two square pieces the same size for the fixed table and the sliding table, then make all dado cuts at the same ripfence setting to ensure that the dadoes align. Glue and screw hardwood runners into the dadoes in the sliding table. These runners should then fit either pair of tracks in the fixed table.

Next bolt down the motor assembly and the fixed table to the base. Shim the fixed table so that the sliding table will be at the proper height relative to the bit. Glue and screw a fence to the top of the sliding table.

The height of the sliding table is not adjustable in this design. This presents no hardship for me because most of my boring is in 4/4 and 5/4 stock. I shimmed the fixed height so that my machine would normally bore 5/4 stock. To switch over to 4/4 stock, I place a sheet of ¹⁄₁₀-in. Plexiglas on top of the sliding table. —*Ed Devlin, Rothsay, Minn.*

Truing a drill-press table

A drill-press table can be leveled easily and accurately with a piece of coat-hanger wire bent into a "Z." Fit one end into the drill chuck, and adjust the height until the other end of the wire just scrapes against the table. Now rotate the wire 180°. If the table is exactly 90° to the drill chuck, then the wire will still scrape the table slightly after being rotated. If it doesn't, adjust the table until it does. The surface is true when the wire scrapes it to the same degree in every position.

—*Lyle Terrell, New Orleans, La.*

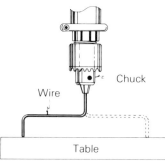

Chuck

Wire

Table

Cutting flutes on curved turnings

For cutting reeds and flutes in curved and tapered turnings, I use a cutter mounted in a drill press, and a special indexing jig to hold the workpiece. Although making the cutter requires some time and moderate metalworking skills (or machine-shop expense), once it is done you can cut reeds and flutes on any shape with minimal set-up and excellent results.

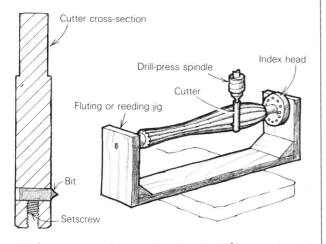

Make the cutter from a short length of ⅝-in. cold-rolled steel. Turn the top 1 in. of the cutter down to ½ in. so it can be chucked in the drill press. Drill a ¼-in. hole through the cutter ½ in. from its bottom, and file the hole square to accept a short length of ¼-in. tool steel for the bit. In the bottom of the cutter, drill and tap a hole for a setscrew, which holds the bit in place. Grind the bit to the shape of the profile desired for the reed or flute.

When the cutter is complete, you will also need a jig to hold the turning and to index the work as the flutes are cut. The jig can be either a simple one-time affair or of a more elaborate, permanent design incorporating an adjustable tailstock. In either case, lay out the round indexing head carefully by dividing the circle into a number of equal angles according to the number of flutes required. For example, if 24 flutes are desired, then the pin holes on the index head will be 15° apart. On a permanent jig, you can use one indexing head for many combinations by laying out several concentric circles of pin holes, each with a different number of holes.

To cut the flutes, first turn and sand the workpiece, then fasten it in place between centers in the jig. With the jig in place on the drill-press table, lower the drill-press quill until the cutter bit is on the centerline of the turning. Lock the quill at this setting. With the drill press running at its highest speed, move the turning into the bit and across the table. The bit cuts the profile of the flute while the cutter body rubs along the turning, regulating the depth of cut. After the first cut, index the turning to the next hole and repeat the process until all flutes have been cut.

—*Kenneth Weidinger, Erlanger, Ky.*

Masking-tape drill stop

The best depth stop for a portable electric drill is a masking-tape flag around the bit stem, as shown in the drawing. Masking tape works on all kinds of bits, is easy to set to the right depth, and never mars the workpiece. The advantage of the flag is that you don't have to strain your eyes to tell when the tape reaches the surface—you simply stop drilling when the flag sweeps the chips away.

—*Richard R. Krueger, Seattle, Wash.,*
and Norman Crowfoot, Pinetop, Ariz.

Preventing tear-out

The problem of excessive tear-out at the bottom of drill-press holes can be solved with a simple metal collar. I discovered the collar solution during a 30-unit production run of a small piece of furniture. Each unit required a drilling operation of eighteen holes in warped 1x12 pine. Without question, the tear-out problems I experienced were because the warped stock was inadequately supported on the drill table.

I'm aware that the classic prevention for tear-out is to support the stock to be drilled with a scrap back-up board. This I wished to avoid because of the hazard, nuisance and expense. I used my small metal lathe to turn a substitute for the back-up board—a steel collar with a 1/32-in. protruding lip to

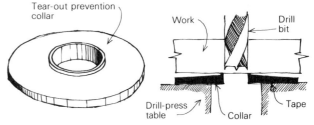

compress and support the wood in the area of the hole. When the wood is adequately supported and compressed in advance of the rotating bit, the result is a clean hole.

The profile of the collar is shown in the sketch. Except for matching the collar's bore to the drill bit used, the dimensions are arbitrary. Turn the bottom of the collar flat (perhaps even a shade concave) to prevent the collar from rocking.

To install the collar on the drill press, put double-sided tape on the bottom of the collar and slip it over the drill bit. With the bit lowered into the table, carefully slide the collar down and press it onto the table. Counterboring the hole in the table will prevent shavings from jamming the collar hole.

—*Carl Hogberg, North Chatham, Mass.*

Drill-press safety switch

If, like me, you've ever been barely missed by a flying drill-press key you inadvertently left in the chuck, you'll appreciate this inexpensive safety device. It consists of a lever-operated

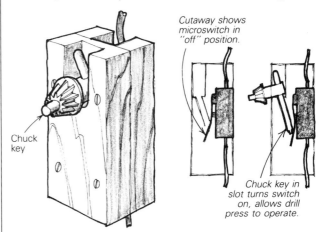

microswitch encased in a box fastened to the front of the drill press. The weight of the key dropped in a slot in the box moves the hinged lever on the switch and closes the circuit. The drill press should be wired through the device so that the existing on/off switch will operate normally only if the key is in the slot. Since several types of switches are available, make sure the one you use is a heavy-duty, motor-rated switch that will carry the amps your motor draws.

—*Wesley Glewwe, West St. Paul, Minn.*

Hole-sawing axle pins

A few days before my daughter's birthday, I discovered I was out of the little axle pins necessary to fasten wheels to the toy train I was building for her. Then I hit on a simple tool that produces pins in abundance. It took only a couple of hours to make, and it freed me from the two-week mail-order delay.

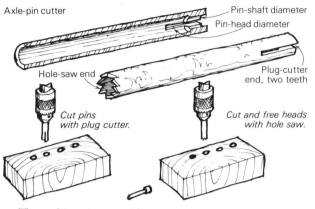

Axle-pin cutter

Pin-shaft diameter

Pin-head diameter

Hole-saw end

Plug-cutter end, two teeth

Cut pins with plug cutter.

Cut and free heads with hole saw.

The tool is a short steel bar that's a plug cutter on one end and a hole saw on the other. Each end is used in turn—first the plug cutter to make the shaft of the pin and then the saw end to free the pin head. To make the tool, start with a 3-in. long section of ½-in. drill rod or round tool steel. Drill a ¼-in. hole through the length, making a tube. Next, enlarge the hole to ⅜ in., stopping about ¼ in. from one end. To make the hole-saw end, file eight deep teeth into the wide end of the tube with a triangular file. To make the plug-cutter end, simply saw a ⅛-in. slot 1 in. into the narrow end of the tube. The slot will allow sawdust to escape. Cut two teeth into this end of the cutter, one on each slot. To finish the tool, dress and sharpen all the teeth, then harden and temper the steel.

To make axle pins, first cut an end-grain block of hardwood a little longer than the pins need to be, ¹⁄₁₆ in. or so. Chuck the tool in the drill press, and using the plug-cutter end, cut all pin shafts in the block. You will likely have to back the cutter out of the hole occasionally to clear chips. When done, reverse the tool and cut the pin heads following each hole. Dress each pin head by chucking the pin in the drill press and filing the head to the desired shape.

—*Robert F. Vernon, Keuka Park, N.Y.*

Electric-cord suspension arm

It is much easier to use portable electric tools if the cord can be suspended from above so it doesn't drag across your workbench. This cord suspension arm is designed to move easily to different heights or to different locations in the shop. The arm pivots on electrical conduit pipe, which is cheap and light but strong enough. The conduit slips into 1-in. screw-eyes spaced so that when the arm is raised, the lower pipe will disengage for removal. —*Pendleton Tompkins, San Mateo, Calif.*

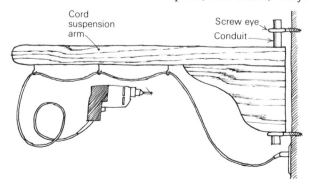

Cord suspension arm

Screw eye

Conduit

Better V-block

I made a flageolet but ran into difficulties in laying out and drilling the holes and in holding the flageolet down while working on it. Although I used a V-block, the slightest jiggle caused misalignments that became painfully evident after all the holes were bored. By adding two clamps atop the block and using a fence for the drill-press table, I was able to drill the holes in successive flageolets precisely and predictably. Mounted in a workbench vise, my modified V-block held the flageolets securely while I worked the windways, channels and slots. To make this V-block, you need less than 2 ft. of con-

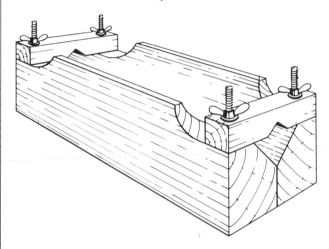

struction-grade 2x4, 6 in. of 1x1 and four hanger bolts with wing nuts and washers. The two 45° bevels that make up the 90° V are planed on the jointer and then carefully aligned before gluing. The clamps and the coves at the end of the body are bandsawn; a spindle or drum sander does a nice job of cleaning up the curves. Most of the dimensions are not critical. —*Bernard Maas, Edinboro, Pa.*

Adjustable slot-mortising table

Recently I rescued an old American 16-in. tablesaw from the junkyard. The machine had a slot-mortising chuck on the end of the arbor and provisions for bolting on a mortising table, which, unfortunately, was missing. So I made a new mortising table using the design principle sketched below. I could

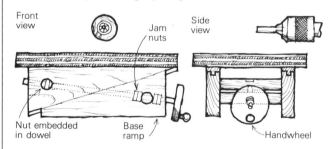

Front view

Jam nuts

Side view

Nut embedded in dowel

Base ramp

Handwheel

have used a hinged table, but a slanted table just felt clumsy to me.

Here's how the table adjustment works. The threaded rod passes through a hole in the dowel in the base ramp, and is held in place by nuts. As the handwheel is turned, the threaded rod screws into a nut embedded in the dowel in the sliding table, thus ramping the table up on the base. The ramp pieces should be aligned using flanges or a slot-and-rail arrangement. —*Bart Brush, Cherry Valley, N.Y.*

Drill-press mortising fixture

Here's a fixture for cutting mortises on the drill press using fluted end-milling cutters. A lateral control mechanism, made from ⅛-in. steel plate, pivots at three points and gives the fixture the back-and-forth movement needed to cut the mortise. The stop mechanism is a ¼-in. rod that passes through a collar piece that is screwed to the base. Two sliding collars, fastened in place on the rod with setscrews, limit the movement of the sliding table. To use, clamp the fixture to the drill-press table. Clamp the work to the fence and set the stop collars for the size mortise needed. Your right hand, on the drill-press feed, controls the depth of the mortise, while your left hand controls the lateral movement for the length of the mortise. —*Mario Rodriguez, Brooklyn, N.Y.*

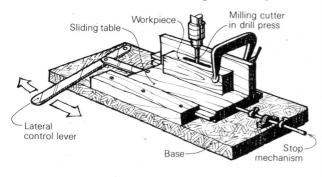

A vise for end-drilling dowels

This vise, shown in the sketch below, makes easy the awkward operation of drilling holes in the ends of dowels on the drill press. The vise consists of a thick wood block and a frame. The sides of the block are keyed to and slide in U-shaped slots in the frame. The block tightens in the frame by means of a hanger bolt screwed into the tail of the block and run through an oversized hole in the frame, as shown in the detail. The vise's jaws clamp the work when you turn a wing nut against the end of the vise frame. A washer at this point helps.

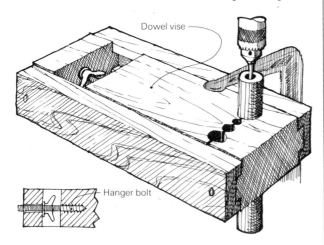

To make the vise, use a 2-in. thick hardwood such as maple or birch. Plane the sides of the frame a little thinner than the center block. This allows the sides to move easily when the center block is clamped in position on the drill-press table.

I use the vise to drill the holes for new ends on broken chair legs and spindles. The four holes in the vise jaws are sized to fit common chair parts (⅜ in., ½ in., ¾ in., 1 in.). To drill the vise-jaw holes, clamp a piece of ⅛-in. scrap in the jaws and drill the four holes centered on the scrap. With the scrap removed, the holes will be undersizd so that the 1-in. hole will grip a 1-in. dowel. —*Leo Myers, Wellington, Ohio*

Mortising table for drill press

Frustrated with hollow-chisel and router mortises, I made this drill-press mortising fixture, which works even better than I expected. Its secret is a pair of precision ball-bearing drawer slides. Precision drawer slides have less play than regular drawer slides, and move so smoothly that I'm sure there are other uses for them in the shop.

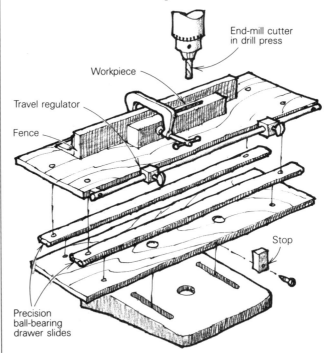

This is how the fixture works. First chuck an end-mill cutter in the drill press, then set the travel regulators to produce a mortise of the desired length. Now position the fence to center the mortise in the thickness of the stock. To cut the mortise to the desired depth, gradually lower the cutter while sliding the table back and forth.

Rather than squaring up the ends of the mortise, I simply round over the tenon with a file.

—*David Grimm, Richmond, Mich.*

Adjustable drill-press fence

This drill-press fence is quickly adjustable for boring holes the same distance from an edge or for routing with the drill press.

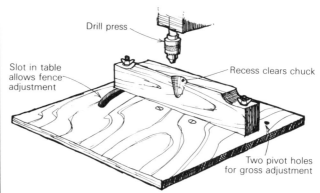

The base is plywood; the fence is hardwood and adjusts using wing nuts and an arc-shaped slot in the base. The sketch shows the details. —*Pendleton Tompkins, San Mateo, Calif.*

Drilling angled holes

For my early American reproductions, such as cobbler's benches and step tables, I have found that splaying the legs about 5° in two directions is just about right.

I recently made a simple fixture for my drill press for boring the holes in the tops of these articles. I used two pieces of ¾-in. plywood, 18 in. square; to each piece I fastened a strip of wood to give me the desired 5° angle. This then works as a compound sine block. The plywood squares are hinged together; if you want the holes flared in only one direction, fold the top piece out of the way.

To determine the height of the elevating strip, I multiplied

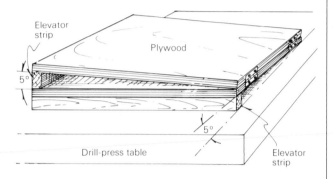

the length of the plywood piece by the tangent of 5° (0.0875) and got 1.575 in., or roughly 1%16 in. I then ripped one edge of two pieces of wood, 18 in. by 1⅝ in. by 1 in., to get 1%16 in. After sanding down the inside edge, I fastened each of these flush with one of the edges of each plywood piece, and hinged the two pieces together, so the angles were at right angles to each other.

I cut the legs to length, with a double 5° angle on each end, before tapering and turning ends to fit holes in the tops. Of course, the angle can be changed by just multiplying the tangent of the desired angle by the length of the plywood pieces, and using the result for the height of the elevator.
—*Eugene Roth, Honeoye Falls, N.Y.*

Horizontal boring jig

My boring jig, which uses a ½-in. portable drill, is similar to a conventional horizontal-boring machine except that the table moves rather than the drill. The jig consists of a base, a hinged drill platform and a sliding table.

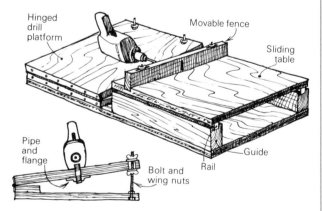

Make the base and sliding table from ¾-in. hardwood plywood. The drill platform should be extra stiff, so laminate two pieces of ½-in. plywood to give a 1-in. thick platform. Spindle elevation is adjusted by raising or lowering the hinged drill platform. Install a piano hinge on one edge and two or three bolts with wing nuts for adjustment on the other edge.

If adjustment is needed over a wide range (say, 3 in.), some sort of pivoting arrangement would be required for the adjustment bolts.

Most ½-in. drills have a threaded handle socket on the top or side that will accept standard ¾-in. threaded pipe. Secure the drill to the platform with a short piece of threaded pipe and a standard floor flange.

Elevating the platform swings the drill through a short arc, so the fence on the sliding table must be mounted through slotted bolt holes to allow for movement. Hardwood rails on the bottom of the table mated with hardwood guide blocks on the base provide the tracking action for the sliding table.
—*Vanessa Skedzielewski, Sierra Madre, Calif.*

Pin router attachment

By bolting a simple router arm and an auxiliary table to my drill press, I can convert it to a pin router. This lets me take advantage of the drill press' quill movement to lower the router into the work. Make the router arm from a 20-in. length of 2x6 lumber. Drill the arm to fit your drill-press quill and feed stop, then notch the back of the arm so it can slide up and down the post. On my drill press the arm is held in place well enough by the drill-press feed-stop collar and the feed stop. Other drill presses might require bolting the arm directly to the housing. In the end of the arm, cut a hole the same size as your router. Then cut a slot in the arm and install a bolt to pinch the router and lock it in place.

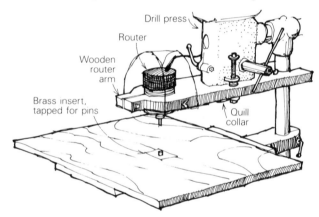

The table is a 20x30 panel of ¾-in. plywood covered with plastic laminate and strengthened by a thick plywood spine on the bottom. A tapped brass plate located in the center of the table accepts different diameter pins (I used standard router pins from Sears).
—*Andrew Makarevich, Villa Park, Ill.*

Drilling compound angles

Here's a simple method for drilling accurately through irregular workpieces, or for drilling tricky compound angles and having the hole exit where you want it. First clamp a board to the drill-press table and drill the board to match a dowel on hand. Point a short length of dowel and insert it in the hole.

Now mark the workpiece for the entry and exit holes, and center-punch the marks. Make the exit punch fairly deep. Place the workpiece's exit punch on the dowel point and drill on the opposite punch mark.
—*George Kasdorf, Ft. Wayne, Ind.*

Shop-made counterbore

Here is an easily made counterbore for bolt heads, nuts and washers. With it you can avoid the problem of centering a second bit over a previously drilled bolt hole. Make the tool from

a length of steel rod the same size as your bolt stock. Find a flat washer that just slips on the rod, saw a slot in it and twist the washer apart slightly. Weld the washer to the rod about 1 in. from one end with the lower edge of the split facing clockwise. File the pilot end of the rod for proper clearance and sharpen the cutting edge of the washer with a file.

—*Carl Meinzinger, Guemes Island, Wash.*

Router Jigs & Fixtures

Chapter 17

Eccentric router base

This router subbase allows me to rout an "in-between" size groove (for various stock thicknesses) without moving the guide fence or changing the setup. Because the subbase is eccentric to the router bit you can change the diameter of the base simply by changing the point of the base that rides against the guide fence.

To make the base, choose plywood, plastic or a 4-ply stack of plastic laminate for the material. You can cut the eccentric shape on a bandsaw or jigsaw, but for a smoother, more accurate base use a router table to machine the base. First drill a $\frac{1}{16}$-in. pivot hole at the center of the blank for the base and another $\frac{1}{16}$-in. pivot hole offset from the center. The offset determines the eccentricity of the base. I used an offset of $\frac{1}{8}$ in. which allows me to cut grooves of up to $\frac{1}{2}$ in. with a $\frac{1}{4}$-in. bit. On a line through these holes drill a $\frac{1}{4}$-in. hole at a radius slightly larger than the radius of your router base. Before proceeding, it's a good idea to locate and drill the mounting holes in the subbase.

To cut the circumference of the base, mount the blank on the router table with the $\frac{1}{4}$-in. hole over a $\frac{1}{4}$-in. router bit. Drill $\frac{1}{16}$-in. holes into the router table through both the center pivot and offset pivot. Put a pin in the center hole, turn on the router and rotate the subbase 180°. Return the blank to its starting position, put the pin in the offset hole and rotate the base 180° in the other direction. You will have to finish the "step" area with a file. Before routing out the center of the subbase, you should pivot the base on the center hole and scribe measurement lines on the base for every $\frac{1}{32}$ in. of diameter change. Use a fine-tip waterproof pen.

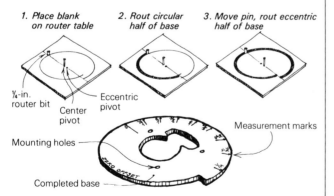

1. Place blank on router table
2. Rout circular half of base
3. Move pin, rout eccentric half of base

$\frac{1}{4}$-in. router bit
Center pivot
Eccentric pivot
Mounting holes
Measurement marks
Completed base

To use the base to cut a $\frac{5}{16}$-in. groove, for example, clamp a guide fence in place on the work and rout a $\frac{1}{4}$-in. groove. Keep the zero-offset part of the subbase against the fence. Now rotate the base until the $\frac{1}{16}$-in. scribe line touches the fence. Keep the $\frac{1}{16}$-in. mark touching the fence and make another pass, taking care not to twist the router. The result is a $\frac{5}{16}$-in. groove.   —Mike Ramey, Seattle, Wash.

Fluted columns

When building a tall clock case I needed two fluted half-columns 44 in. long. Since my lathe is only 36 in. between centers, I had to turn the columns in two pieces. It would have been almost impossible to match the flutes, match the grain and hide the joint had I tried to make the columns look identical through their length. So I borrowed a trick from a piece of furniture I saw in the Philadelphia Museum of Art.

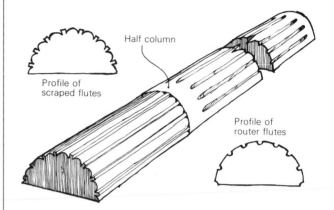

Profile of scraped flutes
Half column
Profile of router flutes

First I glued up two column blanks with paper between (for separation into half-columns later). One blank was turned 35 in. long and fluted with a $\frac{3}{16}$-in. veining bit in the router, stopping the flutes $\frac{1}{2}$ in. from the ends. The other blank was turned 10 in. long and fluted by scraping with an inexpensive wood chisel ground to produce the shape I wanted. These flutes extend the entire length of the shorter piece. After the columns were split apart into half-columns, the longer sections were simply butt-glued to the shorter sections to produce 44-in. long half-columns. The butt-joint is weak but not critical since the half-columns will later be glued and screwed to the clock case.

—Richard M. Watson, Lindenwold, N.J.

Fluting jig

This jig routs accurate and consistent flutes on tapered turned legs. The jig is a U-shaped plywood channel as wide as your router base, mounted to the lathe bed. Dimensions will vary according to your router base and the peculiarities of your lathe bed. Attach two router-support strips to the inside of the jig with bolts and wing nuts through slotted holes so the strips can be angled parallel with the tapered leg.

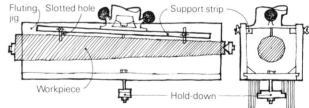

Fluting jig
Slotted hole
Support strip
Workpiece
Hold-down

To use the jig, first turn all legs to shape, then mount the jig to the lathe bed. Chuck one leg between centers, locking it into position with the index head. Now set the router-support strips parallel with the turned workpiece. To do this, simply set a board (as wide as the interior of the jig) on the work and tighten the support strip's wing nuts with the strips resting on the board. Remove this adjustment board and fasten stops to the support strips so each flute will be the same length. Now you're ready to rout the flute. Use the holes in the lathe's indexing head for accurate spacing of the flutes around the leg.   —John Sanford, Camden, Maine

Dadoing guide

Sketched below is a quick setup I use for repeated dadoing operations with my router and portable workbench/vise. It's so simple, yet it's more accurate and quicker to use than the fence-clamped-to-the-board approach. Make the parts from stock the same thickness as the boards you're dadoing. Clamp the fence atop two guide blocks to form a bridge over the work as shown. Shim the fence off the two guides with cardboard or veneer. This should leave enough clearance so the stock will slide in under the fence easily. Now just push the workpiece in under the bridge, snug against the stop. Clamp the workpiece to the workbench somewhere behind the fence, set the router to proper depth and go to town. The guide blocks not only guide the workpiece, they also support the router base near the edge of the board.

—*Josh Markel, Philadelphia, Pa.*

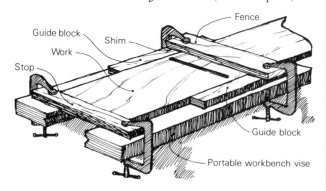

Jig for cross-grain routing

The concept is simple, but this jig is indispensable for routing dadoes in carcase sides, especially when several dadoes are to be made in one board. Once the jig is clamped together you can slide it quickly into position for the next cut.

Make up two *L*-shaped pieces with 4-in. wide plywood strips. Cut the shorter pieces of the *L* 16 in. to 18 in. long (router base plus 8 in.) and the longer pieces 20 in. to 30 in. long (widest carcase plus 8 in.). Face-glue and screw the pieces together taking care to maintain a 90° angle.

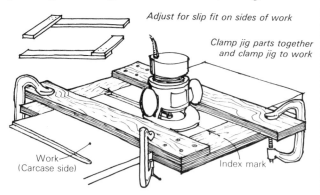

Adjust for slip fit on sides of work

Clamp jig parts together and clamp jig to work

Work
(Carcase side)

Index mark

To use, place one *L* on the front edge of the board to be routed and one on the back edge so that the two *L*'s form a woven rectangle as shown. Adjust both directions to give a slip fit against the router base and against the sides of the board. Then clamp at the intersections of the two *L*'s. Pencil in an index mark on both sides of the jig to simplify lining up for a cut. Clamp the jig to the board before routing the dado. —*Roger Deatherage, Houston, Tex.*

T-square router guide

A couple of years back, I grabbed an old drafting T-square for a woodworking student to use as a guide for routing a dado. When he approached the end of the cut, he stopped and told me that if he continued to the edge of the board, he would rout through the head of the square. Since I had a few spares around, I told him to go ahead. When he was finished, we were surprised to find that we had produced, by routing off the tip of the head, a very useful dado guide. The head of the square, now perfectly sized, could be used to align subsequent cuts with the same router and bit.

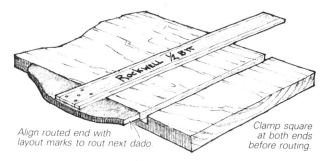

Align routed end with layout marks to rout next dado.

Clamp square at both ends before routing.

Now we have eight T-squares with lopped-off heads, each clearly marked as to the router and bit they go with. Four go with different size dadoes (¼-in., ⅜-in., ½-in. and ¾-in.) on a Sears router; the other four go with a Rockwell router.

The T-squares are handy for other operations as well. We use them with a ½-in. carbide bit in the router to "saw" wide or long boards to length if the operation is awkward on the tablesaw. Nothing could be squarer.

—*Jeff Sherman, Finn Rock, Ore.*

Flip-up router fence

When routing grooves, some people draw a line on the work where the groove will be, then calculate where to clamp the fence. Others draw the line where the fence will be, instead of marking the location of the groove. Both methods have obvious drawbacks. But if you make a router fence that has a hinged extension, you can mark the center of the actual groove on the work, line up the extension with the mark, then flip it out of the way to rout the groove. Make the fence out of a straight, flat 1x4. Now rip another board half the diameter of your router base (measure from the center of the bit to the edge of the base) and secure it to the fence with flat hinges. As shown in the drawing, offset the hinges so that they won't protrude when the extension board is swung up out of the way. —*James F. Dupler, Jamestown, N.Y.*

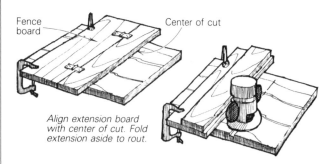

Fence board

Center of cut

Align extension board with center of cut. Fold extension aside to rout.

Variable-width dado fixture

This variable dado fixture will allow fine adjustment of the dado width from bit diameter to double the bit diameter. The fixture works on the principle that one edge of the router base is farther from the bit than the other. To use, clamp a fence in place on the workpiece and make one pass with the wide side of the fixture against the fence. Turn the router around (narrow side to the fence) and make a second pass.

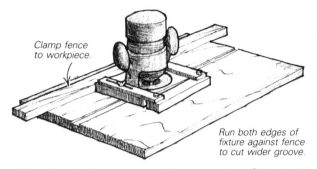

Clamp fence to workpiece.

Run both edges of fixture against fence to cut wider groove.

To make the fixture, cut a 9-in. square from ¾-in. hardwood plywood and rout a ½-in. deep recess in the center to receive the router base. Rip one edge off the fixture and re-attach it with two cleats, as shown. Slot one cleat to allow adjustment. The other cleat is fixed, and the adjustable edge pinned to it so that the edge can pivot. You'll have to trim the corner of the base outside the pivot point so that the adjustable edge won't bind. After the fixture is attached to the router, check to be sure that the distance from the bit to the adjustable edge is slightly (¹⁄₁₆ in.) less than the distance to the fixed edge. If it isn't, saw a little off. Otherwise, slight adjustments over bit size are impossible. —*Jere Cary, Edmonds, Wash.*

Improved horizontal mortiser

This horizontal mortising router jig can be clamped in a vise, but is fully portable and could be clamped to a sawhorse.

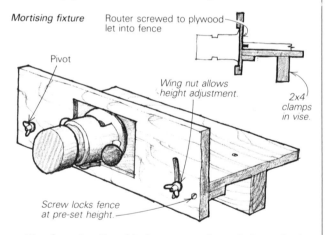

Mortising fixture

Pivot

Router screwed to plywood let into fence

Wing nut allows height adjustment.

2x4 clamps in vise.

Screw locks fence at pre-set height.

The fence is adjustable by means of two bolts and wing nuts, which lets you center the mortise in stock of different thickness. The fence can be locked in pre-set positions (for mortising ¾-in. stock, for example) with a screw through the fence into the frame behind. My version of the jig is made from plastic-laminate-covered particleboard. I mounted the router on a piece of ¼-in. birch plywood recessed into the face of the fence. —*Charles W. Milburn, Weston, Ont.*

Router jigs for making molding

The sketches below show two jigs which, when used with a portable router, can produce both semicircular and straight molding in patterns difficult to produce with a shaper. The first jig is an adjustable router trammel used to make curved molding. The jig's two-part base adjusts by means of a slot-and-track arrangement and locks with a bolt and wingnut. The router is screwed to a ¼-in. hardboard foot which is, in turn, screwed to the base.

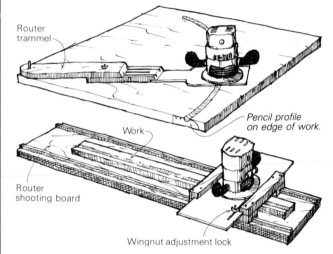

Router trammel

Pencil profile on edge of work.

Work

Router shooting board

Wingnut adjustment lock

The second jig consists of a sliding adjustable router holder and a "shooting board" which has two parallel tracks. The slotted hardboard in the holder allows the router to be adjusted laterally.

To use these jigs, first pencil the molding profile on the edge of the workpiece. Position the work and the jig so the router is right over the molding. Take repeated cuts adjusting the bit depth, changing bits and adjusting the router's lateral position as needed. When all the routing is complete, separate the curved molding from the waste stock with a bandsaw. Some sanding is necessary to finish the molding. —*S. Gaines Stubbins, Birmingham, Ala.*

Scissor-jack fence

After years of enduring the inconvenience of removing and resetting numerous small bolts to adjust the fence on my router table, I made an adjustable fence that makes the whole process simple, rapid and accurate.

The fence is built around a used Toyota scissor jack that I found at an auto wrecking yard. First I spent a few minutes

with a hacksaw to remove the portion of the jack that fits the underside of the car. Next I cut down the base to the width of the jack and bolted it to a ¾-in. plywood backboard. To make the fence, I attached a piece of straight, well-seasoned cherry to the top of the jack. With the careful use of shims, I set the face of the fence exactly perpendicular to the tabletop. The fence is easy to adjust precisely. Once it's in position, I anchor it with small C-clamps on both ends.

I suspect that these readily available scissor jacks could easily be adapted to a wide array of clamping, pressing and fine-adjustment problems.

—*John B. Moon, Mount Vernon, Wash.*

Routing splined miter joints

This router-based method for cutting the slots in splined miter joints is easy to set up and guarantees an accurate fit. First miter the panels in the normal fashion on the tablesaw and clamp them face-to-face as shown in the drawing, below. Wide or bowed panels may require the addition of a stiffener clamped below the miters. Now chuck a spline-sized bit (⅛-in. or ³⁄₁₆-in. for ¾-in. stock) into the router and set the depth of cut (¼ in. to ⅜ in.). Adjust the router guide to be about

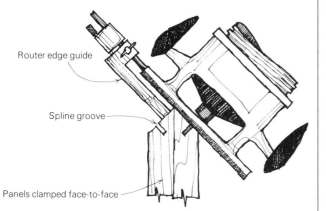

Router edge guide

Spline groove

Panels clamped face-to-face

¾ in. from the bit. Absolute accuracy in depth and guide settings is irrelevant. Rest the base of the router on the peak formed by two panels and rout a spline slot in each panel. To cut a stopped spline slot, just plunge the router.

Although the whole process can be accomplished with little more than eyeball measurement, the right angle formed by the two miters and the constant offset of the cut all but guarantee success.   —*Warren H. Shaw, San Francisco, Calif.*

Circle guide for the router

This fixture for routing circles has several advantages over commercial circle guides: it's cheaper, it cuts circles smaller than the router base and it allows repeat set-ups to precise radii without trial and error.

The guide is easy to make. Screw a piece of ¼-in. plywood to the base of your router, carefully countersinking the screws. The plywood should be as wide as your router base and somewhat longer than the largest radius you intend to cut. Saw or drill a clearance hole for the router bit.

Let's say you need a 4-in. radius circle. Measure from the edge of the bit out 4 in. and drill a small hole at that point. Insert a brad in the hole, point up, to serve as a pivot. Drill a centerhole in a piece of scrap, place it on the guide, rout a short arc and measure the radius produced. You'll be lucky if it is right the first time. Regardless, label that hole with whatever radius it produces, say, 4¹⁄₁₆ in. Then make another hole closer or farther, as the case may be, until you get the radius you want. Remember to mark each hole as you go.

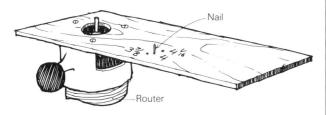

Nail

Router

Since the markings are accurate for only that particular bit, you can divide the guide into sections and head each group of holes with the bit used—½-in. straight, for example.
                        —*Brian J. Bill, Old Bridge, N.J.*

Mortising fixture

The sides of a cradle I built recently were made of slats mortised into the frame. The router-based mortising fixture I built for the project helped me cut all those little mortises quickly and easily. The fixture has three simple pieces: a hardwood clamping lip, a birch-plywood router base and a Masonite hold-down. Bolt the 2x3 clamping lip under the workbench flush with the front edge. To permit deeper mor-

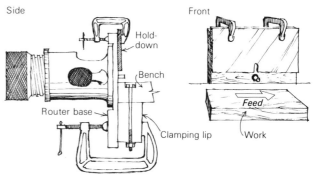

Side

Front

Hold-down

Bench

Router base

Clamping lip

Work

Feed

tises, rout a ⅜-in. recess in the plywood base to fit the router. Mount the router in this recess using countersunk screws driven from the face.

To use, clamp the base to the clamping lip, making sure the bit is the right height above the workbench. Then clamp the hold-down in place. Stand behind the router and, sighting from above, pull the workpiece into the router. A router cut or pencil lines on the hold-down are needed to show the left and right boundaries of the cut. Feed the work from right to left. The router produces mortises with rounded ends, which can be squared up with a chisel. But it's easier to round the tenons with a rasp or sandpaper.
                        —*G.R. Livingston, New York, N.Y.*

Jointing wide planks

Here's a way to joint those monster wide planks that are impossible to true on a jointer no matter how strong you are. Clamp your raggedy edged board over a long, straight guide-stick and trim the edge square with a big (1½-HP, ½-in. collet) router fitted with a flush-cutting spiral trimmer. Position the workpiece to overhang the guide-stick slightly so the whole edge gets machined in one pass. With a hardboard template the same setup can be used to smooth contours.

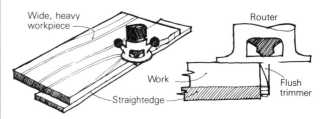

Wide, heavy workpiece

Router

Work

Straightedge

Flush trimmer

Ocemco (1232 51 Ave., Oakland, Calif. 94601) makes a dual-bearing, ½-in. diameter, flush trimmer with two spiral flutes that's ideal. The trimmer, which sells for about $30, is 1½ in. long, limiting its use to 6/4 stock.
                        —*Patrick Warner, Escondido, Calif.*

Routed miter joint

I recently had to make two 24-in. long splined 45° miter joints to join a coffee-table top to its sides. Since the tabletop was too large for me to use my table saw, I devised a way to cut miters and spline grooves with my router and a simple homemade jig.

To make the jig, select a 2x4 slightly longer than the required joint and, using a carbide-tipped blade for smoothness, rip the board at 45°. Glue and screw the smaller piece to the main piece to extend the face of the jig, as shown in the sketch. Rip a ¼-in. groove a little less than 3 in. from the pointed edge of the jig and install a spline in the groove. The spline serves as a straight-edged guide for the router's base.

To use the jig, rough-cut the workpiece at 45°, leaving it about ⅛ in. long. Position the jig exactly on the cut line and

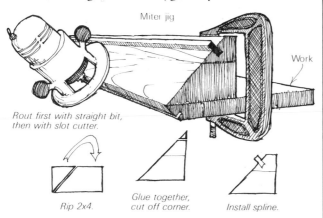

Rout first with straight bit, then with slot cutter.

Rip 2x4.   *Glue together, cut off corner.*   *Install spline.*

clamp in place. Chuck a double-fluted carbide straight bit in your router and feed the router along the jig slowly and carefully. The ends are especially delicate. After the mitering cut is complete, leave the jig in position, chuck a slot cutter in the router and rout the spline slot. For a blind spline just stop the cutter an inch or so from the end. Repeat the process on the matching 45° piece. If the jig is made accurately, you'll be amazed how perfectly the joint will turn out.

—*Paul Darnell, Phoenix, Ariz.*

Making dowels with the router

Here's how to make dowels of any size with a simple router setup. First drill a pilot hole through a 2x4 the same diameter as the dowel you want to produce. Chuck a core-box bit in your router, rout a recess in the front of the 2x4 just above the hole and clamp the router in position. Center the bit right

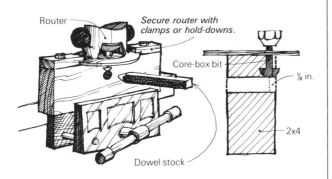

Secure router with clamps or hold-downs.

Router
Core-box bit
⅛ in.
2x4
Dowel stock

over the top of the hole with the shaft of the bit inset about ⅛ in. into the 2x4. Make sure the leading edge of the bit is precisely at the circumference of the hole. Now turn on the router and push the dowel blank into the hole, rotating the blank with a hand drill. Taper the front of the blank for easier starting. —*G. Weldon Friesen, Middlebury, Ind.*

Making dowels

Here's how to make dowels on your lathe with a router. First build a guide box with sides a little higher than the turning stock. Allow about an inch of clearance between the stock and the box walls. Chuck a ¼-in. straight bit in your router and adjust the depth of cut so that when the bit is over the dowel stock it will cut the dowel about 1⁄16 in. oversize. Position the router on the downward side of the stock rotation as shown in the sketch. Turn on the lathe, turn on the router and cut away. Take several light cuts to reduce the possibility of the bit grabbing and breaking the dowel. Lower the bit to the final depth and make one final pass with the router centered over the dowel. —*Lee R. Watkins, Littleton, Colo.*

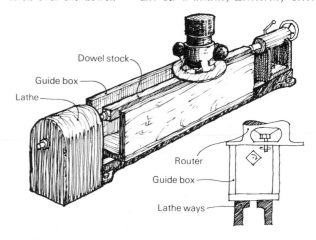

Dowel stock
Guide box
Lathe
Router
Guide box
Lathe ways

Purfling router guide

In stringed-instrument construction the router is commonly used to cut a small shoulder around the perimeter of the instrument. The dado holds an ornamental inlay (purfling) used to cover the glue seam between top and side. The chore requires a precise cut with a router guide capable of following sharp curves. Though I've tinkered with various adjustable guides, I keep coming back to simple, wooden, preset guides.

The guide consists of a wooden finger glued to a crescent-shaped piece of plywood, which ensures proper positioning. A single bolt and wing nut provide fast but secure fastening.

For inlay work I have three guides, each made to cut a rabbet width corresponding to one, two, or three layers of veneer. Thus, for any given thickness of inlay I just bolt on the right guide. No time is lost making practice cuts.

—*George Mustoe, Bellingham, Wash.*

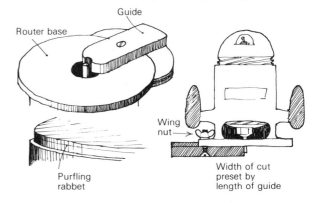

Guide
Router base
Wing nut
Purfling rabbet
Width of cut preset by length of guide

Hole-cutter for speaker enclosures

I have been involved in making professional sound equipment and speaker enclosures for a number of years. The usual construction routine requires me to cut holes up to 18 in. in diameter for speaker baffles. Here's how I used a modified router table to cut the holes accurately, quickly and safely.

My router table is constructed of ⅝-in. Baltic birch plywood. I've installed an aluminum-channel track and pivot assembly on the centerline of the table as shown in the sketch. The standard 1½-HP Makita router bolted underneath the table is equipped with a stagger-tooth cut-out bit (Wisconsin Knife Works #68802).

To cut a circle on the setup I first slide the pivot assembly

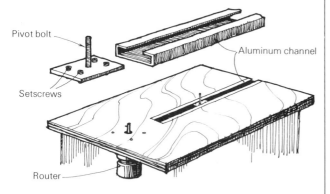

Pivot bolt

Aluminum channel

Setscrews

Router

to the right position for the radius I want. Then I lock the assembly in place by tightening the four setscrews. Next I drill a center-hole in the baffle board and slide this over the pivot's assembly's threaded rod. I secure the baffle board with a flat washer and a self-locking nut. The baffle board should rotate on the pivot with a mild resistance. Next I turn on the router, bring it up through the wood and rotate the baffle clockwise on its pivot point to cut a perfect circle. Once the device is set, you can quickly reproduce duplicate baffles.

—*James Campbell, Orange, Calif.*

Sliding dovetail fixture

While attempting to rout long sliding dovetails on the end of shelving joints, I found it impossible to keep the over-wide and long shelves perpendicular to my router table. Here is a

End of work in table slot

Cut slot in table longer than work.

fixture I devised that, in effect, brings the table to the work. It's a platform with a slot in the middle and two perpendiculars for sandwiching the work. To rout the dovetail, I clamp the work in the jig flush with the top of the platform. Two fences, attached at the proper spacing, guide the router and ensure a consistent dovetail. —*Victor Gaines, Glenside, Pa.*

Raising panels with the router

I wanted to make some raised panels, but I didn't want to invest in a shaper and special cutters. My solution was to raise the panel with a ¾-in., 2-flute helical end mill in my router. All that's needed is a simple jig to tilt the router base to 15°. I fitted outriggers to the sides of my Makita router, as shown in the sketch. Each outrigger is connected to the router by a pair of ¹⁵⁄₃₂-in. drill rods that fit into existing holes in the router base. The rods are fastened to the outriggers with epoxy. The low outrigger acts as a fence against the edge of the panel. In the sketch below, the tongue that will fit the frame's groove has already been milled on the tablesaw, but you could just as well do this step afterward.

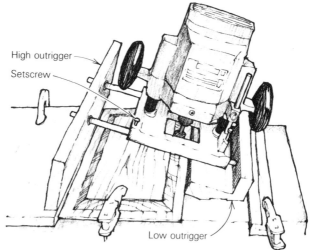

High outrigger

Setscrew

Low outrigger

The high outrigger rides atop the panel or, if the panel is narrow (as in the sketch), atop a board of the same thickness clamped to the bench.—*Edward M. Rosenfeld, Gunley, Ala.*

Routing spline slots in mitered frames

This simple little jig is extremely useful for routing blind spline slots in spline-mitered frames. Nail or glue together scraps of the frame lumber into the configuration shown in the sketch. The workpiece should fit accurately into the slot, where it can be pinched in place with a clamp. A plunge

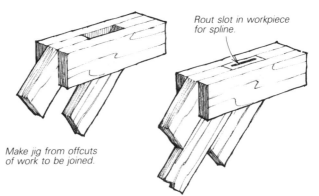

Rout slot in workpiece for spline

Make jig from offcuts of work to be joined.

router is desirable, both for ease of starting the cut and because it has a built-in fence for centering the slot. But I imagine that with a little courage a regular router would do—you could add an integral fence to the jig itself by tacking on more scraps, shimmed with cardboard where necessary. I scribed marks on the jig to show where to start and stop.

—*Jim Small, Newville, Pa.*

Routed box joint

I like the visual results, strength and ease of assembly the box joint allows. I use a router to cut box joints using the following technique. I have installed a guide block on the base of my router that acts as a jig for accurately spacing the finger cuts. The setup does not limit me in width, angle or length of project. I have made jigs to fit several common-size router bits but I usually prefer the ½-in. setup for most work. The sketch shows how to mount the guide block for ½-in. cuts. The ac-

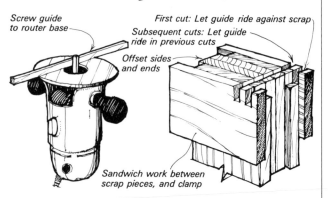

Screw guide to router base

First cut: Let guide ride against scrap

Subsequent cuts: Let guide ride in previous cuts

Offset sides and ends

Sandwich work between scrap pieces, and clamp

curacy of the joint depends on how carefully you position the guide in relation to the bit. Drill the screw holes in the router base a little large to give yourself some adjustment room.

To use the guide, sandwich the box sides and ends between two pieces of scrap, offsetting the sides from the ends ½ in. and the ends from the scrap ½ in., as shown. Now chuck a carbide bit in the router and make the first cut with the guide sliding against the scrap pieces. For the second cut, just slide the guide in the newly cut groove. Continue the process across the ends of the boards for the rest of the cuts. It's like climbing a ladder. Wax the guide to slide easily in the grooves.
—*George Persson, Star Lake, N.Y.*

Routing tongues

I cut the tongues for tongue-and-groove joints with a router. There are faster methods, but the router's precision depth ad-

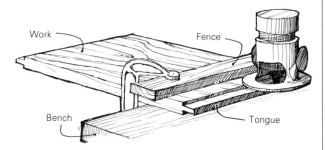

Work

Fence

Bench

Tongue

justment produces a fit that's unbeatable. First set the router depth by trimming the edge of a scrap board. Flip the board over, trim the other side and test the resulting tongue in the groove (which has been previously cut). Make fine depth adjustments and continue to rout test tongues until the fit is perfect. To cut the tongue, first measure the distance from the router base to the bit. Then clamp a fence to the work this distance from the tongue. Gently tap the fence into perfect position with a mallet, checking the measurement with a steel ruler.
—*Jeffrey Cooper, Portsmouth, N.H.*

Routing European-hinge mortises

Several years ago, I remodeled my kitchen. Since I have neither a drill press nor a special bit with which to bore large mortises for the door hinges, I made a router jig that did the job. To calculate the diameter of the cutout in the jig, add the router-base diameter to the mortise diameter, then subtract

Router base cut away
for illustration only

the diameter of the router bit. For example, if the diameter of the router base is 6 in., the mortise diameter $1\frac{3}{8}$ in. and the router-bit diameter ½ in., the cutout diameter should be 6 plus $1\frac{3}{8}$ minus ½, which equals $6\frac{7}{8}$ in.

To rout the mortise, lock the jig in place with handscrews, lower the router base into the cutout, and move the router around and to and fro. To avoid overloading, especially with a light-duty router, make several passes, lowering the bit gradually to final depth.
—*Grant D. Miller, Reno, Nev.*

Producing dollhouse siding

Here's how to produce simulated clapboard siding for dollhouses with a router and an easy-to-make subbase. First, to make the subbase, bevel a ¾-in. thick, 6x10 block on the tablesaw in much the same fashion as you would cut a raised panel. Be sure to leave a $\frac{1}{16}$-in. or so fillet, as shown. Now bore a hole through the block, and mount the router so that a ¾-in. straight bit chucked in it is tangent to the fillet of the

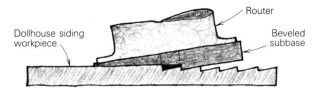

Dollhouse siding workpiece

Router

Beveled subbase

base. After experimenting with the bit depth, you should be able to rout multiple beveled cuts across the workpiece, indexing each cut in the previous cut. For narrower siding, relocate the subbase on the router and use either the same or a smaller bit.
—*Jim and Dan Fortner, Newport, Ind.*

Routing wooden spheres

Last Christmas, I wanted to give my wife a sphere covered with ½-in.-sq. mirrors. Styrofoam was my first thought, but a plastic ball would have cost $32, so I decided to make one from wood, and devised this simple router fixture to do it.

First, glue up a rough sphere by laminating graduated discs of plywood or solid wood; the larger discs should be rings, to save weight and material. Drill a hole through the north and south poles so that the blank can be mounted on a threaded-rod axle inside a box frame, as shown in the sketch. Washers serve as shims to center the blank in the frame.

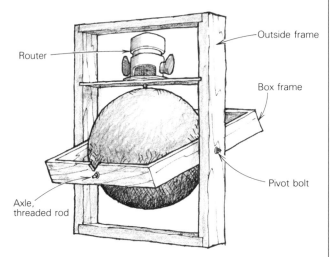

The outside frame is just wider than the box frame, which pivots inside it on two mounting bolts. The sphere should rotate smoothly within the box frame; the box frame should turn smoothly within the outside frame.

Center a router on a platform so that the bit is suspended over the sphere.

To rout the sphere, first clamp the fixture to the bench. Then rotate the rough sphere to find its high spot, and set the router bit a little lower than this. Turn on the router and rotate the sphere inside the box frame, occasionally pivoting the box frame a little within the outside frame. Continue lowering the router bit until the sphere is true. Except for a small area at each pole, the router bit can reach every point on the sphere. The small flat spots at the poles can easily be rounded off by hand.　　　　　　—*Frank D. Hart, Plainfield, Ind.*

Routing dovetail slots for Shaker tablelegs

Although the Shaker pedestal table design has been around for 150 years, its clean lines have a contemporary feel. Inexpensive to build, the table requires only six wooden parts and a handful of screws. The only construction problem is cutting the sliding-dovetail housings for the legs. The jig shown below solves this problem.

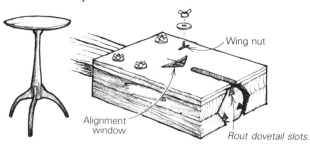

Rout dovetail slots.

To use the jig, first build up a hexagonal turning blank for the table's stem, chuck it in the lathe and turn the lower 5 in. of the stem to size, leaving the remainder of the blank hexag-

onal. Now remove the blank from the lathe, mark out the centerlines for the dovetail cuts on three sides of the stem, and mount the jig in place on the workpiece.

The jig has two halves that mate with the hexagonal part of the workpiece, thereby positioning the turned section under the router guide slot. Be sure that the marked centerline on the blank is correctly positioned in the alignment window.

A bench vise holds the entire setup. Start by hogging out all three dovetail slots with a ⅜-in. straight bit. Use your router's guide bushing to guide the cut. Next, clean out the slots with a dovetail bit. After the dovetail slots have been cut, return the stem to the lathe to complete the turning.
　　　　　　—*Bernie Maas, Cambridge Springs, Pa.*

Pattern jig trims veneers

Matching veneer pieces on a long edge requires a truly straight cutting procedure. Bookmatching is particularly fussy, for any departure from a straight line is doubled when the pieces are positioned. The traditional solution is to clamp the veneers between cauls and hand-plane the exposed edges. It doesn't work very well—the cauls do not distribute pressure properly to the veneers (usually puckered), and planing a three-foot length to a few thousandths of an inch is rarely a happy adventure.

By using a form of pattern routing, employing a piece of ground tool steel as the pattern, the precision cutting of veneer edges becomes routine. The ground stock is available at any tool and die supply house. Although it is expensive (about $25 for the size shown), do not stint on size; accuracy is based on the stiffness of the steel cross section. To avoid distortion, do not heat-treat the bar or machine it in any way. Simply embed and bond to the upper jig section. I used polyester resin, instead of epoxy, to make the ultimate retrieval of the steel simpler. Polyester resin develops about one-third the strength of epoxy on metal.

To clamp the wavy veneers, I use a rubber tube that is simply pushed into a snug groove in the lower board. I suspect that foam weather-stripping would work as well.

The upper jig member should be made of a hardwood (mine is cherry) but the wider lower member can be made of plywood. If after clamping a full load of four veneers there is some visible bow in either piece of the jig, do not be alarmed. The only necessity is support along every inch of the veneer edge. Unsupported veneer will chip off.

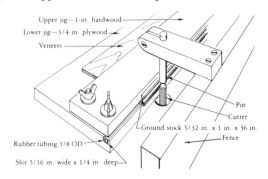

To use the jig, first set your router into a shaper table. Use a straight carbide cutter. Attach a metal pin, equal in diameter to that of the cutter, to the fence so that the pin is centered on the cutter and about ½ in. above it. Great precision is not required; eyeballing the pin location is adequate. With the pin guiding the steel bar, the cutter will generate a nearly perfect edge on the veneers in one pass. Even such hard and brittle materials as Brazilian rosewood are easily cut.
　　　　　　—*Leon Bennett, Riverdale, N.Y.*

Routing multiple mortise-and-tenon joints

After several less-than-satisfactory attempts to construct through, wedged multiple tenons, I designed this router jig for accurate, repeatable results.

The jig consists of strips of plywood or particleboard laminated together as shown in the drawing. The long, continuous pieces correspond to the spacing between mortises. The shorter pieces are glued up to form openings and projections that correspond to the thickness of the stock.

To use the jig, place it over the workpiece to be mortised (or tenoned) and pencil in the outline of the joint. Remove most of the waste. Now clamp the jig in place under the workpiece so it becomes a guide for the bearing of a flush-trim router bit. This results in clean, accurate mortises or tenons with straight sides except in the corners, which must be cleaned up with a chisel. If the jig is accurately lined up with the edge of the workpiece, the spacing of the mortises and tenons will be identical. —*Ed Devlin, Rothsay, Minn.*

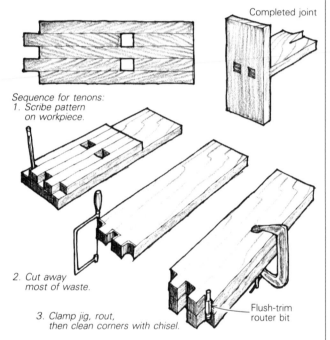

Completed joint

Sequence for tenons:
1. Scribe pattern on workpiece.

2. Cut away most of waste.

3. Clamp jig, rout, then clean corners with chisel.

Flush-trim router bit

Saw fences for router

By mounting a router table to the side of the table saw as shown, you can combine the control of the saw's miter gauge and rip fence with the safe, crisp cuts of the router. You'll find the saw's miter gauge useful in cutting cross-grain dadoes, dovetails and finger joints. Cut mortises, tenons and with-grain grooves using the saw's rip fence. The combination saves shop space and increases the surface area of your table saw. There's no need ever to remove the router table—just lower the bit when not in use. —*Mark Duginske, Wausau, Wis.*

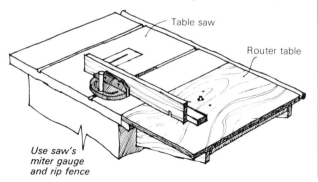

Table saw

Router table

Use saw's miter gauge and rip fence

Two shopmade router subbases

In the woodworking shop at Edinboro State College, we've developed two router subbases that do away with much of the trauma associated with routing dadoes across wide boards and grooving the edges of narrow stock. The subbases all but eliminate wavering cuts, plunge-cut kickouts and awkward balancing acts. Subbase No. 1 is made from ¼-in. Masonite

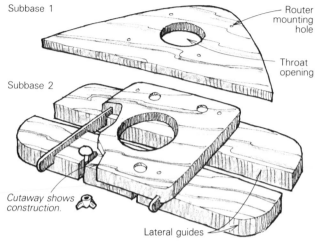

Subbase 1

Router mounting hole

Throat opening

Subbase 2

Cutaway shows construction.

Lateral guides

or hardwood plywood. Mounted to the router in place of the regular base, the straight side of the subbase allows uniform fence pressure for rabbeting and positive control even after the bit has left the workpiece. I curved the other two sides to avoid confusion about which side of the triangle was indexed to the bit.

Subbase No. 2 sits saddle-like atop narrow-dimension stock. The lateral guides are completely adjustable to various stock and groove locations. A simple system of slots with slides ensures rigidity and perpendicularity during use. Hefty ⅜-in. carriage bolts and wing nuts make tightening easy and positive. The lateral guides eliminate plunge kickout and balance problems. —*Bernard Maas, Cambridge Springs, Pa.*

Routing deep through mortises

Here's a simple but effective way to cut deep through mortises. First rout the mortise halfway through from the face edge of the stock. Then drill out the majority of the waste through the member. Mount a ball-bearing flush-trim bit in

Rout mortise to depth of bit.

Drill out waste.

Complete mortise from other side with flush-trim bit.

the router and clean up the mortise from the back edge of the stock. Be sure the trimmer bit's bearing is deep enough to ride on the dressed portion of the mortise. Of course, you will have to square out the corners by hand.

—*Patrick Warner, Escondido, Calif.*

Hinged router table

I suspect that many of us use our routers upside-down, like a shaper, more than we do as a portable tool. I certainly do. But I don't like the flimsy metal stands sold for this use. They are too small and, used on top of the bench, are too high to be comfortable.

Here's a router table I built a few years ago that solves these problems. The table is solid and set at a comfortable height. Because the table top hinges over, I don't have to squat down to remove the router, change cutters or adjust cutter height.

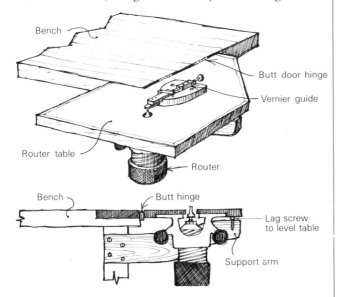

I usually bolt, screw or clamp appropriate guides to the table for straight routing. For irregular contours I use a vernier-controlled guide as shown in the sketch. The vernier adjustment allows me to make two passes, removing most of the wood on the first pass and cleaning up the last $\frac{1}{16}$ in. on a final cut. I make the rub block on the guide from hardboard. Any unusual problem can usually be solved simply by making a new specially shaped hardboard rub block.

—*John W. Greenwood, Dublin, Calif.*

Ball-bearing collars

My wood shaper has a $\frac{1}{2}$-in. dia. spindle. In using spacer thrust collars for irregular edge molding, I found that the edge of the wood gets burned from the friction of the collars.

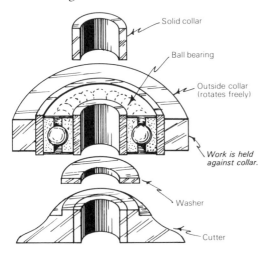

I purchased about a dozen $\frac{1}{2}$-in. I.D. x $1\frac{1}{8}$-in. O.D. sealed ball bearings, $\frac{3}{8}$ in. thick. Next, I machined collars to half a thousandth less than the outside diameter of the ball bearings.

The O.D. of the collars were in steps of $\frac{1}{16}$ in., starting from $1\frac{1}{4}$ in. (the collars are thinner than the bearings). Next, I pressed a bearing into each collar, using the vise to keep the surfaces parallel.

It is very important to use a solid collar that matches the inner ring of the ball bearing above and below the assembly, so that when the shaper nut is tightened the tension will be only on the inner ring—the outside will float. When the wood is pressed against the outside of the assembled collar, the outside perimeter stops rotating and only the spindle with its bearing rotates. I have used a small, thin washer on each side of the ball bearing, which permits the same freedom.

—*George P. Calderwood, Long Beach, Calif.*

Tripod jig

With the aid of this homemade jig, mortises for tripod table legs can be routed while the pedestal is on the lathe, after it is turned cylindrical and before it is turned to shape. The jig consists of a triangular box that fits around the cylinder, with mortises in its faces to guide a router bit. To build the jig, first make a full-scale drawing of the pedestal bottom and construct an equilateral triangle around it. Draw another triangle $\frac{1}{2}$ in. outside the first one. Then cut three rectangular pieces of $\frac{1}{2}$ in. plywood to the width determined by the drawing and about twice as long as the mortises will be. With table-saw blade set at 60° and plywood held vertically against the fence, cut the long edges at a 30° angle. Then cut

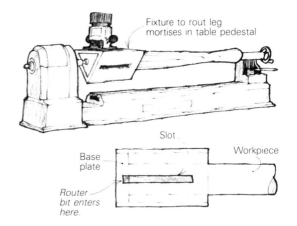

mortise templates in the exact center of each piece—a dado blade simplifies the operation; chisel the ends square. The width of the mortises will vary according to the router bit and template follower you plan to use. For the back piece of the jig, bandsaw an equilateral triangle of $1\frac{3}{4}$-in. thick scrap wood to fit. Then glue and nail the four pieces together.

With the pedestal cylinder held by the tailstock of the lathe, position the jig and center the headstock spur on its bottom plate. Triangular spacers may be inserted between the pedestal and jig base to adjust the length of the mortise. Rout the first mortise, turn jig and pedestal 120°, mortise, and repeat.

To cut dovetail housings, first remove the bulk of the wood with a straight bit the diameter of the dovetail waists, then rout out the sloping sides with a dovetail bit.

—*Lyle Terrell, New Orleans, La.*

Router-table fence for edging discs

I developed the fence shown below to shape the edges of round rings, such as clock bezels, on the router table. The fence can shape both outside and inside edges of circular blanks. When shaping the outside edge, some part of the profile must remain uncut to provide a bearing surface against the fence, otherwise the disc would just keep spiraling smaller. The fence is made by laminating 2-in. wide, ½-in. thick plywood strips into two arms that fit together in a finger joint that pivots on a ¼-in. bolt. The other ends of the fence arms fasten to the router table with wing nuts. Slots in both sides of the router-table top and in one arm of the fence allow adjustment for different size circles and different width rings.

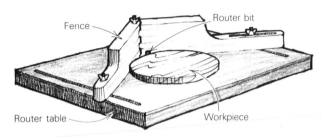

Fence
Router bit
Router table
Workpiece

The dimensions of the fence don't really matter, but I've found that the angle between arms cannot be less than 90° for safety and should not be more than 135°. At angles greater than 135°, the workpiece rolls away from the router bit. These two extremes, therefore, dictate the spread between the two slots in the router table and the length of the adjustment slot in the fence arm. With the setup shown here, the work should be rotated counterclockwise, into the bit's rotation.

—*Robert Warren, Camarillo, Calif.*

Other router-table improvements

I see the advantage of mounting an extra router base under the router table, but instead of groping around under the table to release the router or feel for switches and adjustment knobs, I've installed both an aluminum insert and a switch-controlled receptacle so I can perform all those operations up front with greater convenience and safety.

I made the 10-in. square table insert from ¼-in. thick aluminum plate. I chose aluminum over mild steel because it's easier to drill out the mounting and spindle hole and, if polished, is almost friction-free. The insert is held firmly in place

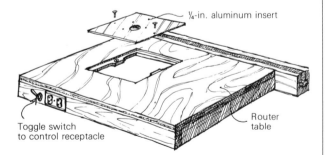

¼-in. aluminum insert
Toggle switch
to control receptacle
Router table

with two countersunk ¼-in. flat-head machine screws into *T*-nuts in the table top. An accurately inlaid insert won't float or vibrate.

I mounted the switch and receptacle on the front of the router table. You can use any type of switch—just make sure it will carry the amperage. You will find plenty of other uses for the switch-controlled outlets (drill, sanders, etc.). Just unplug the router when you don't want it to run.

—*D.B. Neagley, Groveland, Calif.*

Vacuum attachment for the router

Routing produces a lot of dust and chips. It is much more efficient to collect this messy waste as it is produced rather than to sweep it up later. The sketch below shows how I adapted my Sears router to hold my shop vacuum nozzle.

I positioned the nozzle so that it filled the gap near the router's work light. It's supported in place with a wooden

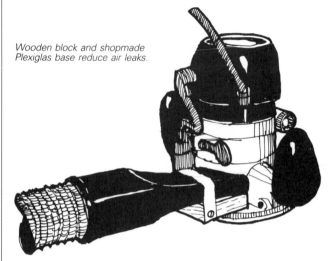

Wooden block and shopmade Plexiglas base reduce air leaks.

block (screwed to the base) and a steel band. To reduce air leakage through the holes in the router base, I added a solid base plate made from ¼-in. clear Plexiglas.

—*Harry M. McCully, Allegany, N.Y.*

Router under saw table

My shop is too small to endure much more big equipment. So when I needed both a router table and additional outfeed support on my table saw, I combined both functions in the extension table shown in the sketch. Since the table is bolted to the saw, alignment between extension and saw table is better and the table is easy to clean under.

I made the ¾-in. flakeboard table 32 in. wide. Added to the saw table, this gives 44 in. of support. Leave a gap be-

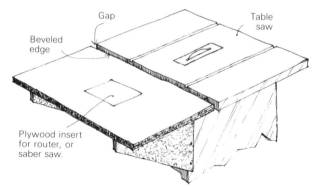

Gap
Table saw
Beveled edge
Plywood insert for router, or saber saw.

tween the saw table and extension so that a plywood panel can be ripped, then crosscut with a saber saw or circular saw without moving the panel off the table. The blade will travel between saw table and extension. Bevel the front edge of the table so it won't catch work as it leaves the saw table. Cut a 10-in. square hole in the middle of the outfeed table to hold a router or saber saw mounted on 10-in. plywood inserts. Cut another insert blank to fill the hole when not in use.

—*W. Davis Smoot, Duncanville, Tex.*

Veneer-trimming guide

Here's the easy and cheap way to trim veneers. Make a guide from ¾-in. stock longer than the veneer, joint the edge straight and band with Formica. Put a lever-acting hold-

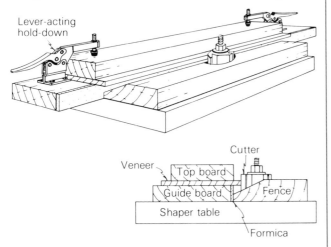

Lever-acting hold-down

Cutter

Veneer

Top board

Guide board

Fence

Shaper table

Formica

down on each end of the guide board. Then set the veneer on the board, put a piece of ¾-in. stock on top and tighten the hold-downs, as shown. Set the shaper or router cutter back $\frac{1}{16}$ in. from the edge of the fence so that the cutter won't nick the edges of the guide boards as it trims the veneer. Trim with the grain of the veneer to prevent chipping, and be careful to hold onto the board. With this method I've joined veneers for 4-ft. x 10-ft. conference table tops with no problems.
—*Jim Sieburg, Chicago, Ill.*

Sander Jigs & Fixtures

Chapter 18

Tool-grinding fixture for the belt sander

We developed the fixture below to take advantage of our belt sander as a wide-surface grinder. Because the sanding belt has much more surface area than an abrasive wheel, the grind is cool, with less danger of overheating the cutting edge. The

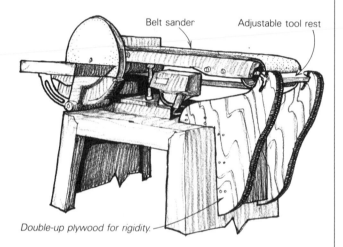

Belt sander   Adjustable tool rest

Double-up plywood for rigidity.

fixture is easily removed, so it doesn't interfere with other, more conventional uses of the belt sander. The tool rest can be reset using a wing-nut/slot arrangement to grind at different bevels, or to give more or less hollow grind.
—*Steve Vetter and Norman Gritsch, Washington, D.C.*

Edge-sanding fixture

Here's a fixture that turns a belt sander into an edge sander. Simply build a wooden fixture that supports and locks your belt sander in a horizontal position. Bolt the fixture to the tablesaw's rip fence as shown, and use the saw's flat cast-iron surface for the work. —*Wayne Hausknecht, Tucson, Ariz.*

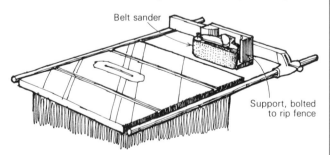

Belt sander

Support, bolted to rip fence

Thickness-sanding on the belt sander

Lacking a commercial thickness sander, I use my standard 6-in. stationary belt sander as shown to face-sand thin strips of resawn stock. The base of the fixture touches the sanding belt. The fence is slightly angled, to provide a wedging effect for pressure. Cross-grain sanding removes wood fast, and the work can't kick back.—*William B. Allard, Tacoma, Wash.*

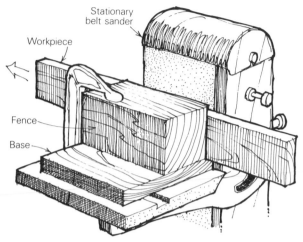

Stationary belt sander

Workpiece

Fence

Base

Making little wooden balls

Faced with having to reproduce a number of ½-in. diameter wooden balls (to replace missing ornamentation on an old fireplace), I discovered a virtually painless procedure using a large belt sander. Build a box frame, open on the bottom, and clamp it to the stationary part of the sander so it sits just off the belt. For ½-in. diameter balls, cut ½-in. cubes and toss them in the box frame. Put a cover on the box (Plexiglas is best) and turn on the sander. The sanding belt will throw the cubes around in the frame like dice on a game table, knocking off their corners and edges until they're perfect spheres.

If the cubes don't tumble about but rather line up neatly against the far wall of the frame, glue a wedge there. If this doesn't work, you could vary the number of cubes, presand

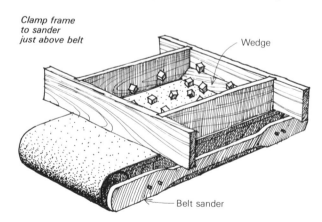

Clamp frame to sander just above belt

Wedge

Belt sander

the corners or throw in a few ball bearings to keep the cubes tumbling. Using this method, I produced a dozen or so perfectly shaped balls in an hour's sanding time. Had I shaped the balls by hand it would have taken longer and the result would have been less uniform. Perhaps laziness really is the mother of invention. —*Charles Reed, Washington, D.C.*

Sanding drum

This homemade sanding drum is sized to fit belt-sander abrasive cloth belts. I use mine on a shaper, running it at less than 1000 RPM, but it would work on a lathe, too. To make it, glue up a slightly oversize round blank as wide as the sanding belt you plan to use. To determine the required diameter, divide the belt length by *pi* (3.14). Turn down the blank so

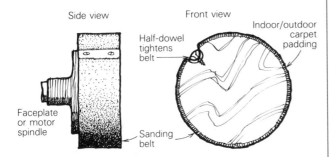

Side view   Front view

Half-dowel tightens belt

Indoor/outdoor carpet padding

Faceplate or motor spindle

Sanding belt

that the belt plus padding fits snugly. To tighten the sanding belt on the drum, rip a ¾-in. dowel in half and install it in a slot in the circumference with flathead screws, as shown.

—Charlie Thorne, San Luis Obispo, Calif.

Boss spinner makes discs

While visiting a woodworking pattern shop I ran across this tool called a "boss spinner." It is used with a disc sander to make wooden discs of varying diameters and thicknesses. As I found it, the unit was made from wood. Aluminum would perhaps give more accurate adjustment.

The boss spinner consists of three main parts: a slide bar that fits the channel in the sander table, an adjustment plate and a swing arm. A slot in the adjustment plate allows gross

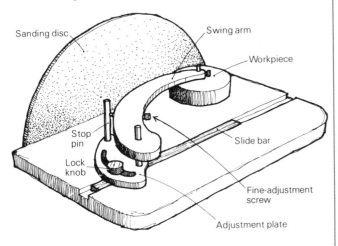

Sanding disc

Swing arm

Workpiece

Stop pin

Lock knob

Slide bar

Fine-adjustment screw

Adjustment plate

circle size adjustment while a screw in the swing arm provides fine adjustment. The sketch shows only one pivot hole and adjustment screw in the swing arm. You can extend the capacity of the spinner by drilling a series of pivot holes and installing a fine-adjustment screw for each position.

To use the boss spinner, first set the rough radius: With the fine-adjustment screw against the stop, rough-adjust the radius of the disc with the adjustment plate and locking knob. Set the rough radius about ¼₆ in. oversize. Now position the circle blank under the center pin. Feed the workpiece into the sander and rotate by hand until the fine-adjustment screw hits the stop. From there, use the fine adjustment screw to reach the final diameter.

—Richard M. Williams, Cleveland, Ohio

Counterbalance improves belt sander

The belt sander can be a valuable tool in the production-shop world of tight schedules and competitive prices. But most belt sanders are designed with a flaw that renders them difficult to control: The motor hangs off one side, throwing the machine off balance. Unless you apply constant corrective hand pressure the sander will gouge or edge-scoop the work. A balanced machine will not scoop and allows the user to concentrate on direction and coverage.

To correct the imbalance I add wood and lead weights to my belt sanders. The amount of weight and position will vary with the sander. Fasten the weight under handles, knobs or whatever. The counterbalanced machines pass my test when they balance on a ¼-in. thick piece of plywood set under the centerline of the belt. *—Rod Goettelmann, Vincentown, N.J.*

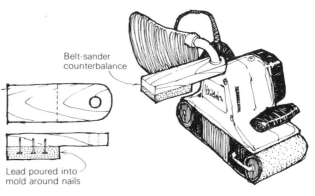

Belt-sander counterbalance

Lead poured into mold around nails

Circle duplicator

My circle duplicator uses ³⁄₁₆-in. thick aluminum for its arm, adjustment cam and base, which is laminated with epoxy to a piece of hardboard that slides in the slot of my disc sander. Start with rough, oversize blanks and position the adjustment cam so that when the swing arm touches it, you have an accurately sized disc. The cam can be locked in position for accuracy. My device handles diameters from 2 in. to 6 in.

—Jay Wallace, Ashland, Ore.

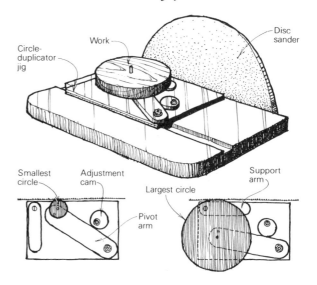

Circle-duplicator jig

Work

Disc sander

Smallest circle

Adjustment cam

Largest circle

Pivot arm

Support arm

Lathe Jigs & Fixtures

Chapter 19

Making sectional molding

Sectional molding for cabinet doors is easy to make on the tablesaw and lathe. Cut the straight sections on the tablesaw with a molding head. To make the semicircular section at each corner, remove the cutter from the molding head and bolt it to a heavy strap-iron handle. This provides a scraping tool for shaping a circle on the lathe's faceplate. Separate the molding from the waste wood with a parting chisel. Then cut each of the four corner sections from the circle at the proper miter angle. —*Duane Waskow, Cedar Rapids, Iowa*

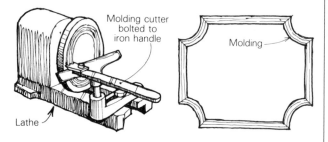

Molding cutter bolted to iron handle

Molding

Lathe

Taping bowls to faceplate

I use a faceplate-fastening method for shallow bowls or dishes for faster and cleaner separation of the finished piece from the faceplate. There is no glue and paper to remove as when the work is glued to a piece of scrap wood with paper between. Nor are there any screw holes to fill as there are when the faceplate is screwed directly to the turned piece.

Screw the top side of the turning blank to the faceplate and turn the bottom of the dish with a recess to accept a wood chuck. After the bottom of the dish is sanded, I apply a polyurethane finish. Next, attach a scrap block of wood to the faceplate and turn it until it fits snugly into the recess on the bottom of the dish. Apply masking tape to the bottom of the dish over the recess in a single layer. Rub the tape with your fingernail to remove air bubbles. Now glue the scrap

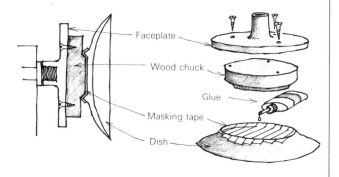

Faceplate

Wood chuck

Glue

Masking tape

Dish

wood chuck (which should fit snugly in the recess) to the taped recess in the bottom of the dish. When the glue is dry, mount the dish-faceplate assembly on the lathe and finish turning.

To remove the dish from the scrap wood chuck, place the chuck in a vise, and, using both hands, gently twist the dish until it separates from the chuck. Alcohol will remove any adhesive left from the masking tape.
—*Dennis Castagna, Southfield, Mich.*

Faceplate taping revisited

Dennis Castagna's procedure for taping bowls on a faceplate prompts me to suggest a similar method using double-faced tape.

First, sand and clean the back of the work to ensure good contact. Then apply a layer of double-faced tape to the faceplate without overlap. Attach the work to the faceplate by squeezing momentarily in a vise. For larger workpieces use two layers for more holding power.

Remove the work by wedging a chisel between the faceplate and the workpiece. —*Max Kline, Saluda, N.C.*
EDITOR'S NOTE: Standard hardware-store "carpet tape" may be adequate only for smaller projects. Kline recommends a special tape manufactured by Nashua Corp., Nashua, N.H., which, because the adhesive is partially cured, softens less during the heat of sanding.

Another proponent of double-faced tape, Russ Zimmerman (RFD 3 Box 57A, Putney, Vt. 05346), recommends Permacel—a thicker, cloth-backed tape with more holding power. Zimmerman sells and ships the cloth-backed tape in 75-ft. rolls.

Zimmerman states that "most people start using this tape cautiously, but confidence builds." He now uses the tape for 15-in. wide, 4-in. thick bowls.

Hot-gluing turnings

A common technique for attaching a turning blank to a faceplate to avoid screw holes is to glue the blank to a waste board with paper in between. The method works well, but the long curing time of the glue is inconvenient.

I have found that a hot-melt glue gun will attach the blank to the waste board rapidly and securely. The glue sets in about 15 seconds, so no clamps are needed—just hand pressure. No paper is needed because the glue bond can be easily broken later with a chisel. Since the glue doesn't become hard, cleanup of the bottom of the turning is easy.
—*John Foote, Clarksville, Tenn.*

Improved hot-glue faceplate technique

To avoid screw holes and to speed assembly, I attach turning blanks using hot-melt glue chips and a torch-heated faceplate. Aluminum faceplates work better for this method because they conduct heat well and cool quickly. If your faceplate is iron, you can attach a thick aluminum face to the faceplate with flat screws.

First, be sure the bottom of the blank is flat. Then heat the faceplate with a torch and place it on the turning blank to warm the wood. Cut thin discs of hot-melt glue (no gun needed) and place them on the heated blank in amounts proportional to the bulk of the blank. Use enough to secure your doubts as well as your wood. Place the faceplate on the blank, and clamp in position until cool.

After turning is complete, aim a torch at the faceplate, heating it enough so the wood falls off with a gentle tap. While the glue is still hot, clean up the faceplate with a rag and scrape the glue from the bottom of the turning.
—*Randy Kalish, Belen, N.Mex.*

Chair-rung chuck

In the Southern Appalachian mountains we turn dowels and rungs from stock that's been riven with a froe, then cleaned up with a hatchet or drawknife. With the device sketched, you can quickly chuck the rough stock in the lathe.

To make the chuck, screw a 1½-in. thick hardwood block to a small faceplate. Turn the block to a 3-in. cylinder with a cone-shaped depression in the face, as shown in the sketch. Stop the lathe and with a V-parting chisel cut four ⅛-in. deep grooves in the walls of the cone 90° apart to grab the corners of square stock.

Prepare the stock to be turned by giving it four quick licks with a hatchet to cut a short, square section on one end. With the square end of the stock in the cone, tighten the lathe's tailstock on the other end and you're ready to turn.

—*W.W. Kelly, Clinton, Tenn.*

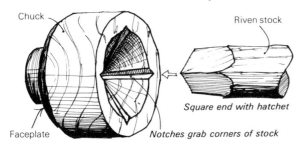

Chuck

Riven stock

Square end with hatchet

Faceplate

Notches grab corners of stock

Expansion chuck

I needed a lathe chuck to hold work without screw holes. This shopmade expansion chuck is invaluable for turning small trays, dishes and vases. A single ¼-in. machine screw pulls a tapered wooden plug into a matching tapered section thereby expanding the chuck and tightening it in a prepared recess in the base of the workpiece.

Make the chuck from a block of hardwood (I used Honduras mahogany) that has been permanently screwed to a small faceplate. Since the wood grain is perpendicular to the faceplate, install three birch dowels in the base of the block to increase the holding power of the mounting screws.

The overall shape of the chuck is somewhat arbitrary, but proper expansion can be achieved only if the webs are thin. After you have turned the outside to shape, carefully hollow the inside to give about ⅛-in. thickness to the web region. Fit the plug blank with a threaded steel insert, then turn the plug to match the taper of the chuck body. A 7° taper is about

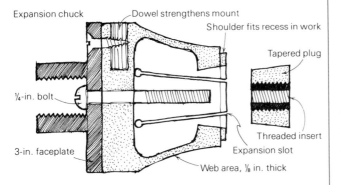

Expansion chuck

Dowel strengthens mount

Shoulder fits recess in work

Tapered plug

¼-in. bolt

3-in. faceplate

Threaded insert

Expansion slot

Web area, ⅛ in. thick

right. After turning is complete, drill stop-holes and cut eight expansion slots in the chuck body.

—*R.E. Hollenbach, Livermore, Calif.*

Another lathe chuck

This easy-to-make lathe chuck simplifies turning small bowls and other faceplate work. Mount a solid-wood block to a plywood base and turn a short cylinder with a flared lip as shown in the sketch. For flexibility, cut a saw kerf nearly through the cylinder. Then cut a mortise through the saw kerf and fit two wedges to the mortise. A dowel or bolt through the cylinder's base will add strength.

To use the chuck, bandsaw the blank to shape and mount

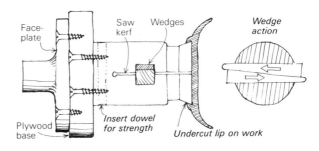

Face-plate

Saw kerf

Wedges

Wedge action

Plywood base

Insert dowel for strength

Undercut lip on work

it on a screw center, screwing into what will be the waste from the concave part of the bowl. Shape the outside of the bowl, then carefully undercut a dovetail recess in the base to fit the lip on the chuck. Remove the stock from the screw center and the screw center from the lathe, attach the chuck, then slip the work over the chuck's lip, carefully orienting the grain to take the pressure. Drive home the two wedges to spread the lips and lock the work in place. For safety's sake, wrap a band of masking tape around the wedges to prevent their flying out. —*W.W. Kelly, Clinton, Tenn.*

Expanding-action bracelet mandrel

Here is an effective mandrel for turning the outside contours of bracelets. You'll need an arbor (made for using buffing and grinding wheels on the lathe), a rubber stopper and a small piece of ¼-in. thick plywood. Turn the rubber stopper to a ⁵⁄₁₆-in. thick, 2⅝-in. wide disc. This diameter works well for bracelets, which usually range from 2⅝ in. to 2¾ in. in inside diameter. Turn also two ¼-in. plywood discs—one to a diameter of 3 in., the other to 2½ in. Assemble the mandrel with the arbor's steel washers to the outside and the rubber disc sandwiched between the plywood discs as shown.

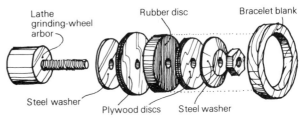

Lathe grinding-wheel arbor

Rubber disc

Bracelet blank

Steel washer

Plywood discs

Steel washer

To use the mandrel, cut the inside of the bracelet blank with a circle cutter, bandsaw the outside to rough shape and slip the blank over the rubber disc. Now tighten the nut. The rubber will expand uniformly to exert enough pressure to hold the bracelet. Turn one side of the outside contour, then reverse the blank and turn the other face.

This method could be adapted to napkin rings and other ring-shaped objects by sizing the rubber and plywood discs to the project. —*Max M. Kline, Saluda, N.C.*

Turning ringed objects

An effective mandrel for turning napkin rings and other annular objects can be made as follows. Choose a suitable hardwood (such as hard maple) and mount the wood to the face-

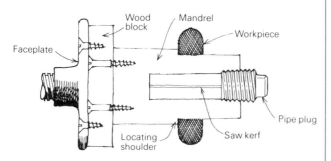

plate with the grain oriented perpendicular to the axis. Turn down the end of the mandrel to give a slip fit with the work piece, leaving a larger-diameter locating shoulder on the base as shown in the sketch. Next, drill and tap the end of the mandrel for a tapered pipe plug of suitable size. First select the recommended tap drill size for the pipe thread and drill into the end of the mandrel ¾ in. or so deeper than the locating shoulder. Then tap the hole so that a pipe plug will thread in halfway. The resulting threads, though rough in appearance, are quite strong if the grain is oriented·as suggested. To complete the mandrel, cut two crossed saw kerfs to the same depth as the hole.

To use, slide on the workpiece and screw the pipe plug in the hole. The plug will expand the mandrel, gripping the workpiece firmly.　　　*—Edward F. Groh, Naperville, Ill.*
and Charles E. Cohn, Clarendon Hills, Ill.

Making toy wheels

Hardwood wheels for toys are expensive, not well sanded and do not come in many varieties of wood. I tried making my own, but the work was prohibitively time-consuming until I came up with the modified screw center I now use. With it I can turn out a wheel every four minutes on production runs.

I started with a standard morse-taper screw center (Sears) that I modified in two ways. First, I drilled and tapped the tail of the screw center to accept a ¼-in. drawbolt which holds the tapered shaft from the back of the headstock through the spindle. The drawbolt is simply a length of threaded rod with a washer and wing nut. The second modification was to remove the center screw itself. This leaves a ¼-20 threaded hole for attaching the work.

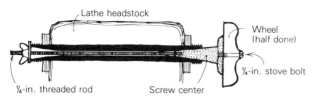

I cut the wheel blanks from scrap using a hole saw with a ¼-in. pilot bit. Then I mount a blank on the modified center with an ordinary stove bolt. It takes about a minute to shape and sand each side. I try to completely finish one side before I turn the wheel around. While shaping, make sure the hub area is slightly thicker than the wheel rim for clearance.

For axles on the toys, I use ¼-in. stove bolts screwed into a hidden nut mortised and epoxied in the vehicle's side. This is stronger and longer-lasting than wooden axles and allows the owner to take apart the toy and put it back together.
—George Pilling, Springville, Calif.

Finishing toy wheels

To finish wooden toy wheels on the lathe, I use a simple faceplate fixture. After I cut the blanks using a hole saw with a ¼-in. pilot bit, I mount the blank on a special wooden faceplate in one of two ways, depending on the work to be done. If I'm smoothing the rim, I install a ¼-in. bolt through the fixture from the back, slide the blank on the protruding threaded shank and fasten the blank in place with a wing nut, for quick changes.

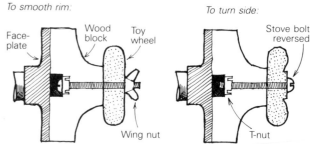

On the other hand, if I'm turning the face of the wheel, I remove the bolt from the back and screw the blank to the fixture from the front, which allows more room. A T-nut installed in the back side of the fixture anchors the bolt. To save time, do one operation on all the wheels before reversing the bolt.　　　*—Carlton M. Herman, Hendersonville, N.C.*

Lathe template fixture

A few months ago, while teaching lathe duplication methods to my cabinetmaking class, I discovered a novel and efficient method of rapidly producing identical turnings. Mount a template of 16-ga. metal on a swinging arm at the back of the lathe. After the stock has been turned round, swing the

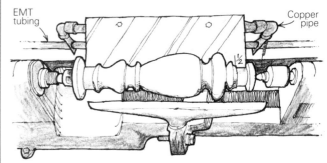

template against it with a light spring, maintaining enough tension to prevent excessive bounce. By cutting from the front in normal fashion and referring visually to the template at the rear, you will be able to quickly and accurately produce any number of identical turnings with few rejects and a minimum of tedious measuring and calipering.

To keep each turning the same diameter, scratch a final diameter reference on a short, straight run at each end of the template. Work each end of the turning to these reference diameters first, then the gap between the reference diameters and the template will show the maximum cut depth to be taken from the workpiece's high spot.

My version of the duplicator is made from ¾-in. copper pipe, copper pipe elbows and a length of ½-in. EMT conduit. Solder up a U-shaped assembly from the copper pipe, flatten the pipe on each of the U's legs and drill to pivot on the conduit. Flatten the crosspiece of the U and drill to attach the template. Adjust the angle at which the template hits the work by heating the joints of the U and turning the template to the proper position.

—Doug Christie, Fort Grant, Ariz.

Bandsaw cuts gauge turnings

Turning copies of a spindle on a hand lathe can be tedious work. Templates, gauges and other gadgets help but don't substantially increase speed and accuracy. In contrast, this method, which uses the bandsaw, is the best turning aid I've found yet. On one face of the square stock, mark out with a template the desired profile and make bandsaw cuts to within ⅟₁₆ in. of the profile at convenient reference points. Bevel the square's corners as you usually do, mount the stock on the

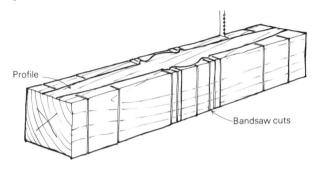

Profile

Bandsaw cuts

lathe and begin turning. The cut lines will be easy to see and will allow quick and accurate shaping without so many stops for caliper checks. The secret to this method is accurate layout and careful sawing. —*Robert M. Vaughan, Roanoke, Va.*

Routing 85 spindles

Here's how I used the lathe and router to make my new deck railing a cut above the usual. Starting with the straight U-shaped fixture used to make dowels, I sawed off a curved section from each end. I screwed a V-shaped block to the bottom of the router base. This allowed the router to follow the profile of the top of the fixture and to transfer the shape to the spinning blank below. The shape I wanted in the railing spindles was similar to the backrest supports in a chair. The fixture helped me produce 85 identical spindles quite nicely. —*Donald B. Sherman, Merrimack, N.H.*

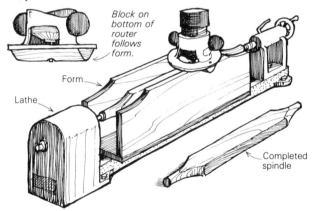

Block on bottom of router follows form.

Form

Lathe

Completed spindle

Duplicate turning gauge

This handy device is invaluable in turning duplicates. Used in multiples, it gives the correct position of control cuts and measures the depth as well. Several of the gauges—the number

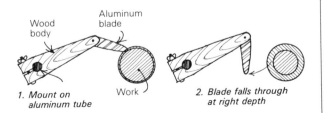

Wood body

Aluminum blade

1. *Mount on aluminum tube*

Work

2. *Blade falls through at right depth*

depends on the complexity of the work—are mounted on a metal tube or dowel fastened behind and level with the work. Select ½-in. hardwood for the gauge body and ⅟₁₆-in. aluminum for the blade. Drill one end of the body to fit the metal tube and slot the other end to fit the blade. The blade should fit loose in the slot and pivot easily on the pin. Set the position of the gauges by sliding along the tube. Then vary the angle of the body to set the depth. In use the blade will ride on the work (in the parting-tool cut) and fall through when the right depth is reached. —*Bayard Cole, Marietta, Ga.*

Hose-clamp lathe chuck

This lathe chuck uses an inexpensive worm-gear radiator-hose clamp to tighten the collar around the work. Four saw kerfs provide the flexibility needed for loosening and tightening the chuck. —*Ernest Moyer, Royersford, Pa.*

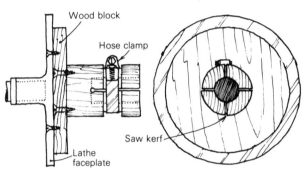

Wood block

Hose clamp

Lathe faceplate

Saw kerf

Roughing out bowls

It is frequently suggested that in bowl turning, one should cut from large diameter to small diameter. I'd like to call attention to a situation where the opposite may be preferable—this is the case when roughing the outside of a bowl with the faceplate attached to what will eventually become the top of the bowl. The method evolved from turning green bowls, where cutting from large to small diameter can be a jarring experience.

For inboard turning, I rough the outside of bowls with my *back* to the lathe, and thus with the headstock to my right. I cut with a deep gouge. Holding the handle in my left hand and resting the butt on my right hip steadies the gouge and supplies considerable power. I work from the base to the side of the bowl, slowly rounding over the nearest corner. The cut goes from small to large diameter with great ease and in my opinion, it's a case of "cutting wood as it prefers to be cut." —*Wendell Smith, Fairport, N.Y.*

Lathe sanding drum

This inexpensive but effective drum sander is made and used on the lathe. Center an 18-in. long 4x4 on the lathe and turn a cylinder of 3½-in. diameter. Carefully reduce the diameter of the cylinder until a standard sheet of emery cloth wraps around the drum without gap or overlap. Glue the emery cloth (I used 100 grit) to the drum with hide glue. Wrap the entire surface with a sash cord and let dry overnight. Turn down the ends of

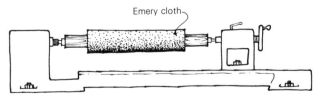

Emery cloth

the drum to about 1½ in. to give free working space. The size of the drum can be scaled up or down for different applications. A smaller open-end drum could easily be made using a screw center. —*Harland Smith, Waterloo, Iowa*

Bowl-turning depth gauge

When turning a hollow, as for a bowl, it is difficult to estimate how deep a cut has been taken. Although the best curves may be made by eye, it is necessary to know the depth to check on the remaining thickness of wood and avoid turning through. A ruler can be held against a straightedge across the rim of the bowl, but that is an improvisation. The tool described here is a more efficient way to check depth.

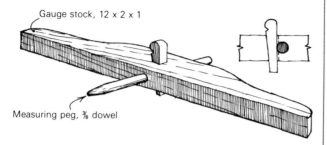

Gauge stock, 12 x 2 x 1

Measuring peg, ⅜ dowel

Make the stock wide enough to span the largest-diameter bowl your lathe can turn. The base must be flat. The other parts can be shaped as you wish, but edges should be rounded for a comfortable grip. It is easier to get the peg hole perpendicular to the base before other shaping is done. The wedge hole can be cut at the same time.

The peg may be a length of dowel rod. Its working end should be slightly tapered and finished with a little doming where it will touch the bowl.

The slot for the wedge has to be made with its edge cutting through the peg hole by a small amount, so pushing the wedge in tightens it against the peg. An overlap of ¹⁄₃₂ in. should be enough. Make the wedge and measure the thickness of the stock centrally on it. From the distance across the wedge at these points, mark the width of the hole at each side. The ends of the wedge can be rounded and decorated, but a plain wedge works just as well.

—*Percy W. Blandford, Stratford-on-Avon, England*

Go/no-go turning gauges

When turning spindles, finials and other pieces having several diameters, it is frustrating to have to reset a caliper to each of

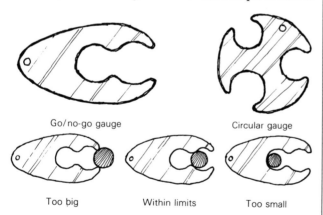

Go/no-go gauge   Circular gauge

Too big   Within limits   Too small

the different dimensions—especially when multiple parts are required. The metalworking industry uses "snap gauges" or "go/no-go" gauges to solve similar problems.

A snap gauge is one whose points are fixed at a given dimension. In precision metalworking, tolerances of one ten-thousandth of an inch are not uncommon. In woodturning the dimensions are not that critical, and a gauge can be readily made to within ¹⁄₆₄ in.

More commonly, a snap gauge is made with two pairs of points and is called a go/no-go gauge (also a limit gauge or

snap-limit gauge). Each pair of points is fixed at a different dimension. The difference between the two dimensions is the tolerance of the dimensions of the workpiece. This is especially handy when turning tenons or dowels.

If you have a good eye for turning and prefer a single set of points (as normally used with a standard outside caliper), several gauge variations are possible. A circular gauge, for instance, can be made to include all dimensions (three in the example shown) for a given turning. Or, a whole set of gauges with, say, ¹⁄₁₆-in. increments can be made.

Infrequently used gauges can be made of ⅛-in. tempered Masonite, but Masonite will wear rapidly if used while the work is turning. For a permanent, accurate gauge (with a touch of elegance) make the gauge from ¹⁄₁₆-in. or thicker hard sheet brass. Mark the size of each set of points and see what a difference a gauge makes.

—*John R. Beck, DeKalb, Ill.*

Laminated bowls

The method I use to make six-sided bowls creates boldly repeating patterns and reduces layout and blank-assembly time. I start by laminating a wedge-shaped beam with 60° sides, sandwiching veneer of various thicknesses between four ¾-in. hardwood boards. The widest part of the wedge (which I make of a highly figured wood) will be the outermost part of the bowl, and 5 in. here will produce a 10-in. diameter bowl. The length of the wedge will determine the bowl's height.

I set the jointer fence at 30° and joint off two sides of a scrap 2x4, leaving a chunk of wood angled 60° on each edge. Then I cut off six thin wafers, arrange them in a circle and check for proper fit. If there are gaps, I adjust the angle of the jointer fence and try again. When the angle is correct, I joint both sides of the laminated beam deep enough to clean out depressions and glue. Then I cut the beam into six equal sections and dry-fit.

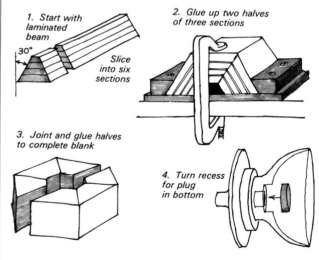

1. Start with laminated beam

30°

Slice into six sections

2. Glue up two halves of three sections

3. Joint and glue halves to complete blank

4. Turn recess for plug in bottom

Now glue up two bowl-blank halves of three sides each. Use a clamping jig. Next, dry-fit the two halves and, if they don't fit perfectly, run the faces of the two sections over the jointer. Glue the two halves together to complete the blank. When you turn the blank, simply make a recess for a round plug to fill the hole in what will be the bottom of the bowl.

—*Roy Ashe, Luther, Mich.*

Reversing lathe rotation for sanding

Here's how I reverse the rotation on my lathe for sanding turned bowls. This approach reduces the problem of the faceplate unscrewing from the spindle, as often happens if you reverse the motor or the drive belt. After the bowl is turned, I cut a pulley groove in the glue block. Then I chuck a plywood pulley mounted on a ¼-in. bolt into my electric drill. I mount the drill to the lathe bed and use a small V-belt to turn the bowl in reverse rotation.

Groove mounting block to fit V-belt.

Be sure to remove the lathe's drive belt before starting up the drill. Otherwise, the drill motor would be fighting the inertia of the heavier lathe motor. This will work on stock held between centers—just leave enough waste stock at one end for a pulley groove. —*Lawrence A. Fortier, Pleasant Ridge, Mich.*

Inlaying veneer in turnings

I use a simple method of inlaying veneer to enhance bowls, jars, lamps and other turned work. This method works for both faceplate and between-center turnings. As shown in the sketch below, start by regrinding an old parting tool or the hardened tang of an old file. Grind the width of the point to the thickness of your veneer, and lengthen the top bevel so that the tool won't bind. Now use the tool to cut a groove ⅛ in. deep where you want to put the veneer.

With a straightedge and an X-acto knife, cut a strip of veneer slightly more than ⅛ in. wide and longer than the circumference of the groove. Bevel one end of the strip and soak in hot water until it's pliable enough to bend around the entire groove. Place the toe of the bevel in the groove and press in the veneer with your fingers. If the water swells the veneer so that it doesn't fit the groove, enlarge the groove slightly with your parting tool. To complete the fitting of the veneer, cut a reverse bevel so that the ends overlap exactly.

Once the veneer is in place, let it dry, then sand or turn it flush with the surface. A coat of shellac or lacquer will cement the veneer into the groove. If your pattern calls for multiple inlaid rings near each other, install the first strip before you cut the groove for the next strip. Otherwise, the wood between the grooves will tear out. —*Bill Vick, Richmond, Va.*

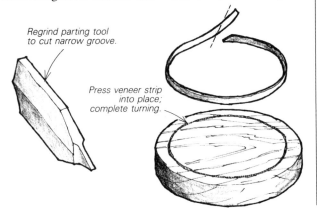

Regrind parting tool to cut narrow groove.

Press veneer strip into place; complete turning.

Machining octagonal turning stock

Spindle-turning goes faster and smoother if you begin with octagonal stock rather than square, but often it seems more trouble to machine an octagon than to simply whack the corners off on the lathe. Here's a tip that lets you easily machine octagonal stock on the jointer. Multiply the width of the square stock by 0.2071. The result is the amount, measured diagonally, that must be removed from each corner to produce eight equal sides. To make the cuts, set the jointer fence to 45°. For a safe depth of cut, you can divide larger measurements into a number of equal parts and make several passes.
—*Robert M. Vaughan, Roanoke, Va.*

Lathe steady rest

This shopmade steady rest can be set up to support the middle of a long, thin spindle, or it can be used as a tailstock for center-boring. Derived from a metalworkers' steady, the rest consists of a rigid plywood upright, three adjustable hardwood bearing blocks, and a base that locks in place on the lathe bed. The bearing blocks adjust by means of ³⁄₁₆-in. eyebolts threaded through tapped right-angle braces screwed to the upright. Each bearing block slides between two guide blocks, and locks in place with a wing nut. Apply beeswax to the bearing blocks for ease of adjustment and to reduce friction on the workpiece. Of course, the base arrangement depends on your particular lathe.
—*Robert L. Koch, Tarkio, Mo.*

Mounting flute blanks

Those of us with limited equipment and money sometimes need merely to think a little harder than those with the equipment we lack. An article on making flutes advised mounting the drilled blank on the lathe with chuck-mounted abrasive cone centers to turn the flute to shape. Those without a chuck and abrasive cones can use this easy trick: Turn a 1-in. blank to the diameter of the bore, leaving about 1 in. at each end square. Cut this piece in half, chamfer the round ends and insert them into the bore of the instrument. This assembly can be remounted on the lathe, using the same live/dead orientation and the same spur indentations. If the live end slips, I suppose masking tape would solve the problem, but I found I didn't need it.

—*Bob Raiselis, New Haven, Conn.*

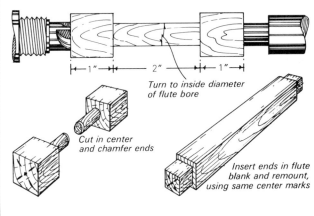

|← 1" →|← 2" →|← 1" →|

Turn to inside diameter of flute bore

Cut in center and chamfer ends

Insert ends in flute blank and remount, using same center marks

Sanding block for lathe work

For years my woodworking students invariably burned their fingers sanding bowls and other lathe work. Then I hit upon the solution—sanding blocks cut from sheets of ½-in. thick rubbing felt. The felt sanding block shapes itself to shallow curves and can be deliberately shaped to match more elaborate forms.

Rubbing felt is available in 1-ft. squares from finishing supply outlets. A similar material, used for typewriter cushions, is available from office-machine suppliers. Cut the pad with a razor knife and rule. One block lasts indefinitely.

—*Russell Anderson, Torrington, Conn.*

Three-jaw "overshoes" for bowlturning

Like many avid woodturners, I use a three-jaw chuck for bowlturning and other faceplate work. With it you can avoid screw holes in the bottom of the bowl or skip the step of gluing on a waste bottom with paper between. But the three-jaw chuck is limited in the size range it can hold, and it contacts the workpiece at only three points, limiting the strength of its grip—if you overtighten it you will mar the work. I overcome these problems by adding wooden "overshoes" to the chuck. The overshoes are simply three 2-in. thick, wooden circle segments. I cut a groove in the back of each segment and bolt the piece to the jaw with two countersunk allen bolts. Annealed chuck jaws, which can be drilled

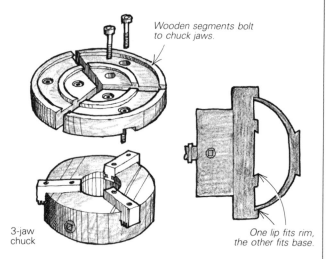

Wooden segments bolt to chuck jaws.

3-jaw chuck

One lip fits rim, the other fits base.

and tapped for the bolts, are available for most chucks; it's handy to have more than one set.

In the face of the wooden overshoes I turn two recesses, slightly dovetailed, to fit the rim and the base of a bowl. I mark both the overshoe segments and their matching jaws—if removed, each overshoe must go back on the same steel jaw it came off.

To use the overshoe chuck, I first mount the bowl blank on a large screw center and turn the outside to rough dimensions, taking care to size the base within a range that will fit the overshoe chuck. Then I reverse the blank, remount with the overshoe chuck gripping the base, and turn the inside of the bowl. When the inside is complete, I reverse the bowl in the chuck, gripping it by the rim to complete the outside. This technique is particularly useful when working green wood, which must be turned rough, dried, then remounted for turning to final shape and finishing.

—*A.R. Hundt, Blackmans Bay, Tasmania*

Faceplate scraping

A curved cabinet scraper works extremely well for the final shaping of bowls and other faceplate turning projects. The scraper easily smooths end-grain areas where turning tools tend to tear out splinter and chunks. It also eliminates the need for coarse grades of sandpaper that put in those hard-to-remove, concentric scratches.

—*John Rocus, Ann Arbor, Mich.*

Two steady-rests

The homemade stabilizer device shown below allows me to turn four-poster beds and architectural columns on my 9-ft. lathe. The stabilizer eliminates the whipping and vibrating that accompany long-stock turning. The brace bolts to the lathe bed at about the midway point. A long upward-pointing handle is hinged to move the cast-aluminum stabilizer

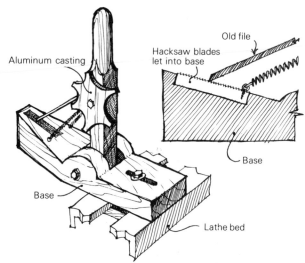

Aluminum casting

Old file

Hacksaw blades let into base

Base

Base

Lathe bed

back and forth so it can ride against the stock. The stabilizer has several different diameters to fit different-sized turnings. The aluminum, coated with a little beeswax where it rubs, effectively carries away the heat. The brace adjusts against the stock through a spring-loaded device that moves an old file against a stack of hacksaw blades.

—*Deloe Brock, Chattanooga, Tenn.*

Here is an economical steady-rest made from three sections of 2x4, a carriage bolt and two plastic casters (drawing, below). Cut and join the wood to fit your lathe bed, then drill the bolt hole the same height as the center spindle. The base clamps to the lathe bed and adjusts in or out for large or small work. The roller arm pivots on the bolt to provide a fine-tune adjustment to the changing diameter of the work in progress.

—*James Ulwelling, Coon Rapids, Minn.*

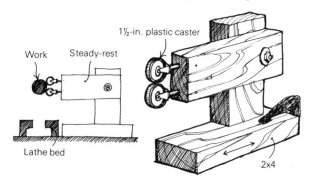

1½-in. plastic caster

Work

Steady-rest

Lathe bed

2x4

Producing round tabletops on the lathe

Here's how I use my lathe and a sanding disc to produce a perfectly round tabletop. First locate the center of the tabletop blank and cut it roughly to shape. Now cut a short length of

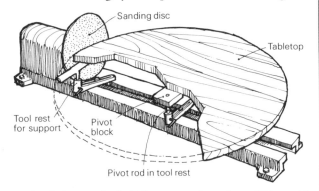

metal rod that can be held in your tool-rest base. Using a bit the same size as the rod, drill partway through a piece of 2-in. scrap. Screw or clamp the scrap block to the underside of the tabletop at its center. Now mount the work on the lathe's tool rest with the block and the rod acting as a pivot. To level and support the work near the sanding disc, mount another tool rest parallel to and about 1 in. from the disc.

Now turn on the lathe and rotate the tabletop against the disc. If the pivot turns out off-center, loosen the tool rest. Advance the work and finish the entire circumference to the shortest radius. —*Robert S. Maxwell, Washington, D.C.*

Turning lamp bases

Here are a couple of tricks to turn tall lamp bases. I don't have a large drill press; I drill the electric cord hole on the lathe with a homemade extended bit and a wooden guide block. To make the long bit, weld the turned-down shank of a ⅜-in. bit in a ¼-in. hole drilled in the end of a 24-in. length of ⅜-in. drill rod. Clean up the weld with a file and sandpaper. Make the guide block as shown in the sketch, screw the block to the stock over the center and carefully drill the cord hole. Back out the bit frequently to remove the chips. The guide block helps keep the hole right on line through the center of the stock.

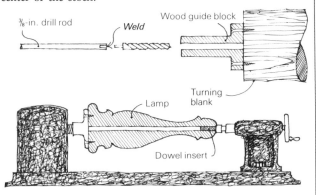

To prepare the stock for turning, glue a short length of ⅜-in. dowel in the top end of the cord hole. Screw a faceplate to the other end of the stock, centering the faceplate over the hole. Now mount the stock in the lathe, centering the tailstock's cup center on the dowel insert. When the lamp base is done, remove the faceplate and drill out the dowel insert. —*Bob Kurz, Hartsville, S.C.*

Auxiliary tailstock for boring

To bore holes through lamp bases and similar turned items, I made an auxiliary tailstock to hold the work so I could pass a long drill bit through the regular tailstock. The key feature of this special tailstock is the bearing from a bicycle crank hanger. This bearing has a 1-in. bore, so I turn a 1-in. tenon on the end of my lamps to fit it. The rest of the device consists of a ¼-in. thick aluminum-plate upright, a short section of a 1-in. angle-iron base to span the lathe ways, and a wooden dog, which tightens under the ways to lock the unit in place. To keep wood chips out of the bearing, I turned a cover for the bearing that also holds the bearing in the upright.

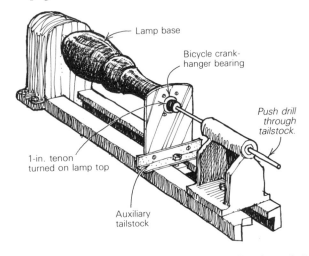

In use, the ram from the tailstock is removed and the drill bit is passed through the tailstock into the lamp, which is supported in the auxiliary tailstock.

—*Ralph Luman, Virginia Beach, Va.*

Bull-nose tailstock

I frequently turn pieces that I have drilled out or turned hollow. To support these pieces for further turning and finishing, I use this large-diameter bull-nose tailstock. To make it, remove the metal center from a 60° ball-bearing center and replace it with a larger, turned hardwood cone. Turn a tenon on the base of the cone to fit the ball-bearing center, as shown in the sketch. I have several hardwood inserts of various sizes to fit different projects. All fit the same, ball-bearing center.

—*Ted Ringman, Barrington, Ill.*

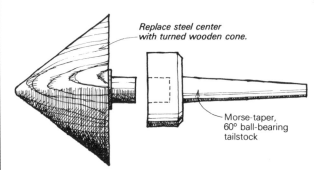

Thickness-sander attachment for lathe

The sketch below shows the thickness-sander lathe attachment I made to sand dulcimer tops and sides. The design is similar to other sanders I've seen, but because the device uses

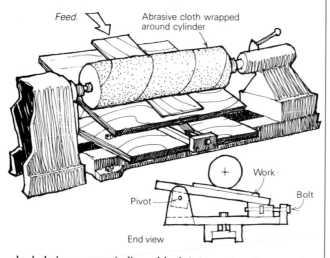

Feed.

Abrasive cloth wrapped around cylinder

Pivot

Work

Bolt

End view

the lathe's motor, spindle and bed, it is much easier to make. By using the lathe's variable-speed pulleys you can always find the perfect sanding speed. The sanding drum is simply a turned wooden cylinder spirally wrapped with abrasive cloth. The plywood and hardwood base bolts to the lathe bed and adjusts with a simple wedge mechanism.

—*Charles R. Adams, Westmoreland, N.H.*

Turning long tapers

Here is an easy way to turn long tapers on the lathe, First, turn the workpiece to a smooth cylinder and mark the length of the taper. With a parting tool, cut the larger diameter on one end and the smaller diameter on the other. Set your outside calipers to the larger diameter and scribe a mark on the caliper knob (so you can count the knob's rotations later). Move the caliper to the smaller end and count the knob rotations as you close the caliper to the smaller diameter.

Suppose, for this case, you counted 5½ rotations. Divide the length of the workpiece into 5½ parts, mark each division with a pencil and return the caliper to the diameter of the larger end. Turn the caliper knob one rotation. This will be the correct diameter at the first line. Use the parting tool to

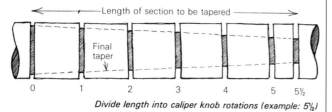

Length of section to be tapered

Final taper

0   1   2   3   4   5   5½

Divide length into caliper knob rotations (example: 5½)

turn the workpiece down to that caliper setting at the first line. Then turn the caliper knob one more rotation and repeat at the second line. Continue the process across the workpiece. Complete the taper with a gouge or skew, using the parting tool cuts as a guide.

For a long, flat taper it might be necessary to base the divisions of the tapered length on half or even quarter-rotations of the caliper knob. This will keep the divisions closer together and facilitate the job of cutting the taper between grooves. —*Frederick C. Weisser, Houston, Tex.*

Shopsmith work tray

This handy work tray, designed to use with the Shopsmith, rests on the tool's tubular ways. It holds lathe tools, work arbors, sandpaper or small workpieces. You can drill holes in the tray for the Shopsmith's allen wrench, drill bits, plug cutters or whatever.

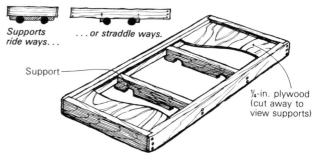

Supports ride ways...

...or straddle ways.

Support

¼-in. plywood (cut away to view supports)

Materials and tray size can vary. My tray (drawing, above) is about 18 in. long, 12 in. wide and 1 in. thick. Semicircular cutouts on the tray's supports let the tray ride the Shopsmith's tubular ways. The supports are spaced so that if the tray is turned 90°, the supports straddle the ways.

—*Billy Hill, Orange Park, Fla.*

Tapered turning head

When lathe-turning candlesticks or other items that have a center hole, the hole can be perfectly centered by drilling it first before turning is started, and then using a tapered turning head, such as the one shown. If the candlesticks are to be

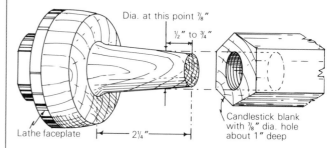

Dia. at this point ⅞"

½" to ¾"

Lathe faceplate   2¼"

Candlestick blank with ⅞" dia. hole about 1" deep

for standard ⅞-in. diameter candles, taper from a large diameter of about 1⅛ in. down to a minor diameter of about ¹³⁄₁₆ in. or slightly less. The important dimensions are ⅞-in. diameter at ½ in. to ¾ in. from the end, along with a smooth, straight taper.

The predrilled wood blank is slipped over the tapered head. Care must be taken not to overtighten, of course, as the taper will split the wood blank if too much force is applied. Making the overall length of the taper about 2¼ in. and using the diameters indicated seem to provide good tightness and good tool clearance for standard candlesticks.

Cutting away stock from the top of the turning adjacent to the tapered head shortens the workpiece and consequently loosens the grip of the head, so if you must cut at that point, be sure to remove only a small amount before stopping the lathe and retightening the tailstock. When finished, the work can be removed easily by backing off the tailstock and moving the work slightly from side to side until loosened. The result is a perfectly centered hole. This method has one other advantage: You proceed with turning *after* you know you've drilled a good clean hole.

The same concept can be applied for other center-hole pieces as well by turning other tapers with different diameters. If you have several tapers, it's best to mount each one permanently on its own faceplate to ensure concentricity.

—*L.L. Chapman, Newark, Ohio*

Making wooden toy axles

When I couldn't find axle pins in the size and length I needed for the wooden toys I make, I devised this lathe tool to make my own. Start with a short length of ½-in. drill rod. Drill a ¼-in. blind hole in the side of the drill rod ⅞ in. from one end. Then drill a ¼-in. hole through the center. Hacksaw out the center portion to produce a ¼-in. slot in the end of the rod. File the sides of the slot smooth, then file the bevels on the leading edge of the cutter as shown in the sketch. Put a ½-in. setscrew collar over the cutter and tighten it up. Without the collar the cutter would open up in use.

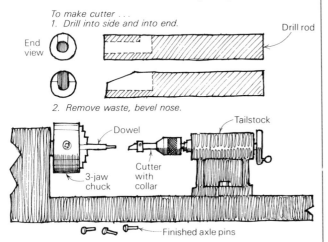

To make cutter . . .
1. Drill into side and into end.

End view

Drill rod

2. Remove waste, bevel nose.

Dowel

Tailstock

3-jaw chuck

Cutter with collar

Finished axle pins

I chuck the cutter in the tailstock and adjust the tailstock clamp so it will slide smoothly on the lathe bed. I use ⁷⁄₁₆-in. dowel stock for the axle pins which I feed through the headstock and hold with a three-jaw chuck. To cut the pin I push the tailstock cutter against the dowel until I have the length pin I need. I then cut off the pin, starting with a fine-tooth saw, rounding off the face with a file and then completing the cut-off with the saw.   *—Stanford LeGath, Clifton, N.J.*

Shopmade tool rests

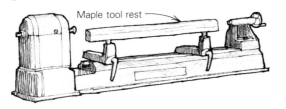

Maple tool rest

Roughing down a whole turning at once is such a pleasure that I have made a series of hard-maple tool rests in various lengths. I use them instead of the skimpy metal rest that came with my lathe. Support the wooden rest with a metal post that fits your current tool rest's base. For long tool rests, you will need more than one base.

—Jim Ryerson, Guelph, Ont.

Planer Jigs & Fixtures

Chapter 20

Hand-feed for the Parks planer

Here's a simple way to get an infinitely variable feed rate on a Parks Model 97 thickness planer, without altering any part of the machine. Simply install a hand crank on the throwout sleeve. Although no planer is 100% tear-proof, it sure makes a big difference once you get used to the feel of cranking wood through by hand.

To make the crank, I started with an old farm machinery crank and fitted it to a short keyed shaft that slides into the center hole of the throwout sleeve. To use it, I simply disen-

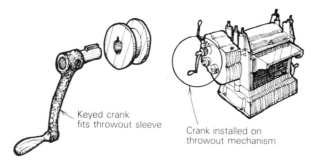

Keyed crank fits throwout sleeve

Crank installed on throwout mechanism

gage the power feed and start cranking. Make sure you remove the crank before you use the power feed.

This idea could probably be adapted to other planers that have a similar feed disengagement mechanism.
—*John Colombini, Pittsburgh, Penn.*

Solution to tear-out problems

If your planer or jointer tears out crossgrained wood, sponge on a light coat of water. The water swells and softens the fibers, packing them tight together to give the cutting edge a little more to push against. Where the grain is steep, more water is absorbed—just where you need it. After applying a light coat of water, wait a minute and take a light cut. If the grain tears out, add more water and let it soak in longer. Since most of the wet wood is planed away, there is little chance of warping the wood.

This trick works best with hardwoods but is occasionally successful with softer woods. Tear-out problems in hand-planing also respond to this treatment, but you must wait until the surface is completely dry before scraping.
—*John Leeke, Sandford, Maine*

Surfacing wide boards

My jointer is small, but that doesn't stop me from surfacing boards wider than 6 in. Say you've found the perfect piece of cherry for a drawer front, but it's 9 in. wide, cupped or slightly twisted. To rip and reglue the board would spoil the gorgeous grain pattern. What I'd do is rabbet the two edges of one surface, run the new narrow width over the jointer, then flatten the top through the thickness planer. Flip the board over and plane the true board to thickness.

Naturally the nature of the cup, bow or twist and the thickness of the finished piece determine the depth of the rabbet. And, if you must rabbet both edges, you'll likely have to remove the regular fence from the jointer to center the work over the blade. —*Donald Leporini, Newton Centre, Mass.*

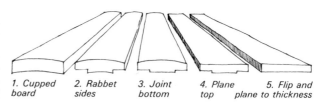

1. Cupped board 2. Rabbet sides 3. Joint bottom 4. Plane top 5. Flip and plane to thickness

Flattening cupped boards

It is difficult to flatten a cupped board with a thickness planer because the downward pressure of the feed rolls will press out much of the cup, thereby not allowing the planer knives to flatten the board. As it emerges from the planer, it simply springs back to its original cup. To counter the pressure of the feed rolls, I tape wooden strips to the concave side of the board. My method is designed for a planer with a single cutter positioned above the board as it passes through the machine.

First run the board through the planer with its concave side up to obtain an even surface along the edges, which will make the next step easier. Now set a straightedge across the board, as shown, to determine the correct thickness for the wooden strips. It is usually easier to use several short strips than one long one, especially if the board is very long or irregularly cupped. With reinforced (cloth-backed) tape, fasten the strips to the board in the area of greatest depth of curvature. Wide masking tape will also work. Now run the board through the planer with the convex side up. The wood strips underneath will prevent the downward pressure of the feed rolls from flattening the cup. Thickness-plane until the convex side is

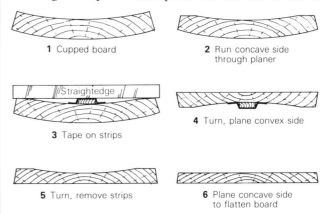

1 Cupped board

2 Run concave side through planer

3 Tape on strips

4 Turn, plane convex side

5 Turn, remove strips

6 Plane concave side to flatten board

flat, then remove the tape and strips and run the board through again, concave side up, until the concave side is also flat. —*Dwight G. Gorrell, Centerville, Kans.*

Smoothing veneer

Here's how I safely smooth resaw veneer on the jointer. I secure the veneer to a flat back-up board with double-stick carpet tape. The back-up board holds the veneer flat and gives it the stiffness it needs. If the veneer is short or narrow I tape scraps of the same thickness to the back-up board to keep it from tipping. Set the jointer for a light cut and proceed slowly. —*Rock Thompson, Centerville, Utah*

Unwinding lumber

Here's a method for recovering short lengths of twisted lumber too wide for your jointer. First tack a strip (wider than the lumber is thick) to one edge. Lay the work on the saw table and tack an identical strip to the other side so that both strips lie flat on the saw table and are precisely parallel. Now run both sides of the work over a dado head (or flat, three-lipped cutter) to obtain a flat board.

—*Pendleton Tompkins, San Mateo, Calif.*

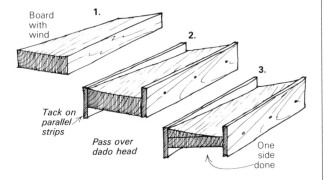

Dressing thin stock

This jig allows you to dress stock to thinner than ⅛ in. on a conventional thickness planer. Without it the thin workpiece will vibrate and often splinter on the ends.

To make the jig, glue 45° beveled hardwood cleats to a length of lumber as wide as and slightly longer than the wood to be dressed. The cleats can be any thickness, since they will be planed down to the final thickness desired, at which time they serve as a rough thickness gauge for subsequent duplicate planing.

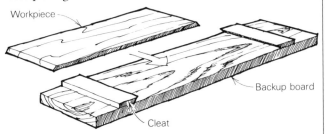

To use, bevel the ends of the workpiece so that it fits snugly under the cleats. Wax the back of the jig, slip the stock in the jig and run the jig through the planer, taking light cuts down to the desired thickness. Push the jig into the planer, then pull it through from the other side to prevent the feed rollers from pushing the workpiece out of its cleats.

—*John S. Pratt, Avondale Estates, Ga.*

Planing thin stock

I have found that the following procedure for preparing small pieces of veneer works well. Bandsaw a ⅛-in. thick slice from the desired veneer stock which has already been planed. Then glue the slice to a scrap board with rubber cement. Apply the rubber cement to both the scrap board and the smooth side of the ⅛-in. thick slice. Press the two pieces together after the cement has dried. With the scrap as a base you can hold the work securely for planing to final thickness. To remove the veneer, insert a putty knife between veneer and scrap; then slide it along the scrap. Rub the veneer with a rough cloth to remove the remaining rubber cement.

—*Alan U. Seybolt, Harwich, Mass.*

Planing end grain

I used to cringe at the thought of sending end-grain slabs through a power planer. I do it often now and end up with cutting boards few people can bring themselves to cut on. Scrap pieces from the table saw are jointed smooth and glued together side to side along the length to form a laminate of different kinds of wood—the more species the better. (1) This laminated plank is planed down until smooth and then cross-cut into strips on the table saw (2). The strips are stood up and then glued to each other. One can shift every other

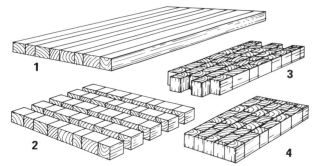

strip a bit for a checkerboard effect (3) or line them all up straight. At least three bar clamps are used for each gluing step. Then run the slab through the planer until it is smooth (4). Then round the corners, bevel the edges, sand and finish with mineral oil. When the oil hits that end grain it will have been worth the effort.

Checkerboards may also be made in this way, using heavier stock. Only with experience have I been able to estimate the size of the finished board—it varies directly with how thick it is made. It helps to have a sharp planer but no matter how sharp, some of the trailing edge is going to be chewed up. This is to be expected and must be compensated for, especially when making checkerboards.

—*James B. Small, Jr., Newville, Pa.*

Skewed jointing

When you're jointing wavy-grained, contrary woods like curly maple, a skewed cutting angle will often produce smoother results with less tear-out than a straight-on cutting angle. To take advantage of this effect simply attach a long wedge to the jointer fence. —*M.W. Uresti, Bryan, Texas*

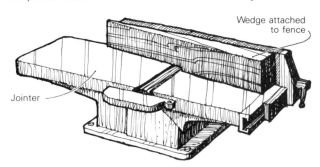

Fixing jointer-knife nicks

If jointer knives get nicked as a result of hitting a nail or whatever, you can slide one knife a fraction of an inch to the right and another knife a little to the left. Leave the third knife in its original position. Because the nicks do not come in line, the jointer will surface lumber as smoothly as it did originally. —*Eric Schramm, Los Gatos, Calif.*

Chamfering tambour strips

Here's a jig I developed to safely chamfer the edges of narrow strips, such as tambours. It consists of a straight piece of scrap as long as the strips and wide enough to be handled safely. Rabbet the bottom edge of the jig a fraction narrower and shallower than the strip, and attach a stop to one end of the rabbet. Now set your jointer fence to the desired angle, place a strip in the rabbet, and run the jig across the jointer. The depth of cut determines how wide the chamfer will be.

—*Greg Forney, Gilcrest, Colo.*

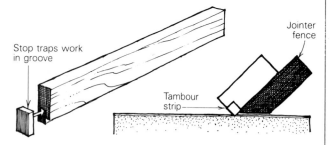

Stop traps work in groove

Jointer fence

Tambour strip

Safe jointer hold-down

A few years ago, after nipping a finger in a jointer, I became preoccupied with the safe operation of this machine. I pored through textbooks and catalogs searching for a hold-down/guard device that would be safe, easy to construct and inex-

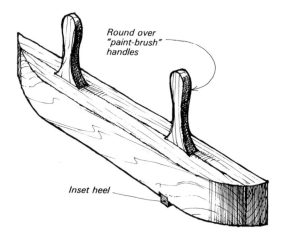

Round over "paint-brush" handles

Inset heel

pensive. I looked for a design that would protect both hands, be rigid, provide firm, steady pressure and allow good control of the workpiece. Finding nothing meeting my requirements, I eventually came up with the design shown above.

I keep three different lengths of hold-downs (24-in., 48-in., and 78-in.) to accommodate various lengths of lumber. Dimensions, however, are not critical and you should adapt them to your needs. Start with two lengths of 2x4. Dress the inner faces and cut dadoes into them to accept the "paint-brush" handles. Mate the dadoes and glue up. After the glue has set, square up the piece and cut the dado into the base to accept the 3/4-in. heel so it protrudes about 1/2 in. Now band-saw the curves in the leading and trailing ends of the unit and sand smooth. These curves allow the jointer's blade guard to open and close with a minimum of blade exposure.

Next set the heel and the handles. If possible wedge the 3/4-in. square heel in place rather than gluing it. It may have to be replaced from time to time. Cut the heel and the handle bases a trifle short so they won't protrude and snag on the jointer fence or the workpiece. The hold-down is now ready for very safe surfacing work.

—*Bernard Maas, Cambridge Springs, Pa.*

Replacing one knife

I solve the problem of a deeply nicked jointer knife by keeping an extra set on hand and replacing only one nicked knife with one from the spare set. Replacing one knife at a time saves on setup time and extends the life of the knives between sharpenings. Of course, all six knives should be sharpened at once, ground to the same size.

—*Arthur L. Fiest, Emmaus, Pa.*

Installing jointer knives

Here's how to replace reground knives in a jointer quickly and accurately. First crank the infeed table all the way down so it's out of the way. Place a knife and a gib in the cutterhead slot, with the screws tight enough to hold the knife in place but loose enough so that it can be moved. The knife should project about 1/8 in. above the outfeed table.

Now place a piece of heavy plate glass on the outfeed table so that it projects over the cutterhead. Manually roll the cutterhead backwards until the projecting knife lifts the glass at the top of its turning circle. Hold the cutterhead in place and gently press the glass down on the outfeed table, pushing the knife down into the cutterhead slot. If the knife was not exactly at the highest point of its arc, it will still be slightly too high. Rocking the cutterhead back and forth under the glass will level the knife with the outfeed table. Now tighten the gib, then repeat the sequence with the other knives.

—*Joe Robson, Trumansburg, N.Y.*

INDEX

Index

Angles, approximating, 4
Ash-splint joints, 29

Balls, making little wooden, 102
Bandsaw, drift-adjustable ripfence for, 80
Bandsaw, increasing throat capacity of, 83
Bandsaw, squaring cuts on, 81
Bandsaw wheels, balancing, 81
Benches, portable, 9
Bending, wooden blanket for ribbed form, 23
Bending iron, 24
Bending wood without steam, 23
Bookends, sliding dovetail, 33
Boring jig, horizontal, 88
Boring machine, horizontal, 84
Boss spinners, 103
Bowls, laminated, 108
Bowls, roughing out, 107
Bowls, taping to faceplate, 104
Bowl-turning depth gauge, 108
Box, book-matched, 26
Brad-setting tool for tight places, 65
Brush, disposable foam, 44

Cabinet-hanging prop, 38
Cabinets, holding in place, 38
Canoe paddles, sanding, 35
Carver's stand, 7
Carving tools, maintaining sharp, 49
Catch, bullet, wooden, 54
Centerfinder for woodturners, Plexiglas, 3
Centerfinders, 4
Chair spindle joint, hammer-eye, 26
Checkerboard, 27
Checkers, making, 26
Chisels, making, 60-61
Chuck, chair-rung, 105
Chuck, expansion, 105
Circle division table, 3
Circle duplicators, 103
Circle guide for router, 93
Circles, cutting, 82
Circles, cutting, revisited, 82
Circles, cutting on bandsaw, 83
Circles, cutting on tablesaw, 75
Clamp grips thin wood, 13
Clamping with bedsprings, 17
Clamping boxes, 17
Clamping a scarf joint, 18
Clamping segmented turning blanks, 18
Clamping wide boards, 16
Clamp-nut, quick-adjust picture-frame, 14
Clamp pads, magnetic pipe, 16
Clamps, bar, 15
Clamps, bench, 15
Clamps, bench-top, 16
Clamps, clothespin, 13
Clamps, deep-throat, 12
Clamps, gain two, 15
Clamps, homemade, inexpensive, 12
Clamps, homemade bench-top, 16
Clamps, long, 17
Clamps, making, 12
Clamps, picture-frame, 14
Clamps, pipe, blocks for, 16
Clamps, rubber, 15
Clamps, Spanish luthier's, 18
Clamps, toolmaker's, 12
Clamps, vacuum-powered, 17
Clamps, wooden, 13
Cleaning with shavings, 44
Collars, ball-bearing, 99
Compass, beam, 2
Counterbore, shop-made, 89
Cracks, repairing, 20
Crosscut fixture, tablesaw sliding, 70
Crosscutting wide panels, 71
Curve, adjustable, 2
Curve, drafting a smooth, 3
Cutoff box, 74
Cutoff table, 68
Cutting table, folding, 8

Dadoes, spacing, 78
Dadoing guide, 91
Dents, raising, 42
Dogs, bench, wood, 11
Dogs, plastic collars for bench, 11
Dogs, spur, for clamping miters, 17
Dollies, plywood, 9

Door bumpers from cue tips, 56
Door joint, decorative, 30
Dovetail cutting on scroll or band saw, 32
Dovetail marking setup, 32
Dovetail saw, sliding, 65
Dovetail square, 32
Dovetail template, 32
Dovetail trimming, 33
Doweling T-jig, 31
Dowels, center-drilling, 84
Dowels, making with hand plane, 32
Dowels, making with lathe and router, 94
Dowels, making with router, 94
Dowels, making with tablesaw, 73
Dowels, reducing diameter of, 84
Dowels, vise for end-drilling, 87
Drawer bottom, bandsawn, 81
Drawer pulls, 56
Drawknife, mini, 65
Drill, hand, 63
Drilling angled holes, 88
Drilling compound angles, 88
Drilling a dowel, 5
Drill press, pin-router attachment for, 88
Drill-press fence, adjustable, 87
Drill-press table, truing, 84
Drills, twist, modifying for wood, 48
Drill stop, masking tape, 85
Drying, in microwave, 24
Drying oven, tin can, 24
Duplicate parts, bandsawing, 81
Duplicating wood parts, 72
Dutchman, cutting a, 45

Edge-banding plywood, 28
Edge-banding plywood joints, 27
Edge-gluing without clamps, 20
Edge-sanding fixture, 102
Edging, applying wood, 26
Edging, clamping with wedges, 29
Edging with a leathercraft tool, 65
Electric-cord suspension arm, 86
Ellipse, drawing, 2, 4
Epoxy mixing, no-mess, 20

Faceplate scraping, 110
Fan, exhaust, portable, 39
Fence, scissor-jack, 92
Ferrules from end caps, 63
File teeth, cleaning, 65
Filler for knot holes, 44
Finger-joint jig, 76
Finger-pressure boards, non-skid, 73
Finish, clearing a clouded, 44
Finish, oil, vacuum-aided, 46
Finish, samples, 46
Finish, testing, 47
Finish for clocks, 44
Finish containers, collapsible, 44
Finishing plywood edge, 29
Finishing tips, auto, adapted to wood, 46
Flattening cupped boards, 114
Flush-hanger plug, 55
Flute blanks, mounting, 109
Flute bores, enlarging, 48
Flute bores, enlarging, revisited, 48
Flute cutter, lathe, 85
Fluting columns, 66, 90
Fluting jig, 90
Froe, homemade, 64
Froe handle, fitting a, 64

Glass, installing for easy replacement, 39
Glue, hot-melt, tips, 82
Glue, masking out squeeze-out, 21
Glue, removing excess, 22
Glue, spreading in sockets, 20
Glue bottle, homemade, 22
Glue lines, darkening, 20
Glue spreaders, 20, 21
Glue-up rack, 21
Gluing table, 21
Graining tool, 46
Guard, tablesaw, 71

Handles, recycling tool, 64
Hand plane, guide blocks for, 60
Handsaw storage rack, 38
Heating the shop, 39
High-chair mechanism, wooden, 55
Hinge, cam, reveals hidden compartment, 55

Hinge, leather, laminated, 55
Hinge, segmented column, 55
Hinge, wooden box, 54
Hinged box tops, aligning, 54
Hold-down, 13
Hold-down, jointer, 116
Hold-down, shaper or molding head, 77
Hold-in, improved, 76
Hold-in, molding head, 77
Hold-in, roller, for resawing, 80
Hold-in, rubber tire, 76
Holding irregular shapes, 19
Hole-cutter for speaker enclosures, 95
Honing, constant-angle, 52
Honing, hazardless, 52

Inlaying with dental silver, 45

Jig, dressing thin stock, 115
Jig, reversible, for radial-arm saw, 68
Jig, tripod, 99
Jig indexing mechanism, 37
Jigs, chamfering tambour strips, 115
Joint, Greeno interlock, 31
Jointer-knife installing, 116
Jointer-knife nicks, fixing, 115
Jointer-knife sharpening jigs, 50, 51
Jointer-knives, replacing, 116
Jointing, skewed, 115
Jointing decorative strips, 30
Jointing on radial-arm saw, 68
Jointing wide planks, 93
Joints, box, routed, 96
Joints, bridle, cutting corner, 31
Joints, curved edge, 82
Joints, drawer, 30
Joints, edge, invisible, 30
Joints, finger, cutting on bandsaw, 81
Joints, lap, three-member, 31
Joints, routed miter, 94
Joints, stretcher, easy, 30
Joints, tusk-tenon, for bed frame, 27
Joints, wedged loom, 29

Knife-making from sawblades, 63
Knife profile patterns, 53
Knife-sharpening fixture, improved, 51
Knots, repairing, 45

Ladder, fold-away, 37
Ladder, fold-away, modification, 37
Latch, wooden, 56
Lathe, bead-scraping tool, 62
Lathe, check-free drying for green bowls, 24
Lathe, drill reverses rotation, 109
Lathe, faceplate taping, 104
Lathe, freeze bowl blanks, 25
Lathe, hot-gluing turnings, 104
Lathe, inlaying veneer, 109
Lathe, jointing octagons for spindles, 109
Lathe, reground parting tool, 62
Lathe, shopmade tool rest, 113
Lathe, steady rest, 109
Lathe chuck, 105
Lathe chuck, hose-clamp, 107
Lathe chuck, shopmade 3-jaw, 110
Lathe sanding drum, 107
Lathe template, 106
Light stands, 39
Locking up tools, 39
Louvers, making, 73
Lumber, straightening curved, 77
Lumber, unwinding, 115

Making stationary tools portable, 9
Mallet, poor man's, 62
Mallet, wooden, 62
Mandrel, expanding-action bracelet, 105
Marking, with chalk, 4
Marking gauge, Archimedean, 2
Marking tips, 3
Marquetry patching, 45
Marquetry veneer, shading, 45
Mill marks, removing, 43
Miter fixture, improved, 67
Miter gauge, enhanced tablesaw, 74
Miter-gauge setting jig, 75
Miter-gauge stop, adjustable, 76
Miter jig, 67
Miter jigs, tablesaw, 74, 75

Molding, making sectional, 104
Molding, ogee, 72
Molding, router jigs for making, 92
Mortiser, horizontal, 92
Mortising fixture for drill press, 87
Mortising fixture for router, 93
Mortising table, slot, 66
Mortising table for drill press, 87

Nails, coating, 40
Notes, taking, 40

Panels, cutting wide, 74
Panels, raising arched, 72
Plane, ball, 59
Plane, chisel rabbet, 60
Plane, English, 59
Plane, mortising, 58
Plane, router, 60
Plane, scraper, homemade, 59
Plane-iron sharpening, 52
Planes, wooden-soled, refurbishing, 58
Planing end grain, 115
Planing stand, 7
Planing thin stock, 115
Plexiglas, cutting, 63
Plug extractor, 40
Plywood-storage bracket, laminated, 38
Pull/catch, wooden, 54
Pumice, easier than, 43
Purfling, router guide, 94
Push stick, 78

Rack, plywood, 37
Radial-arm pin router, 66
Radial-arm saw, cutting angled rabbets on, 67
Radial-arm saw, poor boy's, 68
Rags, replacement for, 43
Raised panels, router method, 95
Reamers, socket, 62
Rests, steady, 110
Reversing switch, 38
Roller support, for ripping, 77
Roller support refinements, 78
Router base, eccentric, 90
Router fixture, dado, 92
Router guide, T-square, 91
Router jig, flip-up dado, 91
Router jig, mortise-and-tenon, 98
Router jig, sliding dovetail, 95
Router jig for Shaker dovetailed legs, 97
Router jig for splines, 95
Router jig for wooden spheres, 97
Router subbases, 98
Router table, hinged, 98
Router table, tablesaw extensions, 98, 100
Router-table fence for edging discs, 100
Router table improvements, 100
Router vacuum attachment, 100
Routing, cross-grain, jig for, 91
Routing deep through mortises, 98
Routing European hinge mortises, 96
Routing splined miter joints, 93
Routing tongues, 96
Rule joint, flush, for oval tables, 27

Safety switch, drill press, 85
Safety switch, tablesaw, 78
Sander, belt, counterbalance improves, 103
Sander, block, from sanding belt, 35
Sander, contour, 34
Sander, disc, with tablesaw, 79
Sander, hand, 34
Sander, homebuilt vertical belt, 34
Sanding block for beaded edges, 34
Sanding block for lathe work, 110
Sanding device, 35
Sanding disc, ersatz, 34
Sanding drum, 103
Sanding mop, 35
Sanding small pieces in clothes dryer, 35
Sanding small pieces, 46
Sanding strips, long-lived, 34
Sandpaper, how to fold, 35
Sandpaper, stopping gumming, 36
Sandpaper sizer, 35
Sawblades, circular, jointing, 53
Sawblades, cleaning, 40
Sawblades, protecting, 40
Saw-dolly, folding, 9
Saw fence, setting, 77
Saw guard, space-age, 71
Saw guide for portable circular saw, 67

Sawhorse, portable, 8
Saws, fixing new, 53
Saw setup, space-saving, 68
Saw-sharpening stand, 7
Saw tables, waxing, 79
Scrapers, cabinet, homemade, 36
Scrapers, glass, 36
Scrapers, recycling old blades as,
   36
Scrapers, triangular, 61
Screws, dip for, 40
Screws, removing broken, 40
Screws, sheet metal, faster in
   wood, 40
Scriber, poor boy's, 62
Sharpening, bicycle wheel, 49
Sharpening, grit-slurry, 53
Sharpening, lineshaft, 49
Sharpening with belt sander, 102
Sharpening jointer knives, 50, 51
Sharpening plane irons, 52
Sharpening a wire wheel, 48
Shaving horses, 6
Shims, playing card, 39
Shine, Mister? 43
Shop-vac, auxiliary tank, 41
Sizing, 33
Slot-mortising table, adjustable, 86
Spade bit, improved, 48
Spindles, turning duplicates, 107
Splines, cutting, 28
Square, checking a miter, 5
Square, trueing framing, 3
Square cuts, 66
Stain, cheap, 43
Stain, shoe-polish, 43
Staining curly maple, 43
Stains, natural, 42
Staved cylinders, assembling, 18
Steady rests, 110
Steam-bending jig, 25
Steamer, pipe, 23
Steamer, tank, 23
Stones and strops from the attic,
   49
Stop, chest lid, 57
Superellipse, 4
Support for tablesaw, 79
Surfacing wide boards, 114

Table feet, adjustable, 56
Tablesaw, portable, 10
Tablesaw jig, trig angles, 75
Tablesaw jointing fixture, 77
Tabletops, recessed, 73
Tabletops, round, producing on
   lathe, 111
Tailstock, auxiliary, for boring, 111
Tailstock, bull-nose, 111
Tape tricks for little sticks, 79
Tear-out, preventing, 85
Tear-out problems, solution to, 114
Tenoner, tablesaw, 70
Tenons, chair-rung, on bandsaw,
   81
Tenons, cutting round, on slats, 69
Tenons, tablesaw, 41
Thickness planer, Parks, hand-feed
   for, 114
Thickness-sander attachment for
   lathe, 112
Thickness-sanding, on belt sander,
   102
Threads, cutting wooden, 33
Threads in end grain, 33
Tool holders, 61
Tool rest, adjustable, 49
Tools, restoring old, 61
Tools, reversing belt-driven, 39
Toy axle pins, making wooden, 86
Toy axles, making wooden, 113
Toy dollhouse siding, router jig for,
   96
Toy log-house joint, jig, 28
Toy shake shingles, for dollhouse,
   61
Toy wheel cutter, 48
Toy wheels, finishing on lathe, 106
Toy wheels, making, 106
Tray, Shopsmith work, 112
Triangle, drafting, to set tablesaw,
   79
Triangle tips, 2
Trim, repairing, 42
Turned goods, decorating, 44
Turning gauge, duplicate, 107
Turning gauges, go & no-go, 108
Turning head, tapered, 112
Turning lamp bases, 111
Turning long tapers, 112
Turning ringed objects, 106
Turnings, polishing, 44

V-block, better, 86

Vee-block, for resawing, 80
Veneer, smoothing, 114
Veneer, trimming, 97, 101
Veneering convex workpieces, 19
Veneering cylinders, 18
Veneering with sandbags, 19
Veneers, blending, 44
Veneer strip thicknesser, 61
Vise, auxiliary, 11
Vise, bench, homemade, 10
Vise, horizontal, 15
Vise, leg, 10
Vise, leg adjustment, improved, 11

Walnut, bleaching, 42
Workbench, inexpensive, 8
Workbench, outdoor, 6
Work station, 7
Worktable, two-level rolling, 8

**Fine Woodworking
Editorial Staff, 1975-1984:**

Paul Bertorelli
Mary Blaylock
Dick Burrows
Jim Cummins
Katie de Koster
Ruth Dobsevage
Tage Frid
Roger Holmes
John Kelsey
Linda Kirk
John Lively
Rick Mastelli
Ann E. Michael
Nina Perry
Jim Richey
Paul Roman
David Sloan
Nancy Stabile
Laura Tringali
Linda D. Whipkey

**Fine Woodworking
Art Staff, 1975-1984**

Roger Barnes
Deborah Fillion
Lee Hov Hochgraf
Betsy Levine
Lisa Long
E. Marino III
Karen Pease
Roland Wolf

**Fine Woodworking
Production Staff, 1975-1984**

Claudia Applegate
Barbara Bahr
Pat Byers
Deborah Cooper
Michelle Fryman
Mary Galpin
Barbara Hannah
Annette Hilty
Nancy Knapp
Johnette Luxeder
Gary Mancini
Laura Martin
Mary Eileen McCarthy
JoAnn Muir
Cynthia Lee Nyitray
Kathryn Olsen
Barbara Snyder

If you enjoyed this book, you're going to love our magazine.

A year's subscription to *Fine Woodworking* brings you the kind of practical, hands-on information you found in this book and much more. In issue after issue, you'll find projects that teach new skills, demonstrations of tools and techniques, new design ideas, old-world traditions, shop tests, coverage of current woodworking events, and breathtaking examples of the woodworker's art for inspiration.

To try an issue, just fill out one of the attached subscription cards, or call us toll-free at 1-800-888-8286. As always, we guarantee your satisfaction.

Subscribe Today!
6 issues for just $29

TAUNTON MAGAZINES
...by fellow enthusiasts

The Taunton Press
63 South Main Street
P.O. Box 5506
Newtown, CT 06470-5506

Fine WoodWorking

1 year (6 issues) for just $29.00
— over 18% off the newsstand price
Outside the U.S. $38/year (U.S. funds, please).

☐ payment enclosed
☐ bill me

☐ Please send me a *Fine Woodworking* books and videos catalog (BBBP).

Use this card to subscribe or to request a *Fine Woodworking* books and videos catalog.

NAME

ADDRESS

CITY

STATE

ZIP

PHONE

I am a
1. ☐ novice
2. ☐ intermediate
3. ☐ advanced
4. ☐ professional woodworker.

Fine WoodWorking

1 year (6 issues) for just $29.00
— over 18% off the newsstand price
Outside the U.S. $38/year (U.S. funds, please).

☐ payment enclosed
☐ bill me

☐ Please send me a *Fine Woodworking* books and videos catalog (BBBP).

Use this card to subscribe or to request a *Fine Woodworking* books and videos catalog.

NAME

ADDRESS

CITY

STATE

ZIP

PHONE

I am a
1. ☐ novice
2. ☐ intermediate
3. ☐ advanced
4. ☐ professional woodworker.

Fine WoodWorking

1 year (6 issues) for just $29.00
— over 18% off the newsstand price
Outside the U.S. $38/year (U.S. funds, please).

☐ payment enclosed
☐ bill me

☐ Please send me a *Fine Woodworking* books and videos catalog (BBBP).

Use this card to subscribe or to request a *Fine Woodworking* books and videos catalog.

NAME

ADDRESS

CITY

STATE

ZIP

PHONE

I am a
1. ☐ novice
2. ☐ intermediate
3. ☐ advanced
4. ☐ professional woodworker.